9/00

WITHDRAWN

KOREAN IMMIGRANTS AND THE CHALLENGE OF ADJUSTMENT

Recent Titles in
Contributions in Sociology

KOREAN IMMIGRANTS AND THE CHALLENGE OF ADJUSTMENT

Moon H. Jo

Contributions in Sociology, Number 127
Dan A. Chekki, Series Adviser

Greenwood Press
Westport, Connecticut • London

Library of Congress Cataloging-in-Publication Data

Jo, Moon H., 1934–
    Korean immigrants and the challenge of adjustment / Moon H. Jo.
       p.   cm.—(Contributions in sociology, ISSN 0084–9278 ; no.
  127)
    Includes bibliographical references and index.
    ISBN 0–313–30918–3 (alk. paper)
    1. Korean Americans—Cultural assimilation. 2. Korean Americans—
Social conditions. 3. Immigrants—United States—Social
conditions. 4. United States—Ethnic relations. 5. Korea—
Emigration and immigration. 6. United States—Emigration and
immigration. I. Title. II. Series.
E184.K6J6   1999
305.8957073—dc21   98–55752

British Library Cataloguing in Publication Data is available.

Library of Congress Catalog Card Number: 98–55752
ISBN: 0–313–30918–3
ISSN: 0084–9278

First published in 1999

Greenwood Press, 88 Post Road West, Westport, CT 06881
An imprint of Greenwood Publishing Group, Inc.
www.greenwood.com

Printed in the United States of America

∞™

The paper used in this book complies with the
Permanent Paper Standard issued by the National
Information Standards Organization (Z39.48–1984).

10 9 8 7 6 5 4 3 2 1

Copyright Acknowledgment

Extracts from *East to America: Korean American Life Stories* by Elaine H. Kim and Eui-Young Yu. Copyright © 1996 by Elaine H. Kim and Eui-Young Yu. Reproduced by permission of The New Press, NY.

CONTENTS

PREFACE

The passage of the Immigration Act of 1965 by the United States Congress permitted tens of thousands of Koreans to immigrate into America every year. Most of these Korean immigrants have adjusted very well to their new country; however, some have encountered difficulties of various kinds in adapting to what, for them, proved to be an alien environment. Many have been terribly disappointed by their experiences in America and have returned to Korea vowing that the American dream is either a sham or a nightmare.

In the recent past, students of race and ethnic relations, particularly those of Korean descent, have studied Korean immigrants in great detail and tested their theoretical perspectives about race relations using the lives of Korean immigrants as their text. My purpose in writing this book is not to raise theoretical issues or to test hypotheses involving Korean immigrants, but to share my knowledge of the adjustment problems of Korean immigrants with other students of race and ethnic studies and those interested in learning about the experiences of Asian immigrants in general and Korean immigrants in particular. To accomplish this objective I have included many first person narratives as anecdotal evidence along with case studies instead of statistical tables and analyses.

There are numerous books and articles about Korean immigrants in America; however, no single book has captured all aspects of the Korean immigrant experience. Some studies on Korean immigrants' lives have focused on histories of particular aspects of Korean immigration, the immigrants' difficulties in making a living, and, to some extent, their difficulties in family adjustment. Economic adjustments, or difficulties with making a living, have been the major focus of most stusdies of Korean immigrants. In this book I have tried to delve more deeply into areas other authors seem to have either overlooked or else neglected. For example, I have devoted extensive space to a discussion of the difficulties Korean immigrants face adjusting to changes in family relationships as a result of their immigration to America. I examined not only the relationship between husbands and wives, but also immigrants and their children, and immigrants and their parents. I have also shown how a knowledge of English has played a vital role in the immigrants' success in America, particularly in securing jobs, making a living, interacting within families, and understanding how American society works. Unfortunately, students of the assimilation of Asian Americans have not examined seriously Korean immigrants' experience with prejudice and discrimination, although they have discussed them in the context of employment discrimination. Therefore, I have allocated one chapter to recounting the immigrants' experiences with prejudice and discrimination.

As the number of Asian immigrants increases and as the United States' foreign and economic policies focus more on Asian countries, Americans' interest in Asians has intensified in recent years. As more children of recent Asian immigrants, including Korean immigrants, have entered college, many universities find that they must meet the demand for Asian-American studies at a time when such ethnic studies programs are under attack. The pressure for such studies comes not from Asian-American students alone, but from those who recognize that offering such studies is a legitimate response to a real need. In addition to textbooks on gender and race, books offering insights into ethnic relations have expanded to include Korean, Vietnamese, Filipino, and Asian Indian groups together with Chinese and Japanese Americans in America. The fact is that the perception that Chinese and Japanese are the only Asians which represent the Asian-American experiences, the view which most native-born academics have held for decades, is no longer tenable.

For many years, only a few universities in the state of California featured Asian-American studies. But this is true no longer. Asian-American studies programs are emerging at major universities in the northeast and midwest. For instance, Yale, Columbia, New York University, City College of New York, the University of Massachusetts, and Northwestern University have established Asian-American studies programs. I hope my modest study will contribute to an understanding of how one Asian-American group adapted to life in an alien culture and thereby add to everyone's understanding of what it is like to be a "stranger in a strange land," and thus serve as a reminder to those whose ancestors' immigrant experiences have been lost in time or else forgotten.

I would like to thank all my Korean immigrant friends who have helped me write this book by answering questionnaires and patiently answering my telephone surveys. In particular I would like to thank Change Bum Oh from the Washington, D.C. area, Sook Lee Ryan and Chong Sun Pak of Chicago, Ji-Hwan Jo of Phoenix, and Young W. Park, Yoon Sam Kim, Soo W. Hong, Jaison Kim from the Williamsport, Pennsylvania area for distributing and collecting questionnaires, and in some cases answering questions themselves. I would especially like to thank Hwan Song, Chairman of the Venice Beach Merchants' Association in Venice, California, and Eui Shik Chung, President of the Korean Senior Citizen's Association in Los Angeles, California for sharing their insights about the adjustment problems of Korean immigrants. Above all, I would like to thank my friend, Daniel Mast of the Department of Languages and Literature at Eastern New Mexico University, who carefully read and edited the manuscript. Without him, it would have been impossible to complete the book.

Finally, I would like to acknowledge my indebtedness to Lycoming College for granting me a sabbatical to write this book. I would also like to say thanks to David Rife who encouraged me to do this book, offered many suggestions, and who provided me with a steady stream of newspaper clippings about Korean immigrants in America.

INTRODUCTION

The century that is rapidly nearing an end will find America's population venturing into hitherto uncharted waters. According to a 1995 Census Bureau report, profound shifts should leave the country older and far more ethnically diverse than ever. By the year 2000 it is estimated that ten million people of Asian and Pacific Islander descent will live in the United States. By 2020 this number is expected to reach twenty million. Midway through the next century, by 2050, the United States will very nearly be a "majority minority" nation; that is, one where the historically dominant population, loosely described as Anglo or Wasp, will make up only about half of the total population, down from three-quarters today. It is estimated that the Hispanic and Asian populations will grow most rapidly on average because of two factors: high immigration rates, and the fact that Hispanic women typically bear more children than do the women of other ethnic groups.

One of the fastest growing Asian American minorities is the Korean-American group. The first wave of Koreans, mostly men and few in number, arrived in Hawaii as laborers in the early 1900s. In 1970 there were an estimated 70,000 Korean residents of the United States; by 1980 the population had grown to 357,393; and the 1990 census shows a total of 787,849. This influx of Korean immigrants is almost entirely due to a liberal immigration policy adopted by the United States government in 1965, but this tide of immigration has come at a cost. Demographic characteristics of the newcomers are much different from those of the early immigrants to Hawaii. Specifically, the recent Korean immigrants brought their children with them. Thus, along with his wife, his family might include infants, adolescents, and his or his wife's parents. As a consequence, intergenerational differences in terms of identity, language facility, and adjustment to the dominant culture are much more pronounced than they were for the earlier, usually bachelor, Koreans.

Korean immigrants are more handicapped in adjusting to the American way of life than other recent Asian immigrants from such places as Hong Kong, the Philippines, India, and Pakistan. To begin with, unlike people from these places, Koreans have not had any form of Anglo-colonial experience; thus, they are generally unfamiliar with the English language in particular and with Western culture in general. As a result, they often feel alienated and culturally ambivalent, engendering within themselves a sense of marginality. Furthermore, their problems are compounded by the fact that most of them came to the United States during a time when the country was experiencing slow or gradual economic growth, and at a time when high-tech and knowledge-intensive jobs were replacing unskilled and semi-skilled jobs, creating a less conducive environment for the newly arrived immigrants, particularly for those who lacked technical skills and English language facility. At the same time, the public attitude toward the newly arrived immigrants has begun to deteriorate in the last decade or so due to the large influx of immigrants not only from Asia in general but a few from Southeast Asia in particular who appear to have become burdens to American society.

Pressured by the public, the state and federal governments—already re-examining the current liberal immigration policy—began toying with ways of limiting benefits to the newly arrived immigrants, a tactic reminiscent of the alien exclusionary acts adopted by the state and the federal governments against Asian immigrants during the nineteenth and early twentieth centuries. Moreover, immigrant bashing—by means of physical as well as verbal assaults against them and vandalism against their property—is becoming as common on the East Coast as it has been on the West Coast. Increasingly, Korean and other newly arrived immigrants are facing an uncertain economic future, and they are finding that members of the dominant group are beginning to exploit them for their own personal gain.

All immigrants in the United States face difficulties in adjustment at one time or another, although the degree of difficulty in adaptation varies from group to group and from individual to individual. However, recent Korean immigrants who are younger, better educated, and comparatively wealthy have a better chance of adjusting to a new society than the elderly, the less educated, and the poor. In part, this ease of adjustment may derive from the fact that these individuals already have some command of English and may have been exposed to Western culture through their contact with Americans in Korea and, thus, are much better prepared for the challenge of adapting to a new way of life. Moreover, the immigrants who had thoughtfully prepared for their emigration anticipated that they would experience problems in adjustment once they arrived in the United States and, therefore, found the transition much easier than did those who were fleeing their homeland because of their straitened financial condition, or those in search of political asylum. Above all, those immigrants who already had relatives and close friends in the United States to welcome them had a better chance of adjustment to life in the United States, at least initially, than those who didn't have anyone to guide them and give them material and psychological comfort.

Among the most frequently mentioned difficulties of adaptation to the United States by Korean immigrants are the language barrier, finding a means of earning a living, family stresses, social isolation, cultural conflict, and the consequences of their children's education. Some of these difficulties, such as the language barrier, making a living, and family conflict are far more pressing problems than other adaptive difficulties for most Korean immigrants and demand immediate resolution as they are not only directly linked to the immigrants' quality of life but also their survival. Although the seriousness of other adaptive problems should not be minimized, the solution to these problems is less urgent than the language problem and finding a livelihood. It should be noted that some of these difficulties are interrelated. For example, difficulty in making a living almost always contributes to family conflict. And the immigrants' language difficulties create problems in finding, and keeping, employment, in absorbing American culture, and in understanding their children who are not only rapidly becoming Americanized but who are becoming monolingual in English. The immigrants also become easy targets of discrimination and prejudice because of their lack of fluency in English.

A plethora of studies have been made on the experiences of Chinese and Japanese immigrants because of their long history as immigrants and because of the extreme hostility they faced from members of the host society, especially in the west. However, the study of the Korean immigrant experience is still inchoate because most Korean immigrants are regarded as recent immigrants, most of them arriving as they did in the 1970s. Their assimilation and acculturation process, the conflict between generations, and their experience of discrimination and prejudice remain to be explored. Furthermore, the American public's attitudes toward Korean immigrants or Korean Americans are still vague as they are not adept in differentiating Koreans from Chinese, Japanese, or other Asian groups. In fact, most public opinion polls do not even include Koreans in their study of public attitudes toward various Asian racial and ethnic groups, although these include Chinese and Japanese.

Americans know little about Koreans, one of the fastest growing ethnic groups finding a home in their midst, nor do they seem particularly interested in why Korean immigrants came to the United States, or even how they came. About all of which they are aware is that their towns and neighborhoods are changing in character, seemingly overnight. They have made little or no effort to learn more about their new neighbors or to try to meet and welcome these strangers into their midst. As a result, the Korean immigrants are left to muddle their own way through the maze of problems they encounter in surmounting the language barrier, social isolation, family tension, and the challenge of earning a livelihood. No one save the newcomers are aware of the successes they have achieved in the process of adaptation to life in a strange culture and in a new society.

Thus far, the study of Korean immigrants has been eclectic at best. It has largely focused on the history of Korean immigration, their economic adjustments, the well-known Korean-black conflicts, the story of Korean War brides, and other topics which had attracted the interest of researchers in the past. This may be due to the fact that, as I indicated earlier, much of Korean immigrants' life is still unfolding. The economic adjustment of Korean immigrants has been more intensively studied by social scientists than any other area. Recent works such as *Blue Dreams: Korean Americans and the Los Angeles Riots* by Abelmann and Lie and *Caught in the Middle* by Min are excellent examples of studies of the Korean immigrants' economic struggle. In time, studies of various other aspects of Korean immigrants' life will emerge and eventually lead to a broad consensus about Korean immigrants' experiences.

For decades social scientists have relied on standard social science research guidelines in their study of the immigrant experiences in the United States: surveys and case study methods. The drawbacks of the survey method, particularly the questionnaire survey, are well known. They include a low rate of return and answers to questions that are too cryptic or too terse to be meaningful. The result is superficial research. However, the survey method does have some advantages over other case study methods. For instance, it can cover a large geographic area and is capable of sampling the opinions of a large number of respondents. This method is also particularly convenient for immigrants who would rather check items in the questionnaire they otherwise might not have answered at all. This was particularly true in the case of Korean immigrant respondents.

On the other hand, the case study approach, based as it is on in-depth interviews, can catch some of the feelings or emotions of the immigrants' experience, but it also raises the real problem of how to choose subjects who accurately represent a true cross-section of immigrants. In addition, in the case study or biographical approach to the immigrant experience, researchers normally select a few subjects and let them speak for themselves, then add their own observations and analyses to their subjects' insights. Frequently, researchers choose the case study approach when they believe that either the subjects' own words are much more powerful, or when they lend validity, rather than simple interpretation of the immigrant experience based on quantitative data, or else they wish to present the life experiences of immigrants in understandable fashion without the encumbrance of sociological jargon. The drawback of the case study is that it is difficult to cover many cases without spending enormous time, effort, and financial resources. Rarely do in-depth case studies cover more than fifty respondents in a particular research project.

Confronted with choosing a questionnaire survey or case study interview, I chose to combine a questionnaire survey with interviews. I constructed a questionnaire covering very broad and general areas which would require both time and some effort to complete. The questions covered the immigrants' motives for immigration, areas of difficulty in adaptation, experiences with prejudice and discrimination, and how they viewed their prospects. I used the same questions for personal interviews. I delivered fifty questionnaires to each of the regional distributors located in the Washington, D.C. area, New York City, Los Angeles, Chicago, Phoenix, and Albuquerque. I specifically instructed these regional distributors, who were my friends or relatives, to distribute the questionnaires to Korean immigrants who came to the United States as adults. In some cases I included Korean immigrants who are young adults and adults who came to the United States as young children (they are often referred to as 1.5 generation) in the sample. However, I eliminated Korean women who had married Americans from my research consideration because I assumed these people who came to America as dependents would have a completely different experience from that of most of the adult Korean immigrants who came to the United States alone or who came as a family group and have struggled to establish new lives and businesses or professions from scratch.

Only about fifty questionnaires were returned and some of these were not even complete. I later learned the reasons for the low return rate. Some respondents said the questions were too broad; or else they preferred close-ended questions, as they didn't want to spend the time writing lengthy answers. Some felt the questions invaded their privacy. Some were so preoccupied with their work that they would not waste their time filling out questionnaires. I expected a low return rate, considering the amount of writing required to answer the questions. I immediately set out to personally interview the respondents as I had originally planned and tried to augment a small sample size by interviewing fifty adult Korean immigrants around Washington, D.C., in the Los Angeles area, and in Philadelphia by asking the respondents the same questions I had incorporated in the questionnaires. Even though some store-owners were very cooperative, interviewing most store-owners proved to be difficult as they were constantly interrupted by customers and co-workers.

Although I preferred to have a large sample, I was not very much concerned about the actual sample size since I was going to augment this study by drawing upon my own experiences as an immigrant. As a Korean-born, naturalized American I have lived in the United States for more than four decades, and I have extensive acquaintances among Korean immigrants, many of whom are close friends. Because of my fluency in Korean and because of my strong affinity with Korean immigrants, I have visited members of the Korean immigrant community frequently. At the same time, they have kept me abreast of what has been transpiring in their community. Thus, I have an intimate knowledge of the Korean immigrants' experiences which few non-Korean-speaking researchers have. In fact, the first-hand knowledge I have gained about the Korean immigrants' life in this manner has proved to be as invaluable as the data I collected through my questionnaires and interviews. Because the expression in Korean of their experiences may include subtle nuances, moods, and tenses, I intend to take great care to try to capture the full range of the Korean immigrants' life, something that simply cannot be captured through questionnaires or by hurried interviews.

The book is divided into seven chapters. The first chapter traces the history of the Korean immigrants' migration, along with their migration patterns, to the United States from its beginnings to the present. The second chapter delves into motives of the recent Korean immigrants for migrating to the United States. Specifically, it will examine the prevailing conditions in Korea that might have pushed people to leave their homeland and also those conditions that appeared to exist in the new land to pull them into the unknown. It also compares the motives of those who came in the early 1900s with those of the immigrants who arrived in the United States since the early 1970s. For example, to the recent Korean immigrants, personal reasons for immigration such as marriage, reuniting families, and retirement are as important as political or economic reasons that drove earlier immigrants.

Since most Korean immigrants face enormous difficulty in overcoming certain hurdles—specifically the language barrier, finding a means of making a living, and stresses in the family—I chose to discuss the language barrier in chapter three, making a living in chapter four, and family conflict in chapter five. Other difficulties which were mentioned frequently by my respondents; such as social isolation, cultural conflict, and children's education, will be explained sparingly throughout the book in the context of how Korean immigrants deal with these difficulties as it is appropriate and as their stories are needed to illustrate a particular point.

Chapter three explores how the language barrier has affected the Korean immigrants' search for employment, their underemployment, their acculturation, their relationship with their children, their economic mobility, and even their self-esteem. Further, it also examines how the dominant group exploits Koreans' language deficiencies to reap economic benefits from them.

Chapter four discusses the ways Korean immigrants have found to make a living in America, particularly recent adult Korean immigrants, many of whom are ill-prepared to make a livelihood in one of the most industrialized societies in the world. Underemployment of Korean immigrant professionals, the immigrants' difficulty in gaining access to venture capital with which to start businesses, their lack of understanding of and inexperience with American business practices, their dilemma in doing business in the black community, the severe competition they develop with their compatriot store owners, and coping with downward social mobility will be highlighted.

Chapter five deals with how Korean immigrants cope with strains in the family, most of which are caused by the Korean immigrants' adjustment to a more egalitarian American family system than that to which they were accustomed in Korea. Some of the sources of strain and conflict in the Korean immigrant family include wives gaining economic power and independence at a time when many husbands are experiencing downward social mobility. Then, there is a weakening of the bonds between children and parents because of the language barrier and the children's acculturation. There is the need to cope with loneliness, not necessarily because most immigrants have few relatives or friends with whom to socialize, but because their almost compulsive devotion to work, sometimes seven days a week, leaves little time for family activities. There is the deteriorating relationship between adult immigrants and their parents, who feel completely at sea in the new world. In particular male Korean immigrants, who grew up in a patriarchal, extended family environment, are not easily amenable to changes taking place in their families. Sometimes their unhappiness leads to divorce; at other times, sadly, it may be expressed in the form of physical violence.

Chapter six provides the Korean immigrants' perceptions of race relations in America and their own experiences with prejudice and discrimination. Surprisingly, experience with prejudice and discrimination may not be immediate concerns for the most recently arrived Korean immigrants as their economic and social activities are typically confined to the Korean community. A Korean immigrant who lives in Koreatown in Los Angeles mentioned that he doesn't feel he is living in America as he can't differentiate between living in Los Angeles or Seoul, Korea. However, the longer Korean immigrants reside in America, the more they become aware of or are likely to have experienced prejudice or discrimination. This is particularly true for the Korean immigrants who arrived early. Korea immigrants who came to America as students in the 1950s and 1960s were not too much concerned with the problem of discrimination and prejudice as they were too busy studying and establishing their careers. Only now are many of them discovering that America is a land of opportunity, but not equal opportunity, as many of them find themselves stuck in the middle management level at their work place at the peak of their career. This chapter also examines Korean immigrants' experiences with both subtle and overt discrimination and the different experiences of professionals and entrepreneurs. While immigrant professionals are likely to experience discrimination in hiring, promotion, pay, and discriminatory treatment in the work place, Korean store owners have their own experiences of prejudice and discrimination to relate.

In the closing section, Prospects, I will examine the Korean immigrants' assessments of their current status and their future plans. I will relate their successes as well as their failures and disappointments. As Korea becomes more industrialized, it needs highly trained professionals. Today, Korea's economy is the eleventh largest in the world according to the World Bank. Korea's booming economy will undoubtedly affect Korean immigration rates which were already dropping from a peak of 35,849 in 1987 to18,185 in 1996. Indeed, Korean professionals who never gave a thought of returning to Korea are giving serious consideration to returning to Korea. They have begun comparing the advantages and disadvantages of living in Korea and the United States. In many cases, Korean firms can match the salaries offered in the United States in order to attract Korean specialists trained in the States. Improved communication between Korea and the United States and reasonable travel costs between these two countries have allowed an increasing number of Korean immigrants to visit and revisit their homeland and assess their future in America in the light of the improved economic prospects of Korea. Many Korean immigrants realize that they are ambivalent about living in the United States for the rest of their lives. While many expressed this ambivalence, they had many reasons (rationalizations) for remaining in the United States for the foreseeable future. Ironically, others plan to stay in America because they anticipate difficulty in adjusting to life in Korea.

Chapter 1

HISTORY OF KOREAN IMMIGRATION

Korean immigration to the United States began shortly after the start of the twentieth century and has continued to the present, although the flow of immigration has not been smooth and has been halted from time to time to conform to shifts in United States immigration policy. These interruptions in the flow of Korean immigrants usually reflect prevailing American economic conditions and the temper of the political climate which also resonates to the prevailing sentiment. In particular, two major events and a major immigration policy instituted by the United States government were very influential in affecting Korean immigration to the United States. The first of these events was a shortage of laborers on Hawaii sugar plantations brought on by the prohibition against importing Chinese and Japanese laborers as a result of the Chinese Exclusion Act of 1882 and the "Gentlemen's Agreements" between Japan and the United States in 1905. To replace them, Koreans were permitted to immigrate to Hawaii as laborers.

The second event which spurred Korean migration to the United States was the Korean War (1950–1953). Immediately following the cessation of hostilities, Korean war brides, orphans, and other dependents began coming to the States. Another important group were Koreans with student visas who came for an education but who remained and became naturalized citizens after completion of their education. Then the 1965 Immigration Act abolishing the quota system based on national origins opened the "floodgates" of the third, modern Korean immigration, and this Korean migration still continues. For example, in 1965, 3,130 Korean immigrants came to America; a decade later, the number had reached 28,362.[1]

Although Korean immigration can be divided into three broad time periods, as I have indicated, the third period actually overlaps the second because Korean orphans are still adopted by Americans, and American servicemen who have been stationed in Korea still bring their brides back to the States while students regularly come to the United States to study.

Each successive wave of newcomers has differed in their demographic composition and characteristics, the circumstances surrounding their migration, and the kind of treatment they received once they arrived in the host society. Consequently, their experiences of adjustment and adaptation in the United States are markedly different, depending on whether they were early immigrants or more recent immigrants. Historically, however, regardless of the circumstances surrounding the time when immigrants from the different Asian countries migrated, they had much more difficulty in adjusting to life in America than those immigrants from largely Protestant western European countries, such as England, Germany, and others.

THE FIRST WAVE

Needed by Hawaiian sugar plantation owners who found themselves unable to replace Chinese laborers excluded from the islands after the implementation of the Chinese Exclusion Act of 1882, the first wave of Korean immigrant workers came to Hawaii as contract laborers. The Act became permanent in 1902 and led to a ban on the immigration of all Asians in 1924. Following hard on the heels of the Chinese Exclusion Act came a series of progressively more exclusionary "Gentlemen's Agreements" between Japan and the United States in 1900, 1905, and, finally, in 1908, when no Japanese laborer could get a passport. Furthermore, the Japanese workers, who constituted two-thirds of the total plantation work force in the islands, had become militant and were engaging in work stoppages and spontaneous strikes. The sugar plantation owners in Hawaii turned to Koreans as a possible source of labor. At about the same time a series of events in Korea, including a severe famine, a cholera epidemic, heavy taxes, and government corruption prompted many Koreans to look for relief outside Korea. Even employment on a Hawaiian sugar plantation had a greater appeal to many Koreans than remaining where they were.[2] Between 1900 and 1905, in hopes of making enough money to return to Korea and enjoying relatively comfortable lives, approximately 7,000 Korean immigrants found work laboring under harsh conditions for long hours on sugar plantations or as cooks, janitors, and launderers at subsistence wages within the confines of the plantations.[3]

After 1905, however, the number of Korean migrations to Hawaii dwindled drastically as the Korean government became reluctant to permit further migration after learning of the poor working conditions on the plantations in Hawaii. In 1905 Korea had become a protectorate of Japan and the Japanese government began to influence Korean foreign policy. One of its first acts was to use its power to discourage Korean immigration to the United States for fear that the Korean immigrants would compete with Japanese immigrant workers already in Hawaii before the "Gentlemen's Agreements" were enacted. However, all Korean immigration to Hawaii and the mainland United States effectively ended when the United States Congress passed the Immigration Act of 1924. This Act created an apportionment formula for the allowable number of foreigners into the United States based on national origins. Northern and western Europeans were allotted fairly large quotas while all Asian nations were given token annual quotas of 100.

Unlike the recent Korean immigrants who came to America since 1965, the first wave of early Korean immigrants had strong emotional ties to their homeland, and when they emigrated to Hawaii they did it almost exclusively for economic reasons. They were sojourners with no desire to assimilate into the host country; their intention was to return to their homeland as soon as they were financially able to do so. They became very active in their ethnic community's functions, usually held in Korean-language schools, churches, and social and political gatherings. Their concern for their homeland grew stronger when their country was annexed by Japan in 1910. Most Korean organizations concentrated on the creation of an independence movement dedicated to freeing their homeland from the Japanese, and some even offered military training for those who anticipated participating in the armed liberation of their homeland. The Japanese annexation of Korea not only gave a *raison d'être* for many Korean organizations but also helped develop a strong collective consciousness among the Korean immigrants who became inconsolable in their isolation in what was, to them, an alien land. Some donated large sums of their hard-earned money to the independence movement while others were ready to lay down their lives to achieve their homeland's freedom from Japanese rule. This devotion to the cause of independence was so fierce among many of the early Korean immigrants that they could not tolerate anyone who was supportive of Japanese control of Korea. When Durham Stevens, an advisor to the Foreign Department of the Korean government, stated that Japanese control of Korea was working for the good of the Korean people, he was physically assaulted by a number of Korean immigrants and died from his injuries.[4]

In contrast with their great expenditures of time, energy, and money on political activity, the daily life of the typical Korean worker on the sugar plantation consisted of mind-numbing routine physical drudgery. However, during World War I, some of the Korean laborers were able to leave their back-breaking field work and become carpenters, tailors, store operators, and laundrymen at Hawaiian military bases as the military shifted to a wartime footing. As their living standard improved, some non-plantation workers were able to afford to bring picture brides from their homeland. About 800 picture brides came to Hawaii around 1920 to marry immigrant bachelors.[5] At the beginning most of the early brides were recruited by relatives and close friends of the Koreans working in Hawaii. But soon professional matchmakers arranged marriages for the lonely, desperate Koreans.[6] Such marriages made men become more responsible and desirous of stability in their lives. As their chances for returning to the independent Korean homeland appeared to dwindle as the years passed, some men began to drift to the mainland with their families in hope of finding better jobs for themselves and their families. There were 1,677 Koreans living on the mainland in 1920, 1,800 in 1930, and 1,700 in 1940.[7] The majority of Koreans settled in either San Francisco or Los Angeles. Most of them found employment in farming, railroad construction, mining, and fishing, while some soon ventured into various mercantile occupations, such as grocers, greengrocers, or launderers as their financial resources grew. In fact, some Koreans were able to engage in large scale farming. In Willows, California, Korean farmers cultivated 43,000 acres, for instance, and the total income for one year was estimated at 1.3 million dollars.[8]

With the defeat of Japan in 1945, the Korean nationalist movement so carefully nurtured by the early Korean immigrants floundered as Korea became independent. Some of the early supporters of the independence movement had died by this time, but others were able to return to a free Korea. A number were content to remain in the United States. Then, political strife led to the division of Korea and the Korean War. This quite naturally put many of the early immigrants' plans on hold. Now, too, they had American-born children they were reluctant to leave behind. The patriotism and concern for the welfare of their homeland never diminished in the breasts of the expatriates, however. They were saddened to watch their homeland being devastated by the war and the deep political division resulting from the armistice. They were further disheartened to see their former compatriot, Syngman Rhee (1875–1965), the first president of the Republic of Korea, contribute to the political instability in Korea and forced from office and into retirement in Hawaii in 1960.

Meanwhile, descendants of these early Korean immigrants began to take their place in the United States as American-born citizens. Although they remembered and honored their fathers' love of homeland and their involvement in the Korean nationalist movement, their feeling of a bond with their fathers' homeland was once removed, and thus more remote and detached. Their major concerns were assimilation, or the lack thereof, into the mainstream of American society and in pursuing professional careers which were rarely available to their fathers. Most of them not only identified themselves as being of Korean descent, but also as Asian American.

Ironically, children of the early Korean immigrants had one of the highest rates of interethnic marriages in Hawaii. Between 1960 and 1968, 80 percent of the Koreans married non-Koreans, compared with a 40 percent out-of-ethnic-group marriage rate during the same period for Hawaii's other ethnic groups. In the 1970s, the interethnic marriage rate actually reached 90 percent.[9] A curious set of facts emerged from these intermarriages. Korean women generally chose Caucasian husbands, whereas Korean men generally chose Japanese wives. As a consequence, it was not unusual for some of the Korean men who chose Japanese wives to be ostracized or disowned by their parents because of the deep resentment harbored against the Japanese for their colonization and annexation of Korea and their treatment of the subjugated Koreans. A seventy-eight year-old son of early Korean immigrants who settled in Los Angeles still remembers how his parents' resentment toward the Japanese affected his socialization in his teen years in the 1930s: "When it came to socializing, each ethnic group was totally separate. My mother forbade me to play with the Japanese Americans. They were always upset when they saw me with any Japanese—Chinese maybe, but Japanese under no circumstances. We couldn't even eat Japanese food. We couldn't afford to eat out often, but if we did, we had to choose either Mexican, Chinese, or Italian."[10]

The experience of the early Korean immigrants in Hawaii and on the mainland was primarily focused on matters related to the liberation of Korea from Japanese rule, and only secondarily to various ethnic-centered activities such as the importation of brides, the birth of children, and a new generation that would know little of Korea except what they were told by their parents. Although a few of the early wave of immigrants became assimilated and successful in business, most of the early Korean immigrants were eagerly preparing to return to Korea when the Japanese occupation ended in 1945. A historian of Asian immigration, Chan, observes that the plowing of so many resources into efforts to liberate Korea by the early Korean immigrants also retarded the development of Korean immigrant communities in the United States. For unlike the Chinese and Japanese, who opened stores to cater to the needs of their compatriots and for whom ethnic enclaves became a channel of upward socioeconomic mobility, only a small number of Korean immigrants went into business. The donating of so much of their savings to the nationalist effort meant that little capital could be accumulated.[11] With virtually every avenue of access to the larger society blocked, their fierce involvement in the Korean independence struggle was at once a cause and a result of the circumstances under which they lived. Korea became independent in 1945, but for many of these people, sadly, their return to their homeland never came to fruition because death overtook them before they could realize their dream.

THE SECOND WAVE

The "second wave" of Korean immigration began in 1951 after the outbreak of the Korean War (1950–1953) with the number of immigrants gradually increasing to 15,050 by 1964. The passage of the Immigration Act of 1965 led to a further dramatic increase in Korean migration to the United States. The demographic characteristics of Korean immigrants coming to the United States between 1951 and 1965 were markedly different from those of Koreans who came to the United States in the early 1900s and those who came after 1965. The Koreans who came to the United States between the 1950s and 1965 are often referred to as the "second wave" by students of Asian-American studies.

Unlike the first wave, the second wave of Korean immigrants consisted of wives of American servicemen who participated in the Korean War, orphans, and students. The McCarran-Walter Act of 1952 and the Korean War helped to ease the Korean immigrants into the United States. Although the McCarran-Walter Act was a continuation of the national origins model, it removed all racial and ethnic bars to immigration and naturalization and provided for family unification. The Korean War also had the effect of establishing close ties between South Korea and the United States as a result of the casualties suffered by these allies in their fight against a common enemy, the North Korean communist regime. The plight of South Korea almost devastated by war, as well as by the marriage of Korean women to American GIs, the sight of 100,000 orphans, and many bright students whose education had been interrupted because of the war created great sympathy among Americans. After the war the United States government not only offered material aid to South Korea for restoration of the devastated land, but it also opened its doors for Koreans willing to emigrate to the United States.

Often overlooked or forgotten, yet perhaps the largest single group of Koreans who emigrated to the United States between 1950 and 1964 were war brides. In 1952 only one Korean woman was admitted as the wife of a U.S. citizen, but in 1964 that number increased to 1,340, ultimately reaching 3,000 in 1971. Korean wives of American servicemen who had come to the United States made up more than 40 percent of all Koreans admitted as legal immigrants between 1950 and 1964.[12] As a result, the overall number of female Korean immigrants increased markedly when compared with the numbers of their male counterparts. During the 1960s, some 70 percent of all Korean immigrants were female, and women outnumbered men significantly in almost every age cohort.[13] The immigration of Korean women married to servicemen apparently will continue as long as the U.S. army is stationed in Korea. It has been estimated that a total of 53,629 Korean wives of U.S. military personnel were admitted to the United States prior to 1981.[14]

How well these war brides adapted to life in the United States was unknown for many years. They proved difficult to study as they were dispersed throughout the country and most tended to be migratory, following their husbands from station to station. Recently, social scientists began to shed some light on the nature of the problems of adjustment faced by these war brides in the United States.[15] Their findings indicate that, except for a small minority, war brides' introduction to life into America had been difficult and their future had not been promising. Besides the usual problems most immigrants face, such as culture shock and the language difficulty, the Korean war brides faced additional challenges which the early Korean immigrants never had to face. Both American and Korean cultures are not immediately open to racially-mixed couples, especially when there are so many barriers to understanding such as differences in language, customs, manners, and traditions, as well as matters of social status and educational level. As a result, interracial couples found themselves isolated from both American and Korean communities with attendant pressures leading to unhappiness, dissatisfaction, and other stresses in their family life.

Most of these Korean women married to servicemen came from the lower socioeconomic levels of Korean society. Many of these women, particularly during the Korean War and immediately following the war, were barmaids or prostitutes who worked in bars and restaurants that attracted a large U.S. military clientele.[16] In Korea they had limited opportunities for education. Consequently, few had any technical or professional skills; certainly they were not prepared to deal on an equal footing with people from the outside world. Most of them came from rural areas where there were few economic opportunities; therefore, they drifted to large cities in search of jobs where they eventually met American soldiers who seemed to have plenty of money and a willingness to spend it. Although many women found jobs in factories and small businesses, their ignorance of English and their misunderstanding of the motives of the American soldiers interested in them and their culture made them doubly susceptible to the strange and exotic new way of life offered by men off duty and off base. In fact, one of the studies of Korean wives of Americans indicates that almost half of American soldiers came from unstable families resulting from death, desertion, separation, divorce, and marital conflict. To the servicemen, the Korean women not only offered comfort and companionship in a strange land, but also made them feel "important." In turn, the women considered marriage to servicemen as an excellent way out of their insecure socioeconomic position.[17]

While the American military tried to put obstacles in the path of marriages between Americans and Koreans, once a GI married a Korean woman, a whole new set of problems were introduced, particularly after they had returned to the United States. Now the roles were reversed. The GI was once again on familiar turf, but his wife was in a strange, alien land. Suddenly, it was the wife who was cast adrift, ill-equipped to make a place for herself in this new environment and badly in need of support, which was rare or else unavailable. If she was marginally equipped to deal with life in Korea, she was severely handicapped in the States. Lacking the necessary command of English, and far from the usual family support, she essentially had nowhere to turn for support. As stresses built up within her marriage, the typical Korean wife found herself frequently neglected and even physically abused by her American husband and helpless to do anything about it. Yet, she often persevered despite her emotional deprivation and social isolation, believing that perseverance is still a better option than desertion by her husband—her most feared concern.

It has been reported that there have been many cases of physical abuse, alcohol abuse, suicide, attempted suicide, and a resulting high divorce rate among the couples. According to Min, the divorce rate of Korean women is twice as high as that of Korean men in the United States, and he attributes the high divorce rate among all Korean women largely to the high divorce rate of the Korean women married to U.S. servicemen.[18] In recent years, a much more sinister side of the problems of these women has been occasionally reported in major media. Although these reports are not based on scientific surveys, such major newspapers as the *New York Times* and the *Los Angeles Times* have occasionally reported that a large number of Asian women working as massage parlor girls have, in fact, been identified as divorced Korean women formerly married to American servicemen. Recently, an article under the subheadline "Korean Prostitutes Doing Business in the Suburbs" appeared in the *New York Times*. The article reported on the work of a Korean sociologist who had studied the sociology of prostitution around military bases. The sociologist described how Korean women who had married American soldiers and moved to the United States often turned to the oldest profession when their husbands, their sole source of support, became abusive and neglectful and ceased to support them.[19]

One should not assume, however, that all marriages between Korean women and U.S. servicemen are doomed to failure. Considering the backgrounds of couples, their motives for marriage, and the race mixture, Korean wives and U.S. servicemen husbands may face enormous adversities which most endogamous married couples would not encounter. Although it is difficult for the Korean wives to overcome a new set of challenges once they arrive in the United States, some do manage to make an adjustment to life in America with a strong determination to work out their problems so that their racially mixed children could make a better living than they have had. For them the failure of marriage places them in a terrible dilemma. First, the possibility of returning to their homeland and starting a new life with a failed marriage to a foreigner in their past is not a viable choice. On the other hand, with their limited educational background and occupational skills, they stand little chance of landing good jobs in their adopted homeland.

Even as American servicemen were marrying Korean women, so were American couples adopting Korean orphans. Between 1955 and 1966, about 6,293 Korean orphans were adopted by American couples in the United States. Roughly 46 percent of these orphans had white fathers, 41 percent were full Koreans, and the rest were black Koreans.[20] The study of the adjustment of the Korean adopted children becomes more problematic considering this mixture of races, particularly in a race-conscious society such as the United States. Few studies are available on the subject of whether children of white fathers adjust or assimilate better than children of black fathers, or whether full-blooded Koreans do better. In general, the full picture of the assimilation and adaptation of the Korean orphans is still not clear, although one particular study indicates that they are doing very well. It suggests they are well supported by their adoptive parents and seem to have a healthy self-concept. The study found, among other things, that most adoptive parents were white, Protestant families who live in rural and small communities. Their main motives for adoption of Korean orphans were religious and humanitarian, though there were childless couples who simply wished to adopt children and Korean orphans were available. The study found that, in general, the adopted Korean children had an average age of fourteen years and one month and the length of their placement was four years at the time of study. These children had relatively little "Korean" identity and identified themselves as "Americans," or more frequently as "Korean Americans," regardless of their racial background.[21]

Although there are no systematic studies on adjustment of adopted Korean children, it seems that as they grow older and become aware of their race and ethnicity and understand the dynamics of their relationship with their parents, friends, and society, they tend to experience confusion over their racial and ethnic identity.[22] As they become more clear about their racial identity, they do begin to question who they are, where they belong, and with whom their loyalty should lie. A Korean adoptee, who is now a college student, expresses her feelings about this predicament:

> The older I get, the more I realize I can't avoid being Korean. Every time I look into the mirror, I am Korean. When I look at family pictures, I feel that I stand out. I guess it shouldn't bother me, but sometimes it does. Even though I may seem very American, which I am—just like anyone who immigrates can be American—I want to be distinctly Korean. I know I'm not in terms of having all the Korean traditions, but I don't want people to see me and say, "Because she grew up in a Caucasian family, and because she's very Americanized, she's white." That's not what I want anymore. When I was younger, maybe that was what I wanted, because I wanted to fit in and didn't want to be different. But the older I get, the more I don't want to be part of that ignorance that labels people and does not allow them to be who they are.[23]

However the adoptive parents may wish their children would be like them, they cannot prevent their children from recognizing the racial difference that exists between themselves and their adoptive parents. The problem of dual identity, or banana identity as it has been called (the Korean equivalent of the "oreo cookie"), is a nagging source of confusion for the adoptees when they begin to discover that they are not like their "parents" and wonder what they are doing in America. These identity problems become more acute as they grow older and become conscious of their racial identity particularly when they begin dating and marrying. The identity problem is not just limited to adoptees, but is also pertinent to any children of racially mixed marriages between Asians and non-Asians. A professional golfer, Tiger Woods, who is the son of a Thai mother and a black father mentioned to reporters after winning a major golf tournament that he is Asian American. This caused quite a stir among black fans who thought he was black. On the other hand, an adult son of a Korean mother and a black soldier had no problem of identifying himself as black:

> Most of the time I consider myself African American. Because of the way I was raised on army bases by a Korean mother, I don't have the same speech pattern as other African Americans. This was always pointed out to me while I was in high school. African Americans pretty well accept me as one of them, even though I talk a little bit different. When I meet Koreans, I know I am not one of them, at least culturally, although I have never been treated badly by Koreans.[24]

The third group in the second wave of Korean immigration between 1951 and 1964 is composed of those who voluntarily came to the United States. This group consisted of non-immigrant students, temporary visitors, businessmen, and others engaged in commerce. Of the more than 27,000 non-immigrants admitted during this period, according to the Immigration and Naturalization Service, a large proportion were students. An estimated 5,000 of these immigrants are still in the country today. Many of them became professionals in academe or in American corporations. This may partly explain why Koreans seem to be overrepresented on the faculties of American colleges and universities. In 1968 the South Korean government reported that over a fourteen-year period, only about 6 percent of the Korean students who finished their advanced studies in America returned to South Korea.[25] How well they have adjusted to and been assimilated into the host country, when compared with those in the first wave and more recent Korean immigrants, is still unknown, as there are few studies devoted exclusively to this segment of Korean immigrants. Still unknown is how well they have fared in the professional world in the United States, although some of these professionals are speaking out more and more about their frustrations as they encounter subtle and overt prejudice in their career path. Some of their frustrations will be examined in chapters four and six of this book.

Ironically, the Korean professionals, who have obtained advanced degrees from American universities and have lived in America three or four decades, are frequently regarded by recent Korean immigrants as members of an intellectual elite group who are least concerned about the problems of recent Korean immigrants. A Korean immigrant store owner in Los Angeles said: "They really don't care about how we are doing, particularly during and after the Los Angeles riot in 1992. They live in the suburbs and are only concerned about their careers and being accepted by the white community." A Korean professional responds to such charges by saying: "I came to America in 1958 and received my undergraduate and graduate degrees from American universities. Now I am a director of a social agency. A recent Korean immigrant couple live right across from my house. I talked with them occasionally and found that I have nothing in common with them. Their major interest seems to be centered around business, church activities, and Korean politics. None of these subjects are my favorites. I am sure they find me boring, too. I became much closer to a white elderly couple, who live next to a Korean couple. I visit the white couple frequently, but I seldom visit the Korean couple, although we say 'hi' when we encounter each other in our neighborhood." The students who came to America after the Korean War and became professional after many years of training are much more interested in American sports, American education, American politics, American music, American movies, and American social issues and problems than Korean's. A naturalized Korean-born mathematics professor who came to America in 1956 and who has been teaching at a major state university in the United States for the past thirty years was always amazed when visiting professors from Korea assumed that he knew everything about what was happening in Korea. He says:

> I left Korea about forty years ago and during these years I visited Korea only once when my mother died. All my relatives are in the United States. My children were born in America and some of them are married to Americans. Although I don't feel I am accepted fully by my American colleagues after all these years, I still feel more comfortable talking and socializing with my American colleagues than with recent Korean immigrants. When I was invited to a Korean social gathering, which does not happen often, I feel I am out of place. At a gathering, they sing songs which I never heard of, discuss politics of certain Korean politicians, whom I never heard of, and envy Korean millionaires and billionaires, whom I never heard of and am not interested in knowing. They are more familiar with business investments, such as real estate and stocks in Korea, not in the United States. I am not being snobbish by not showing any fascination with these matters. On the

other hand, why should I associate with Koreans just because I am Korea-born, in spite of vast differences in interests, goals, and philosophy?

Already some of these early students-turned-professionals are reaching retirement age. Most of them know they are not going back to Korea, although some do contemplate returning to Korea for their retirement. During their career years they have associated with both their American colleagues and frequently with Korean professionals. In many cities there are few Korean professionals where they are employed. A Korean-born college professor who teaches in a small college in a small town in Pennsylvania for thirty years is a good example. He knows he and his wife will not fit into any Korean community where recent Korean immigrants are heavily concentrated. Yet they are hesitant to retire to a community where the retirees are white. The dilemma of where to retire has been a frequently discussed subject at regional and national Korean sociological society meetings in recent years. It will be interesting to know how these college-educated people, who have spent most of their lives in American establishments and corporations, adjust to their retirement. Will they make an easy transition from their professional careers to retirement as most native-born American professionals do? Or are they going to continue to feel marginal (as many of them felt during their careers) where they are neither fully accepted by the Korean community nor by the American retirement community after their retirement? A Korean-born medical doctor who has been practicing in a small town in New York State made a few trips to Korea to assess the possibility of retiring there, but soon discovered that he didn't fit into the Korean society. On the other hand, he is not willing to move to a large city, just to meet Koreans with whom he may have nothing in common. He doesn't want to remain in a small town after his retirement. He says the best alternative will be finding Korean professionals who have similar backgrounds and are faced with a similar retirement dilemma. He opines: "If a well-to-do Korean businessman would build a retirement community in warmer climate areas just to cater to these types of Korean professionals, I will definitely retire there."

THE THIRD WAVE

The "third wave" of Korean immigration was a result of the Immigration Act of 1965 which removed "national origins" as the basis of immigration into the United States. At President Lyndon Johnson's request, Congress passed the most liberal immigration act in American history in 1965. It not only ended national origin quotas, but it also authorized the annual admission of 170,000 Asians and 120,000 Latin Americans in addition to those with close ties to families already in America. The Korean share of the total U.S. Immigration rose from 0.7 percent to 3.8 percent between 1969 and 1973, which meant that, in only four years, more than 71,000 Koreans a year were admitted to the United States.[26] By 1980, eight out of ten of the Koreans living in the United States were foreign born. Between 1976 and 1990, 30,000 to 35,000 Koreans a year were admitted.[27] Although the official count of Korean immigrants in the 1990 census was close to 800,000, there is reason to believe that some Koreans came to this country as visitors and remained here illegally, but there is no way of knowing how many are here illegally. Therefore, the actual number of Koreans living in the United States may have reached one million. At any event, the number of Korean immigrants has increased ten-fold over the last twenty years and they are still migrating to the United States. Their numbers are estimated to reach 1,853,000 by the year 2010.

Using Public Use of Microdata Samples (PUMS) based on the1980 U.S. census data, Barringer, Gardener, and Levin analyzed and presented demographic characteristics of all Asian groups in the United States. For the Korean population, they presented the following demographic characteristics. About 82 percent of Koreans in America are foreign-born, the median age sex ratio is 71.5. Most of the Koreans live either on the West Coast (44.4 percent) or in the northeast (22.8 percent). Only about 7 percent of Koreans live in rural areas; the rest live in urbanized areas, which include central areas of cities, or else on the fringes of urban areas. Sixty-six percent of Koreans are married, 28.8 percent are single, and the rest are either widowed or divorced. About 35 percent have completed four years of college or more, and more than 20.6 of the rest have had some college education. Thus, as a group, Koreans are well educated. More than 55 percent have either attended college or else completed their college education and hold at least a bachelor's degree. About 20.5 percent speak only English at home, while 76.8 percent speak Korean.[28]

Although these characteristics may change as some 20,000 new Korean immigrants arrive in the United States each year, still the typical Korean immigrant can be classified as young, married, and relatively well educated with a preference for living in urban areas on either the West Coast or in the northeast. For example, according to Min, nearly 260,000 Korean Americans settled in California in 1990, of whom 200,000 settled in the Los Angeles-Long Beach metropolitan area. On the East Coast, of the 82,000

Koreans who moved to New York state, fully 80,000 settled in New York City.[29] Korean immigrants most prefer to settle on the West Coast and least prefer the midwest and south. According to the 1990 U.S. census, 44.4 percent Koreans settled on the West Coast, 22.8 percent in the northeast, 13.7 percent midwest, and 19.2 percent in the south.[30]

Most Korean immigrants are settling in large cities because there are more business opportunities than are in small cities or rural areas. It helps that there is an established resident group of Korean Americans who have more or less successfully made the transition to life in the United States. Their presence helps ease the transition to life in America for Korean immigrants with a limited knowledge of English, as well as help them find employment. Although their number is small, immigrant professionals and semi-professionals, such as doctors, dentists, lawyers, insurance agents, real estate agents, auto salesmen, mechanics, and other skilled workers who are unable to effectively communicate with the general public because of their lack of fluency of English language also gravitate into the large cities where they hope to attract Korean immigrants as their clients and customers.

Unlike the early Korean immigrants, many of this third wave of immigrants came to the United States as families, consisting of at least a husband, wife, and one or more children. Moreover, these newly arrived Koreans are able to find homes in established Korean communities in most of the large cities throughout the United States. As a result, they have not had the immediate experience of anti-Oriental hostility with which most of the early Asian immigrants have had to deal, although this, too, has been changing even as this is being written. Furthermore, living and working with their family members as, for example, small storeowners, gave them a greater sense of security than that experienced by the first and second wave of Korean immigrants. In Los Angeles' Koreatown, where an ethnic enclave economy has grown rapidly during the last two decades, Korean immigrants operate grocery stores, restaurants, gas stations, liquor stores, and real estate offices. In East Coast cities, such as New York and Washington, D. C., Koreans have also become prominent in produce retailing and other small businesses. They also tend to remain within the community even after the more successful of them sell their start-up businesses to new arrivals.[31] In addition to innumerable business enterprises, the Korean communities have erected an impressive number of community institutions: newspapers, schools, churches, and a number of cultural organizations.

Korean immigrants' labor participation is also higher than that of the general U.S. population. When compared with the 75 percent employment rate of the male labor force, Korean men had an employment rate of 78 percent, while Korean women had a rate of 55 percent, compared with a 50 percent employment rate among the general female population.[32] However, the actual percentage of employment by Korean women is difficult to include in official statistics because it is next to impossible to measure. Furthermore, the number of hours Koreans put into their work is substantially higher than that of workers in the general population because most Korean workers, particularly store owners, put in long hours of work every day, sometimes seven days a week.

Although the influx of the Korean immigrants to the United States has somewhat abated in recent years (the total Korean immigration in 1987 was 35,849 compared to 18,026 in 1993), Koreans' assimilation into the host society has been a slow process. Their strong ethnocentrism, the language barrier, self-employment in an ethnic enclave, and both subtle and overt racism by the dominant group have not facilitated their full participation in American life. For instance, as with many other Asian immigrants, not many Korean immigrants have shown much interest in participating in the American political process either as voters or by running for political office, although they have been reminded by some Korean social activists of the importance of such participation if they want to claim the rights and privileges of full citizenship. As a result, newly arrived Korean immigrants' requests for assistance have been frequently ignored by native-born elected officials. Ironically, however, many Korean immigrants are keenly interested in the politics in Korea. In fact, Korean politics is a major topic of discussion among Koreans at social gatherings, particularly among gatherings of adult males. Nor have they been full participants in the full range of economic opportunities because most Korean immigrants have resigned themselves to operating small businesses within the confines of the Korean communities or within black and Hispanic ghettoes. Socially, however, most Korean immigrants have not been able to free themselves from the protective circle of their Korean friends and relatives. Their tendency to limit their association to Koreans whom they have met at church, at work, and at social gatherings further delays their assimilation process.

Immigration trends and characteristics of Korean immigrants are changing as the South Korean economy continues to improve and the U.S. immigration laws add new provisions. Beginning in the latter part of the 1970s and continuing through the 1990s, South Koreans' standard of living has improved dramatically with rising per capita income every year. As a result, many professionals and economically established Koreans are no longer yearning to leave their country the way their predecessors did in the 1960s and the early part of the 1970s. At the same time, the U.S. Immigration Act of 1976 restricted occupational immigrants, particularly medical professionals, who wished to immigrate to the United States. For example, between 1961 and 1965, 71 percent of Korean immigrants were listed as professionals and that percentage dropped to 40 percent between 1974 and 1977.[33] The 1976 U.S. Immigration Act also made it easier for immigrants to bring their family members. In fact, since 1976, 90 percent of Korean immigrants have been admitted each year based on family reunification.[34]

Korean immigrants who have been admitted for family reunification are assumed to have much lower socioeconomic status than previous immigrants. It is assumed that their motive for immigration is to improve their living standard, which they were not able to do in South Korea. A survey conducted in Seoul recently indicates that lower-class Koreans had a stronger preference for immigrating to the United States than middle-class Koreans.[35] Consequently, immigrants who came to America in the 1980s and 1990s have been characterized as representing the lower socioeconomic group, while Korean immigrants who immigrated to the United States in the 1970s belonged to the middle and upper-middle class. One should keep in mind that this is a general trend in Korean immigration. Many professionals and middle-class Koreans still immigrate to the United States under the provisions of the family reunification. Most, however, are dissatisfied professionals who want to pursue different careers in America, or middle-class Koreans who feel uneasy about their current social status because of the rapidly changing political and economic environment in Korea.

How well the Korean immigrants are able to adjust to their new country depends not only on the immigrants' own initiative, effort, and willingness to overcome difficult challenges, but also the prevailing socioeconomic conditions and political climate of the host country, and the sentiment of the American public toward newcomers. For some time now, public attitudes toward any new immigrants has vacillated as American economic and political conditions have fluctuated. During the 1970s and the 1980s, Korean immigrants have been relatively well received when they chose to settle in ghettos, usually already populated by blacks and Hispanics, and began renovating the run-down communities. Further, Korean immigrants in health-related fields stepped in to help alleviate the shortage of health personnel in America. Since the beginning of the 1990s, however, the public's attitudes toward and perceptions of the Koreans and other newly arrived immigrants have deteriorated as they are perceived to be recipients of welfare benefits instead of contributors. Furthermore, the immigrants who are productively employed are now widely regarded as economic competitors to

American workers, as they crowd unskilled and semi-skilled native-born workers who have fallen victims of downsizing and other economic measures taken by large corporations. More and more large corporations are turning to high technology and hire only highly skilled personnel. Unemployed and underemployed native-born American workers, who usually disproportionately represent minority groups, now compete with immigrant workers who are not selective in their choice of work. They also regard immigrants as interlopers who are taking their share of welfare benefits which they believe should be reserved for them.

The concept of pie-sharing or resource-sharing among laid-off unskilled workers, blue-collar workers, and newly arrived immigrants galled many average, native-born American citizens. During the 1996 presidential campaign, the subject of immigration, particularly with regard to limiting the number of immigrants admitted into the United States and distributing benefits to the immigrants, became an important political issue. Sensing the anti-immigration sentiment sweeping through America for the past decade, Republican presidential candidate Pat Buchanan suggested that the U.S. government should impose a moratorium on immigration for a few years. Even the governor of California, a state that has always been a bellwether in matters related to immigration, has tried to make an issue of both legal and illegal immigration and even used the issues in an unsuccessful bid to become the Republican nominee for president. The Congress has been reexamining the current liberal immigration policy and considering ways of limiting benefits to the newly arrived immigrants. Meanwhile, increasingly the new immigrants as well as the early immigrants, particularly from non-European countries, are faced with a rising tide of anti-immigrant sentiment.

NOTES

1. Immigration and Naturalization Service, *Annual Reports* (Washington, D.C.:U.S. Government Printing Office, 1960–1979).

2. Harry H. L. Kitano and Roger Daniels, *Asian Americans: Emerging Minorities* (Englewood Cliffs, N.J.: Prentice Hall, 1995), 114.

3. Yo-jun Yun, "Early History of Korean Immigration to America," in *The Korean Diaspora*, ed. Hyung-Chan Kim (Santa Barbara, Calif.: Clio Press, 1979), 33–46.

4. Bong-youn Choy, *Koreans in America* (Chicago: Nelson Hall, 1979), 110.

5. Ibid., 124.

6. Juan L. Gonzales, Jr., *Racial and Ethnic Families in America* (Iowa: Kendall/Hunt Publishing Co., 1992), 73–74.

7. Warren Y. Kim, *Koreans in America* (Seoul: Po Chin Chai Printing Co., 1971), 26.

8. Choy, *Koreans in America*, 126.

9. Harry H. L. Kitano, Wai-tsang Yeung, Lynn Chai, and Herb Hatanaka, "Asian American Interracial Marriage," *Journal of Marriage and the Family* 46 (1984): 179–190.

10. Quoted in Elaine H. Kim and Eui-Young Yu, *East to America: Korean American Life Stories* (New York: The New Press), 298.

11. Sucheng Chan, "European and Asian Immigration into the United States in Comparative Perspective, 1820s to 1920s," in *Immigration Reconsidered*, ed. Virginia Yans-McLaughlin (New York: Oxford University Press, 1990), 48.

12. Pyong Gap Min, "Korean Americans," in *Asian Americans: Contemporary Trends and Issues*, ed. Pyong Gap Min (Thousand Oaks, Calif.: Sage Publications, 1995), 202–203.

13. Roger Daniels, *Coming to America* (New York: Harper Collins, 1990), 365.

14. Eui Hang Shin, "Interracially Married Korean Women in the United States: An Analysis Based on Hypergamy-Exchange Theory," in *Korean Women in Transition: At Home and Abroad,* ed. Eui-Young Yu and Earl H. Phillips (Los Angeles: Center for Korean-American and Korean Studies, California State University), 251.

15. For studies on Korean wives of Americans, see Bok-Lim Kim, "Casework with Japanese and Korean Wives of Americans," *Social Casework* 53 (1972): 273–279; Bok-Lim Kim, "Asian Wives of U.S. Servicemen: Women in Shadows," *Amerasia Journal* 5 (1977): 23–24; Daniel B. Lee, "Marital Adjustment Between Korean Women and American Servicemen," *Korean Observer* 20 (1989):321–352; B. W. Ratliff, H. F. Moon, and G. H. Bonacci, "Intercultural Marriage: The Korean American Experience," *Social Casework* 59 (1978):221–226; G. J. Jeong and W. Schumm, "Family Satisfaction in Korean/American Marriage: An Exploratory Study of the Perceptions of Korean Wives," *Journal of Comparative Family Studies* 21 (1990): 352–335.

16. Shin, "Interracially Married Korean Women in the United States: An Analysis Based on Hypergamy-Exchange Theory," 251; Kim, "Asian Wives of U.S. Servicemen: Women in Shadows," 23–24.

17. Ibid., 276–277.

18. Pyong Gap Min, "Korean Immigrant Entrepreneurship: A Multivariate Analysis," *Journal of Urban Affairs* 10 (1989): 197–212.

19. Doreen Carvajal, "Oldest Profession's Newest Home," *The New York Times*, (May 26, 1996): 29–30.

20. Won Moo Hurh, "Marginal Children of War: An Exploratory Study of American-Korean Children," *International Journal of Sociology of the Family* 2 (1972): 10–20.

21. Don Soo Kim, "How They Fared in American Homes: A Follow-Up Study of Adopted Korean Children," *Children Today* 6 (1977): 2–6, 31.

22. Don Soo Kim and Sookja P. Kim, "A Banana Identity: Asian American Adult Adoptees in America," Paper presented at the annual program meeting of the Council on Social Work Education, Washington, D.C. (Feb., 17, 1985).

23. Quoted in Kim and Yu, *East to America: Korean American Life Stories*, 309.

24. Ibid., 316.

25. Choy, *Koreans in America*, 222.

26. Immigration and Naturalization Service, *Annual Reports* (Washington, D.C.: U.S. Government Printing Office, 1950–1978).

27. Immigration and Naturalization Service, *Statistical Yearbook* (Washington, D.C.: U.S. Government Printing Office, 1979–1992).

28. Herbert Barringer, Robert W. Gardner, and Michael J. Levin, *Asians and Pacific Islanders in the United States* (New York: Russel Sage Foundation, 1993), 170, 187.

29. Min, "Korean Americans," 207–208.

30. U.S. Bureau of the Census, *1990 Census of Population, General Population Characteristics, United States* (Washington, D.C.: Government Printing Office, 1992).

31. Edna Bonacich, Ivan Light, and Charles Wong, "Koreans in Small Business," *Society* 14 (1977): 54–59.

32. U.S. Census of the Population and Housing, *Foreign Born Immigrants: Koreans* (Washington, D.C.: Government Printing Office, 1984).

33. Won Moo Hurh and Kwang Chung Kim, *Korean Immigrants in America* (Cranberry, N.J.: Fairleigh Dickinson University Press, 1984), 53.

34. Min, "Korean Americans," 206.

35. In-Jin Yoon, *The Social Origin of Korean Immigration to the United States from 1965 to the Present* (Honolulu: East-West Population Institute, 1993).

Chapter 2

MOTIVES FOR IMMIGRATION

As with many other immigrant groups, Korean immigrants' motives for leaving their homeland are manifold. Their desire to leave their country is largely the result of a careful assessment of circumstances and conditions which exist both in Korea and the United States. Those who have had to weigh social, economic, and political conditions in Korea vis-à-vis the United States before they decided to emigrate to the United States know how difficult the decision is to make. Their final decision is usually based on their perception of the many advantages of living in the adopted country when compared with the many disadvantages. Therefore, any marked improvement in living conditions in their homeland would have immediate effects on their decision to leave their country. Korean immigration peaked in the 1980s, for example, reaching an average yearly flow of 33,000 people whose destination was the United States when Korea's economy was growing but relatively unstable and while the government was still ruled by an authoritarian military regime. However, in the latter part of the 1980s and the early part of the 1990s Koreans experienced drastic improvement in their living standard as their country's economy blossomed. At the same time Koreans elected a civilian-controlled government in 1992, ending a 16–year-long military dictatorship. In 1991, over 26,518 Korean immigrants arrived in the United States, but in 1996 that number dropped to 18,185.[1] The emergence of a favorable political, economic, and social climate in Korean society had an immediate effect on Koreans' decision to emigrate.

No single motive stands out for Korean immigration into the United States. However, particular periods of time seem to have influenced Koreans' motives for immigration. For example, while economic motives dominated the reasons given by the first Koreans to immigrate to Hawaii, educational and professional career opportunities for professionals and students were the leading motives for Korean immigration in the 1970s. In the 1980s and the 1990s, however, economic opportunities for small entrepreneurs, as well as efforts to reunite families, were the primary motives for Korean immigration. And while there are a variety of motives for Korean immigrants coming to the United States, other factors, such as shifts in the U.S. government's policies, undoubtedly influenced the decisions of certain would-be immigrants.

As with many other immigrant groups, most Koreans who came to the United States did so with specific goals in mind. However, whether they were able to realize their original ambition is an entirely different matter. For example, many Korean immigrants who came to America with the intention to pursue professional careers, but who were unable to overcome the language barrier, professional restrictions, or other obstacles, were forced to find and pursue alternative careers, such as small-store owners. Currently, an estimated 75 percent of all Korean immigrants are small entrepreneurs. There has always been a discrepancy between what the immigrants' original intentions were and what they are currently doing. Frequently, one hears Korean immigrant cab drivers or swap-meet stall owners complain that they did not come to the United States to do these kinds of work. On the other hand, there are some Korean immigrants who wanted to be small store owners but became accountants and ministers instead.

SOME COMPARISON OF MOTIVES FOR IMMIGRATION OF EARLY AND RECENT KOREA IMMIGRANTS

The motives of Koreans who have immigrated to the United States since 1965 are strikingly different from the motives of those immigrants who came to Hawaii in the early 1900s. Contemporary Korean immigrants, unlike the early immigrants, are rarely destitute. They have not come to America to escape poverty as the early immigrants did. The early immigrants had a "sojourner" mentality; never fully participating in American life, they dreamed of their return to Korea, and participated in clubs and activities that kept the homeland alive in their thoughts. Their main motive for immigration was purely economic; most of them left their homeland reluctantly but with the belief that their "sojourn" would be of short duration. Their love of their homeland and their desire to return to it remained strong throughout the length of their stay in America. Recent immigrants, however, brought their families with them when they came to America. Many of them had long-range goals in mind before they set sail for America. Of course, the economic motive was but one of many on the minds of contemporary Korean immigrants: many had a desire to seek careers in professions or else to start businesses of their own.

Then, there is the political motive for leaving Korea. Although the early Korean immigrants who came to Hawaii were politically active when Korea was annexed by Japan in 1910, they did not leave their homeland because they were discontented with the political climate in Korea. Many of the more recent immigrants, however, particularly professionals and students, or intelligentsia who valued civil rights and political freedom, disliked the authoritarian political regime created by military dictatorship that prevailed in Korea from the 1960s through the 1980s, and one of their primary reasons for coming to America was to live in a free and democratic society. During periods of political instability in the military-run government, some high government officials and ranking military officers found it expedient to seek political asylum in the United States. The irony is that, while the early immigrants wished to return to their homeland and help rebuild a democratic society, many of the immigrants in the 1970s and 1980s have apparently chosen to abandon Korea.

Finally, society in America was much more racially and ethnically segregated in the early part of the twentieth century. This meant that early Korean immigrants found their economic and educational opportunities severely restricted. After 1970, however, when most of the recent immigrants began to come to the United States in large numbers, American society was much more open in terms of race relations and receptivity to immigrants. As a result, the recent immigrants quickly learned they would have many more chances to be enterprising than were open to the earlier immigrants. Consequently, unlike the early immigrants, the recent immigrants to America have many more reasons to want to stay in this country.

It is easy to understand and admire the strength and resolve of the Korean laborers who migrated to Hawaii at the turn of the century because of the many social and economic hardships they faced, but grasping the motives for immigration of recent Korean immigrants becomes more difficult, not only because of the increase in the number of immigrants, which makes understanding their motives for immigration more difficult, but also because the newcomers are continually influenced by rapid changes in political and economic circumstances and by shifts in public opinion in both the United

States and Korea. Particularly, changes in the American people's perception of immigrants result in shifts in U.S. immigration law with far-reaching consequences for people seeking to immigrate. In light of the strict U.S. immigration guidelines and quotas and other obstacles built into immigration law that Korean wives of American servicemen had to overcome in order to follow their husbands back to the U.S. immediately following the Korean War is a measure of their determination. The guidelines and quota system in effect at that time specified what kinds and how many immigrants from Asian countries were permitted to enter the United States. The question always remains, however, whether the U.S. government preference for certain kinds of immigrants necessarily results in attracting the kinds of immigrants the U.S. government originally intended to attract. Right after the Korean War, the American government permitted Korean students to study at American universities but only if they returned to their homeland; however, many of them managed to become naturalized American citizens. The 1976 Immigration Act prohibited professionals from coming to the United States, particularly physicians, unless they had genuine job offers from U.S. employers, but many came to the United States as students or trainees and stayed on.

THE DECLINE IN PROFESSIONAL OCCUPATIONS
AMONG THE IMMIGRANTS IN THE 1970s

The decline in the number of immigrants with professional credentials beginning in the latter part of the 1970s and the rise in the number of entrepreneurial immigrants in the 1980s seems to have been affected by changing political and economic circumstances in both the United States and Korea. Some of the changes that occurred in the United States and which directly influenced Korean immigration in the early 1970s include the fact that the United States entered a period of recession with a corresponding high unemployment rate. Fearing further deterioration of the U.S. economy, the federal government passed the Eilberg Act and the Health Professions Educational Assistance Act in 1976. The Eilberg Act required alien professionals to have job offers from U.S. employers before they could gain admission as legal immigrants. The Health Professions Educational Assistance Act removed physicians and surgeons from eligible categories of labor certification. Beginning in the late 1970s, the U.S. Department of Labor discouraged other types of occupational immigration by not issuing labor permits to many otherwise well-qualified prospective immigrants. This meant that, rather than restricting by race and ethnicity, the United States had begun restricting immigration by occupation. As a result, immigration of Koreans in certain occupations almost came to a halt in 1976. However, people with professional occupations were able to find ways around the new obstacle. For instance, if they had family already established in the U.S., they could take advantage of the family connection or they could marry an American citizen, and there were various other business connections they could use. They could appeal for admission for the purpose of receiving further training, or to acquire an American professional degree or certificate. Once here, they could always hope to find employment in their professional field.

Meanwhile, the Korean economy experienced tremendous growth. With Korea an important economic force in Asia beginning in the mid-1970s, and with an expanding international trade, there was a corresponding clamor for professional people in Korea. As a result of the economic boom, many potential professional immigrants decided to remain in their homeland. An expanding economy makes it possible to absorb some professionals, technical, and skilled workers. Furthermore, the Korean government dampened interest in emigration among the well-to-do by amending its emigration policy in 1975. Specifically, the new law prevented persons owning properties valued at more than $100,000, military officers and retired generals, and high-ranking government officials, incumbent or retired, including national assembly members, judges, presidents of national corporations, and other similar status from leaving the country.[2] Although the amendment of 1975 was not specifically aimed at doctors, engineers, professors, and other specific professions, many of them were included because of the positions they held in the military, the government, or business. If a professional person somehow evaded the Korean law, he or she probably ran afoul of the Eilberg Act or the Health Professions Educational Assistance Act. Yet thousands of professionals were persuaded to immigrate to the United States largely because of the appeal of their families to start all over, so to speak, in a new line of work in a new country.

A third likely reason which has influenced professional Koreans to remain in Korea probably stems from the many stories carried in the mass media about difficulties immigrants were encountering in America, as well as tales told by their immigrant friends. They heard that many Korean professionals were unable to convert their Korean credentials into U.S. licenses and, therefore, were unable to practice their profession. In addition, the difficulties of mastering English and speaking with sufficient fluency made it hard, if not impossible, for them to practice their profession. They also learned that there was a strong prejudice against them among the American professionals; moreover, there was an abiding distrust among American professionals toward non-American professional degrees, particularly degrees from Asian universities. Rumors and facts about troublesome experiences which Korean professionals were encountering in America reached many likely professional immigrants and led them to reconsider their decision to immigrate to the United States.

Although these three reasons are by no means the only ones which slowed the number of professional Koreans applying for admission into the United States since the mid-1970s, changing the U.S. immigration law in 1976, rapid growth of the Korean economy, apprehension by Korean professionals about the feasibility of utilizing their professional skills in America all contributed to slow the flow of professional immigrants. However, one must not forget that many professionals and other middle-class Koreans are still immigrating to the United States, not necessarily to pursue their profession, but with the intention of finding some other line of work. Some argue that continued growth of the Korean economy in the 1990s will eventually improve quality of life for all Koreans and the consequence of Korea's increasing prosperity will not only keep professionals in Korea, but will also lure back professionals who are already in the United States. Whether this trend of reverse migration ever takes place remains to be seen.

THE RISE OF ENTREPRENEURIAL IMMIGRANTS IN THE 1980s AND 1990s

Even as the number of professional and highly skilled immigrants declined, entrepreneurial Korean immigrants increased rapidly after the 1980s. About 90 percent of Korean immigrants who have been admitted to the United States each year since the passage of the 1976 Immigration Act were based on family reunification.[3] Although a large segment of the immigrants of the 1980s were entrepreneurs who tended to be from lower socioeconomic backgrounds, this group included people with diverse occupations, including those middle-class immigrants who were concerned about limited social mobility in Korea. The economic expansion experienced by most Koreans also created great class—and status—gulfs between professional middle class, white-color workers, and those who did not get to partake of the economic boom, such as manual workers, and farmers. Yet the middle class worried about the security of their position as the rapid expansion of the Korean economy helped create a new rapidly expanding, urban, middle class. As a direct result, many in this class experienced a widening gap between their expectations of upward mobility and the limited opportunities available in Korea.[4]

In the 1980s, Koreans' main motive for immigration seems to have been to secure some sort of business, usually one that is labor intensive. They were invariably invited by their relatives who already owned an established business in a major metropolitan area. There is a double benefit from this arrangement. By settling near kinfolk and friends, the new immigrant received not only economic advice from their relatives, but social support as well. If they chose Los Angeles, for instance, they not only had the reassurance of being near their kinfolk, they became part of the largest Korean-speaking economy in the United States. Light and Bonacich call this process of migration chain migration.[5] Although there are many reasons why Koreans migrate to large cities such as Los Angeles, New York City, Chicago, and Atlanta, the concept of chain migration helps us understand one of the major reasons why Korean immigrants concentrate in large cities or urban areas, and this behavior is directly linked to immigrants' motives for coming to the United States. A Korean electronic repair shop owner in Los Angeles comments:

> When my sister invited me to immigrate to America, I was very much concerned with how I could make a living in the United States because I couldn't speak English and I didn't have a particular skill to sell except some knowledge about electronics. My sister told me that I didn't have to speak English as I will be working in a Korean town and most of my customers will be Korean. I opened an electronic repair shop in a Korean town when I arrived in this country. Indeed most of my customers are Korean, and I am able to run my business without much knowledge of English. I am barely making a living by running an electronic repair shop. But I can't relocate to anywhere outside the Korean community because of my poor English speaking ability.

There are, however, many Korean merchants whose customers are mainly non-Koreans. For example, Korean shopkeepers in Venice Beach, California, deal with the general public and have acquired some basic knowledge of English in order to conduct ordinary business transactions. Yet over sixty stores operated by Koreans are concentrated side by side along the beach. They have established a business network with other Korean store owners for the purpose of mutual support. In the event that one shop owner should decide to move on to other things in other communities, he will in all probability sell his business to some Korean newcomer. This seems to be a customary business practice among Koreans. Korean-owned businesses, such as laundries, restaurants, gas stations, and small supermarkets, even those located outside Korean enclaves, still depend on establishing a Korean business network as these businesses are frequently bought and sold through the mediation efforts of other Korean entrepreneurs. Therefore, Koreans who are planning to emigrate to the United States usually acquire not only knowledge of the feasibility of making a living with limited knowledge of English, but also learn about buying affordable businesses through a Korean business network or through their families or friends.

For the many newly arrived Koreans, the social support offered by their compatriots is sometimes almost as important as economic survival. Establishing a connection with members of the Korean community is quite easy. All one has to do is reach out to other Koreans at churches, at sport events, at picnics, and at many other Korean community-sponsored activities. The comparative ease in establishing connections is an important consideration for immigrants trying to reach a decision about coming to America, and it may help explain why Koreans tend to congregate in certain locations. A Korean laundry store owner in the Washington, D.C. metropolitan area relates:

> For a few years after my arrival in America, I was frenetic about making sure my laundry business survived. My wife and my two children assisted me in my business to minimize overhead and offer streamlined services. In spite of hectic years establishing my business, I was fortunate to have my family and to be a part of Korean community. I seldom missed Korean community functions. Although I was not religious in Korea, I am seriously involved with Korean church activities. Now I am a deacon of my church and a choir conductor. I don't think I can relocate to any other part of the United States where there is no Korean community, because it is too lonely to do so. My sister-in-law and her husband are living in a small town in Pennsylvania and they told me they would move to a large city if not for their jobs. My cousin and his family are immigrating to America. I have warned them many times not to settle in a small town where few Koreans live.

For most Koreans who grew up in a close-knit family environment in a small country, coping with their social and cultural isolation and loneliness and being unable to find a friendly face is very taxing, particularly for those who have limited knowledge of English. The stress of living in isolation can lead to depression, mental stress, and sometimes odd behavior. For example, it is not unusual for Koreans who settle in small towns for business or career reasons to pick up a local telephone book and look up all Korean surnames they can think of and then call these strangers at random. In large cities, where most Korean immigrants concentrate, Korean organizations, ranging from high school alumni associations to golf and to professional associations abound. These associations and organizations provide important mechanisms for coping with social isolation for the unassimilated Korean immigrants. It often happens that people thinking of becoming immigrants frequently ask their relatives many questions about social isolation in America as it is a very important factor in reaching their decision about their emigration.

GENERAL PUSH AND PULL FACTORS

There are some commonly mentioned reasons for immigration which cut across the ranks of professional immigrants in the 1970s and entrepreneurial immigrants since the 1980s, although some reasons are more frequently mentioned by immigrants who came to America during a particular time period. They include: economic factors, educational opportunities for their children and themselves, concern with their families' security, and politics. Unfavorable economic and political conditions and lack of educational opportunities in Korea set the stage for tens of thousands of Koreans immigrating to the United States every year where better economic prospects, a more stable political climate, and educational opportunities exist. However, not all Korean immigrants are equally concerned with these reasons. To some, one particular issue is paramount, while others weighed a combination of reasons before they decided to emigrate to America.

Economic Push and Pull

As early as 1911, Fairchild, in his study of immigration to the United States, observed that economics was the earliest and by far the most important cause of immigration.[6] This is particularly true in the case of Korean immigrants. The desire to improve their economic condition was far more influential than others in their decision to leave their country. In his study of reasons for Koreans immigrating to the United States in Chicago and Los Angeles, Yoon found, among other reasons, the appeal of economic opportunities in the United States was the dominant reason for Korean immigration.[7] Every year tens of thousands of Koreans graduate from liberal arts colleges and universities and professional schools in Korea. South Korea, however, which is about half the size of Florida, was unable to absorb these highly educated young people into the labor force, particularly during the 1970s when Korea was still in the early stage of industrialization. Tens of thousands of nurses, medical technicians, and physicians chose to emigrate to Europe and the United States. From 1963 to 1974, 17,000 nurses and miners migrated to West Germany.[8] In spite of the expansion of the Korean economy, according to the Korean Ministry of Education, about 33 percent of male college graduates from 1981 to 1990 could not find employment after graduation and about 54 percent of female college graduates could not find employment during the same period.[9] Korean college graduates had similar difficulties in finding employment after their graduation between 1970 and 1980. For these college graduates, finding new employment opportunities in the United States has always been one of young immigrants' primary motives for immigration. In many cases, almost half of the elite medical college graduates left their homeland to practice medicine in the United States. This is a brain drain on a large scale.

The opportunities for female health professionals were further restricted in such a traditional, gender segregated society. Gabaccia observes that the varying rates of female immigration to the United States always has been closely connected with economic and political conditions, the customary division of labor and authority in the households, and the functioning of social networks in immigrants' home country.[10] Because Korean women are prone to suffer from gender inequality and discrimination in practically every institution and are eager to find a place where the gender barrier is less pronounced in the work place and in society, the United States presents an attractive choice. A professional woman who graduated from Seoul National University and came to the United States in 1960 to pursue graduate study comments:

> I looked for a job everywhere in Korea after college before I came to the United States. There was absolutely no job for me. I was willing to take any kind of job, even a clerical job. I am certain that my gender was an important factor for my failure in obtaining a job because pursuing a professional career was not common for women. For women, getting married and starting a family was a norm for even college graduates. In the United States I always had a job. In graduate school, I had a research assistantship. After my graduate degree in biology, I had an immediate job offer. Ever since then, I have always had a job

and never been unemployed. I am grateful to America for what it has given to me. Although I received an advanced degree from an American university to pursue a career, I am always reminded of how lucky I am every time I visit South Korea and see my female college classmates who have not utilized their college education.

In a highly competitive society where there may be few job openings every year, Korean college graduates and professionals must try every tactic to find a job. The names of universities, even high schools, from which a person has graduated, one's regional origin, knowing someone who is important in government or in a corporation, even the cost of searching and finding employment frequently determine one's employability. For those who are salaried employees in large bureaucratic organizations, promotion and pay raises may be few and far between. It is common for senior employees to stay in place as long as they can because Korean corporations have been very slow to adopt such practices as pension plans and social security, things most American workers take for granted. Some retired senior employees, who are still in their early sixties, have immigrated to America and started new careers as employees of Korean stores or else open their own stores because they cannot offord to retire in Korea.

Chances for economic mobility in America appealed to all segment of Koreans. Professionals were willing to take a chance coming to America for the professional opportunities this nation offers. Even when they could not practice their profession in America because of problems getting the appropriate governing body to accept their Korean credentials, they were ready to try their luck at any kind of business or work. Occasionally one hears the tale of an immigrant whose life takes an unusual twist. That was the case when a Korean dentist was unable to practice his profession; he began working as a janitor and did other odd jobs and eventually saved enough money to buy a large apartment complex.

The entrepreneurial immigrants, however, frequently cited unprofitable businesses, a lack of economic opportunities, and little chance of economic mobility as their reasons for immigration. Korea's business management has been more centralized with industrial power more highly concentrated in big business groups. Big business groups dominate the financial system, making it hard for small-sized and medium-sized companies to get funding. Weak or lax enforcement of fair-trade laws makes small companies vulnerable to predatory practices. Although the big groups were the backbone of the first stage of Korea's economic evolution, they have stifled entrepreneurship and creativity. Entrepreneurs who had operated medium-sized businesses in Korea mention that selling products to wholesale buyers rarely involved cash but promissory notes because the buyers had so little cash. Even medium-sized businesses, such as engineering firms or construction companies, found it costly to get cash to meet daily expenses. The cost of doing business was just too high in Korea. For them, coming to America was just an alternative business opportunity in the never-ending quest for economic security. Some of these entrepreneurs also seem less apprehensive than one might expect about their chances for success in America. A small-business entrepreneur commented that he came to America because he had nothing much to lose in Korea, and he supposed that, if he did not succeed in business in America, he could always go back to Korea.

Elderly Koreans are often unable to save enough money to retire. They could either continue to work or they could joint their children in America, In fact, some elderly immigrants have been very reluctant to emigrate to the United States knowing they would not only be dependent on their children, they would face great difficulty in adjusting to a new culture, not to mention the fact that few are able to speak English. An elderly gentleman in Los Angeles remarks:

> I never thought I would ever come to America and spend the rest of my life in a strange land. I knew I would be faced with a language barrier, have to make new friends, adjust to new culture, and live with my daughter, son-in-law, and their children. I knew also I would lose my freedom and independence. Yet I didn't have much choice but to come to America because I have little if any pension or retirement funds to draw on. Furthermore, my health was deteriorating and I was not getting adequate health care. Now in America, I don't have to worry about health care because it is covered by Medicaid. Also, my daughter and her husband are working hard and making a living. My wife and I babysit for our grand children. I miss my native country terribly. But what choice do I have? I would like to visit Korea often. Again, it costs a lot of money and I can't afford to do it.

Not all entrepreneurial immigrants had unsuccessful businesses or careers in Korea. There were a few successful businessmen who decided to immigrate to the United States with their families because they were too successful. They left their homeland when they found maintaining a high-profile image of success became too burdensome. A businessman in New York explains:

Korea is a small country. If you are successful in business, everybody in the community knows you are wealthy. Friends, relatives, and business colleagues respect you and sometimes kowtow to you. At the same time, you must also maintain a certain life-style to show that you are indeed successful by driving an expensive car and living in a big house. After awhile you begin to realize that keeping up with a high standard of living for the sake of others becomes burdensome. Yet it is difficult not to do once you are in that mold. Remember, Koreans are not only status conscious but also very provincial and almost everybody somehow belongs to a particular group or groups based on connections, which includes far reaching distant relatives, high school and college alumni, place of birth, and any other connections you can think of. Once you are known as a wealthy or successful businessman in your circle, you have to keep up your life-style commensurate with your reputation lest you want to lose your "face." America is a big country and you are free to do whatever you want to do without feeling peer pressure. This aspect of American life motivated me to come to America.

On the other hand, some immigrants were poorly paid salaried workers, such as office workers, school teachers, salespeople, middle-level soldiers, middle-level government officials, and social workers, who came to America in the hope of an improved salary and better working conditions. Some of these salaried employees struggled constantly for a livelihood as their salary seldom kept up with the high cost of living. They did not come to America determined to be merchants operating businesses in Hispanic and black neighborhoods. Many of them actually ended up doing what originally they did not intend to do. It is not unusual that laundry operators, small grocery store owners, restaurant owners, and liquor store owners are college graduates who left careers in teaching, or as government bureaucrats, and middle managers in large corporations. To them, the possibility of securing financial stability in America is much more important than holding onto their careers in Korea.

Not all entrepreneurs who came to America wanted to stay in America. There have been a few immigrants who said that they have lived in America as business representatives of Korean companies for many years. During this time, their children were born in the United States and became acculturated to the American way of life. Returning to Korea with their Americanized children proved to be too much of an adjustment for their children; consequently, they decided to stay in America permanently. Still a few others in the import and export business mentioned that becoming a permanent resident or American citizen would give them an advantage in their business, although they are not much interested in living in America permanently after their retirement. Some of these resident aliens make frequent trips to Korea, and their affinity with Korea remains strong.

American capitalism built by immigrants from all over the world continues to attract immigrants who have entrepreneurial spirit and who are willing to work long, hard hours. Most Korean immigrants know what difficulties they will encounter in America. According to a sample of U.S. visa applicants in Seoul in 1986, the majority expected little improvement in their economic status in the short run, but expected to do well over the longer term. In fact, the three lures of the United States were higher wages, rewards for hard work and ability, and a more favorable political environment.[11] The Korean entrepreneurial immigrants who were lured to this country in the 1980s and 1990s fits into a rather predictable pattern. They usually buy labor-intensive businesses such as laundries, restaurants, liquor stores, or vegetable stands either in a Korean community, or in another minority community. The chance of building a new life and a new business on their own is extremely challenging and difficult, yet worth the risk. A former business executive who operates a laundry in Chicago describes his elation at finally being an independent entrepreneur, although his business does not have the same status as his previous occupation. In spite of the fact that almost everything seems designed to exclude the newcomer, many Korean immigrants still believe America is the land of opportunity, one of the reasons they were attracted to America in the first place. Nugent notes that America's exceptionalism, that is, the exceptional capacity of America to absorb people of diverse backgrounds because of its vast available lands, had always appealed to potential immigrants from all over the world in the latter part of nineteenth century,[12] and it is equally attractive to Korean immigrants who are willing to endure various setbacks until they reach their goals.

Educational Push and Pull

The second most frequently mentioned reason for immigrating to the United States was education for their children and themselves. Many Korean professionals, such as college professors, researchers, medical doctors, engineers, dentists, and others came to America with the intention of studying at American universities and then returning to Korea. However, many remained in the United States and brought their families to America. As a research professor at one of the elite universities in Korea mentioned:

> I came to America to study at an American university because research facilities were not adequate in Korea. After the completion of my study, I decided to remain in the United States and bring my children to this country for their education. Although I am no longer in academic line of work—in fact I am a gardener—I am happy because my children are getting an excellent education at the University of California.

Thousands of Korean students come to the United States to study. According to the Institute of International Education, there were 37,130 Korean students studying in the United States during the academic year of 1996–97.[13] A large proportion of the students who came to America to study since the 1950s have decided to remain in the United States after their graduation, although the proportion of students remaining in America dwindled in the 1980s and 1990s as demand for professionals in Korea increased with its rapid industrialization. Again, the motive of Korean students for entering American universities include a variety of reasons. Some enter American universities and professional schools to get better jobs at American firms. Some enter American universities because tuition and fees are sometimes not only cheaper than they would be in Korean universities, but also students are able to choose fields of study not available in Korea. Further, students who failed to enter one of the top universities in Korea because they were unable to pass the rigorous entrance examination and selection process look to American universities which are at least as reputable as well-known universities in Korea.

Many immigrants who came to the United States in the 1980s and 1990s because of economic opportunity stated that their children's education was as important a reason for immigration as their economic reason. They learned that their children could be educated at prestigious American universities for less expense than they could at the top Korean universities. Not only did they discover that American state universities are cheaper, they learned these schools are as good as noted universities in Korea, if not better. They also knew that if their children did well in school, there were plenty of opportunities to receive scholarships even at the best universities. This would lighten the financial burden on their parents who strongly believe that educating their children is their major responsibility. Some parents immigrated to the United States purely for the sake of their children's education. A recently retired immigrant in the Washington, D.C. area remarks:

> My child failed his college entrance examination to enter one of the three best universities in Korea. My son was not much interested in entering one of the second- or third-rated universities in Korea as he knows he is not going to "make it" after graduating from one of these universities because they are not the "right" kind of universities. When I learned that my son could enter a very good university in the U. S. with his high school grades, my wife and I decided to emigrate to the United States with him. My son enrolled in one of the top prestigious state universities, and we are very happy with his studies and with his university. Unlike Korea, there are so many excellent public and private universities from which a student can choose if she or he has very good grades. Now the problem is my wife and I have to look for something to do. Boredom is killing us.

Immigrants' efforts and sacrifices on behalf of their children's education have not gone unnoticed. In the last decade or so, the high percentage of sons and daughters of Korean immigrants who have graduated from American universities has been well publicized in America. In many ways, their children's achievements have fulfilled one of their fondest wishes. In fact, Light and Bonacich believe that one of the reasons, besides chain migration, why Koreans are attracted to the Los Angeles area is that California offers a superior state-run university system at reasonable cost, and they believe this factor persuaded many potential Korean immigrants to come to the Los Angeles area.[14]

Political Push and Pull

The third most frequently mentioned reason which motivated Korean immigrants to leave Korea was political repression, instability of the government, and a dislike of military-dominated authoritarian regimes. Although the difficulty in dealing with an unreliable and repressive government was more frequently expressed by those who immigrated in the 1970s than in the 1980s, anti-government sentiments were expressed by both groups of immigrants. Granted that, in most cases, their antipathy toward the authoritarian government did not stem directly from their own experiences, the idea that the government has been controlled for almost a half century by one devious ruler after another is difficult for many otherwise patriotic immigrants to accept. They still remember how the authoritarian military regimes ran the government through suppression of dissenting political activities, stifling citizen unrest, and by control of consumer goods and censorship of the media. The military government of Park Chung Hee in the 1960s nationalized banks, borrowed money abroad, and funneled it at cheap rates to favored export industries. The recent exposure of seamy symbiotic relationships between large corporations and the government ended with the imprisonment of the last two military generals turned presidents.

Still Korean economic policy under the civilian president since 1992 is a command economy that has often crossed the hazy line between industrial policy and central planning, with industrial power concentrated in huge privately owned business conglomerates that took cues from government. This often created doubt in the minds of Koreans about the stability of the Korean economy as the industrial complex depends so much on government favors. People blame both business conglomerates and their government when they feel the widening gap in earnings of average citizens and that of the business elite. In January 23, 1997, Hanbo Steel Industry Co., a flagship of the Hanbo group, the nation's fourteenth-largest conglomerate, went bankrupt after building up $6 billion in debt, mostly from government-controlled bank loans. Ten people, including a Cabinet minister, were indicted a month later on charges of taking or giving millions of dollars in bribes to arrange the loans. As a result, radical students demanded the resignation of the president Kim Young-Sam. He publicly apologized on national television for a bribery scandal wracking his administration.

For many decades, Koreans have been citing or recalling cases of how some people became rich and powerful through political favoritism and lived in luxury and comfort, while average workers either struggled for a bare existence, or else clung desperately to their slipping middle-class status. Those who immigrated prior to 1990 recall how difficult it was to find employment in the government or private sector without knowing someone influential in government or in industry. Finding employment, getting a promotion, running for political office, and operating businesses are largely done through connections and pull. Who you know and how much you can afford to spend often decide everything. Those who didn't have the right connections, proper educational credentials, and family background felt doomed to failure in trying to climb the economic ladder and sought to emigrate to the United States in the hopes of bypassing these barriers.

Entrepreneurs also expressed the belief that their unhappiness with an authoritarian government was one of the leading reasons they had for immigrating. Although most of entrepreneurs of medium-sized and small-sized businesses probably never felt any direct interference from the government, they were fully aware of how large corporations operated in collusion with the government, and they probably perceived they were left out. Small business entrepreneurs also remember how they used to give gangs or other seedy characters a small amount of "lunch money" to "protect" their businesses. Getting permits or licenses for their businesses and passing various inspections for their business operations also required "lunch money" for officials who were supposed to issue permits and licenses. A dry cleaning store owner in the suburb of Washington, D.C. area, who came to America in the early 1980s comments:

> When I opened a dry cleaning store, a fire department official came to my store to inspect for fire hazards. After checking every corner of the store and dry cleaning equipment, he told me to clean or dust off the top of some of the machines. He said he would be back in two weeks for reinspection. I thought I was going to be ready with "lunch money" when he returned for another inspection. But I didn't have to. The inspector came back two weeks later and inspected my store again with courtesy and told me that everything was all right and left. I began to realize how lucky I was living in America without worrying about how to deal with government officials. Most Americans take a small matter like this for granted; it was not so when I was living in Korea.

An example of an egregious violation of his property rights was recalled by an entrepreneur who came to America in 1981. He was prompted to come to America when in 1966 he was forced to relinquish all his property rights to the government. With nothing to lose he came to America when his sister sent him an invitation. Although it is difficult to gauge how extensively this type of drastic maneuver by the government had affected property owners at that time, many entrepreneurs who emigrated in the 1970s and even the early 1980s were discontented with their government's dealing with citizens' personal assets and property.

Their mistrust of the government is not only deeply embedded in the minds of average entrepreneurs who immigrated to America prior to the 1990s, but also in the minds of otherwise successful industrialists. Their reasons for immigrating to America were not so much based on economics as it was on their suspicion and fear of their government and its continual instability. A successful businessman in New York City explains his reasons for coming to America:

I was a military officer, a government employee, and an executive of a large corporation. I accumulated some wealth, although it would not amount to too much compared to other wealthy Americans. But I was not comfortable living in Korea with my wealth. Although the Korean economy and political system have significantly improved since the election of a civilian president in 1992 and the country is moving toward being a democratic nation, I can't forget how corrupt our political system was under an authoritarian regime and how the economy was controlled by a few who had connection with high ranking government officials. I always felt that I would live more peacefully in my retirement years in the United States than in Korea as I would not be encumbered in my day-to-day activity by anyone. I intend to invest in American companies and live on the profit from the investment.

Even in the 1970s, there were rumors and stories circulating among Koreans about wealthy Koreans immigrating to the United States because they were concerned that the Park regime might collapse at any time, and how a change of government might create civil chaos, putting their lives and wealth at risk. Because they could not openly transfer large sums of money into the United States, they were forced to resort to a variety of stratagems. For instance, some smuggled money into the United States by something as simple as hiding it in pickle jars because the Korean government, as is true with many governments, had restrictions on the amount of cash one could take out of the country. They were also believed to legally send as much money as they could to their relatives. Once they were safely in the United States, they often invested in such things as apartment buildings, restaurants, and other businesses with cash they had smuggled into the country. When these wealthy Koreans suddenly began driving expensive cars and living in expensive homes in the most exclusive areas of the city, average Korean immigrants were stunned, but the experience reaffirmed their beliefs that a few people who had connections in high places in the government made that kind of money in dishonorable ways and then fled to the United States.

American democracy, freedom of speech and press, and respect for individual rights are frequently cited reasons given by Korean immigrants in the 1970s and 1980s for being drawn to America. Some confessed that their understanding of America was heavily influenced by the pictures they saw in the mass media while they were growing up, especially in movies which portrayed America as rich, freedom-loving, and glamorous.[15] For them, coming to America was a form of wish fulfillment which they had harbored from their childhood. Although some were aware that their original perception of America as an ideal democratic country was unrealistic, many pointed to significant differences between American democracy and the form of government they were accustomed to in Korea. Words like "democracy," "freedom," "human rights," and "due process" are frequently used when they cite their reasons for their attraction to the United States. A Korean immigrant, who came to America in 1975, observes: "The fascination of America for the Korean immigrants is to come to a free and abundant country, and breathe in its air of freedom, and to make plans for a new life such that they are changing their destinies, which were fatalistically determined by tradition and history in the old country."[16]

For many Korean immigrants who immigrated to America before 1990, American democracy is a new experience. The civilian-controlled military and police, accountability of government officials, stability of the government, and the power of voters taken for granted by most American-born citizens, are new to many Korean immigrants. The immigrants' perception of American democracy which includes the civility of police officers, standard procedures in acquiring business permits or driver's licenses, the ability to lodge complaints against government officials, the right to due process, and paying taxes based on earnings with no regard for the status of the individual are fascinating to most Korean immigrants, at least in the initial stage of their lives in the United States. An immigrant who came to America in 1960 recalled that, one night shortly after he had arrived in America, a Korean friend invited him to take a stroll in Chicago. As they walked, he saw two police officers coming toward them. His friend quickly reassured him: "Don't worry, they are just civil servants." Although his friend's statement has no significance to most Americans, he felt he tasted democracy for the first time when he heard the word *servant,* and he still cherishes that word after living in America for thirty-seven years. Immigrants' impressions of American democracy and justice are quickly relayed back to potential Korean immigrants in Korea. While American democracy is not perfect, it became one of the motives for Koreans coming to America in the 1960s, 1970s, and even the 1980s.

Security Push and Pull

The fourth push factor frequently cited by the immigrants was their concern for security and peace. Those old enough vividly remember the Korean War, initiated when the North Korean government suddenly invaded South Korea. The fact that Korea was divided and the South was continually threatened by Communist North Korea with the result that there was the perennial presence of U.N. soldiers, constantly reminded citizens that Korea has never been neither secure nor fully independent. Furthermore, even before the beginning of World War II, the government always had been headed by either a corrupt civilian president or by authoritarian ex-military generals who were inflexible and self-centered. Frequent demonstrations in the streets for political democracy and human rights are stitched into the fabric of everyday life. In short, political unrest was a staple of Korean life. The unrest was punctuated by periodic military coups and arrests and trials of high government officials adding to the sense of uncertainty and insecurity in the minds of many citizens. In a small country such as South Korea, every turnover of governments brings about new uncertainties in the people as they wait to find out what the new government will be like. Although the election of President Kim Young-Sam in 1992, the nation's first genuine civilian government in thirty-two years, has heralded the establishment of a "New Korea," immigrants who came to America before 1990 remained pessimistic about their future given the long history of unstable governments in Korea. Their need for security for themselves and their families, especially their children, is more important for those who are older, and who are well educated, than it is for the young and less well educated.

If some Korean immigrants were uneasy living in the halting democracy of South Korea while under constant threat of invasion from North Korea, the United States has always held out the promise of a safe haven for immigrants and their families. The United States' economic and political stability, together with its super power status, holds great appeal for many potential immigrants, particularly for those immigrants who had lived through the Korean War, the instability of their nation's shaky government, and the forced division of their homeland. Many immigrants stated that the United States symbolizes stability, security, peace, and political calm, which gave them tremendous psychological comfort, particularly for those with growing children. The immigrants were told while they were in Korea that, once their economic struggle is over, the immigrants could find peace of mind in America. To live with peace of mind has an enormous psychological appeal to many Koreans and gave added impetus for emigration. An immigrant who came to America in the early part of the 1980s and lives in Arizona expresses this sentiment:

> Although my wife and I are working in the laundry department in a big hotel for more than twelve years, we feel very comfortable living in America. With our salaries, we bought a house which was auctioned

by the federal government at reasonable price, bought a nice used car, and sent our child to a community college. In Korea, I remember that our family was always concerned with the shortage of rice. In America, rice is one of the cheapest food items. I keep on buying bags of rice every time I shop for groceries and accumulate them in our pantry. Somehow I feel comfortable knowing I have enough rice in the house. Furthermore, I don't have to worry about job security, politics, status, congestion, pollution, college tuition for our kid, and many other things, which I used to be concerned about in Korea. In Korea, everybody, particularly men, talked politics. Who is going to run for president and what drastic changes he will bring about to the government if a new president is elected? Gossip compounded with worries are major topics of everyday conversation. In this country, I don't waste my energy on Korean politics, although occasionally some of my relatives egg me on to participate in Korean political talks. I just wish they would leave me alone.

Family Invitation

Immigration through family invitation is, on its face, really quite simple. A Korean who has become a naturalized citizen writes to a relative still living in Korea inviting him or her to come to the U.S. Brothers invite their brothers and sisters, sisters invite their brothers and sisters, husbands and wives invite their spouses, children invite their parents, parents invite their children. This process of family reunion through invitation began with the liberalization of the U.S. immigration law in 1965. But the family invitation is not necessarily a motivational factor in itself, although an invitation from their relatives in America may trigger some reluctant potential immigrants to seriously consider emigration to America. For example, an auto mechanic said he liked America because of what the mass media told him about it and from letters he received from his brother. While he had thought of visiting America, he had never taken any action in that direction. Thus when his brother suggested that he immigrate to America, he remembered how excited he became at the thought of living in America. However, in most cases, an invitation from their relatives in America is simply offering an opportunity for Koreans to emigrate to the United States. Once the potential immigrants receive an invitation from their relatives in America, they carefully examine the pros and cons of emigration in terms of economic opportunities, educational chances, political climate, security, and other numerous conditions before they decide to emigrate to the United States. For economically hard-pressed Koreans, an invitation from their relatives in America is in many cases a godsend. This is also true for college students who are struggling to pay tuition at an expensive Korean university.

Some immigrants do express regret about coming to the United States by saying that they made a mistake leaving Korea for the United States. They say making a living in America is much more difficult than in Korea. Had they not been invited by their relatives, they would have stayed in Korea. They shake their heads and complain how they have burned their bridges. Now it is too late to go back to Korea because they sold everything, including their businesses, before they left Korea. There are many Korean immigrants, however, who pointed out that, without an invitation from their relatives in America, they would have stayed in Korea and suffered economic hardship. Even though making a living in America is difficult, there are always opportunities for immigrants who are willing to do any kind of work. An immigrant observed: "I am glad I was invited by my brother. Not only do I have a good job as a maintenance man, but also my wife has a good job at a sporting goods store. Also my children are attending state universities at very low tuition rates. All of these things could not happen to me if I remained in Korea. I am grateful to my brother."

Some immigrants came to America just to be reunited with their relatives. An elderly woman in Los Angeles who runs a small dress shop specializing in Korean-style dresses explains her reasons for coming to America.

I am sixty-three years old and my husband passed away a few years ago. I have an only son who lives in Los Angeles. I became so lonely in Korea when my husband died and I missed my son very much even though I was surrounded with my relatives. When my son invited me to come to America, I was so elated and happy. Although I am not making a lot of money running this store, I am just happy to be with my son. Now, my son, who is an accountant, is not happy living in Los Angeles and is thinking about emigrating to Australia. I will follow him wherever he goes.

Obviously, family ties exert a strong pull. Not all Korean immigrants, however, accepted invitations from their American relatives without reservation. Not only did reluctant parents follow their children knowing what they would be confronting in the strange new land, but there were also a few cases of reluctant children following their parents and housewives their husbands when they decided to emigrate to the United States. For example, a housewife comments that she was content living in Korea surrounded by her many relatives and friends, but when her husband decided to emigrate to America, she didn't have much choice but to follow him. Then there are the immigrants who came to America for a short visit, met someone they soon married, and before they knew it they had become residents. Others emigrated to America because all of their close relatives already lived in America and joining them was reasonable and logical. Some Koreans were in poor health and needed care that could be provided only by their relatives in the United States. Still others joined their relatives in the United States because they were constantly being urged by their relatives in America to emigrate for the purpose of forming a joint business venture. It happens sometimes that Korean Americans living in some small town where they may be the only Koreans urge their relatives to join them in America to relieve their loneliness, or isolation, and to see a friendly face. Thus, not all immigrants who came to America for reasons of family unity did so willingly.

Reasons for immigrating to the United States vary according to a particular person's circumstance in a particular time, and while each immigrant's reasons are peculiar to his or her situation, taken as a whole the immigrants' reasons do have certain common denominators. On the other hand, some individual's reasons for immigration are unique, and are, therefore, difficult to classify. In fact, Abelmann and Lie discuss a host of reasons which motivated many Koreans to immigrate. For example, American Christianity appealed to both Christian and non-Christian Koreans alike because it is associated with modernity, clean living, gender equality, enlightened thinking, and its modern family structure.[17] Moreover, it is perceived as having a moral superiority over other faiths. The authors also discussed the role of the Vietnam War in relation to Korean immigration. A significant number of Korean Vietnam War veterans made their way to the States either directly from Vietnam or later from Korea. They were allowed to enter the United States because they had fought as allies of the American soldiers. By doing so, they gained familiarity with American culture and society, which, in turn, heightened their desire to emigrate to America and eased their transition into the United States.

To reiterate, the Korean immigrants came to the United States for different reasons, at different times, and by different means. Yet most of them were attracted by the promises of economic opportunities, democracy, security, and peace in the United States. At the same time, they were driven by a lack of economic and educational opportunities, blocked social mobility, and an unfavorable political climate. Their coming to America was a result of an anticipated better future as well as lack of fulfillment with their life in Korea. In this sense, their reasons for coming to the United States do not differ appreciably from those of previous groups who came to America to seek a better life. The immigration of any nationality is not an instinctive action. The Korean immigrants have come to the United States in complex political, economic, and ideological contexts where no single factor is determinant.

NOTES

1. Immigration and Naturalization Service, *Statistical Yearbook* (Washington, D.C.: U.S. Government Printing Office, 1979–1997).

2. Illsoo Kim, *New Urban Immigrants: The Korean Community in New York* (Princeton, New Jersey: Princeton University Press, 1981), 82.

3. Pyong Gap Min, "Korean Americans," in *Asian Americans: Contemporary Trends and Issues*, ed. Pyong Gap Min (Thousand Oaks, Calif.: Sage Publications, 1995), 206.

4. In-Jin Yoon, "The Changing Significance of Ethnic and Class Resources in Immigrant Business: The Case of Korean Immigrant Businesses in Chicago," *International Migration Review* 25 (1990): 303–332.

5. Ivan Light and Edna Bonacich, *Immigrant Entrepreneurs: Koreans in Los Angeles 1965–1982* (Berkeley: University of California Press, 1988), 153–154.

6. Henry P. Fairchild, *Greek Immigration to the United States* (New Haven: Yale University Press, 1991).

7. In-Jin Yoon, *On My Own: Korean Businesses and Race Relations in America* (Chicago: University of Chicago Press, 1997), 127.

8. Kim, *New Urban Immigrants: The Korean Community in New York*, 53–54.

9. Korean Ministry of Education. 1965–90. *Statistical Yearbook of Education.* (Seoul, Korea: Kyoyuk Tonggye Yon'gam).

10. Donna Gabaccia, *From the Other Side: Women, Gender, and Immigrant Life in the U.S. 1980–1990* (Bloomington: Indiana University Press, 1994).

11. Insook Han Park, J. T. Fawcett, Fred Arnold, and Robert Gardner, *Korean Immigrants and U.S. Policy: A Predeparture Perspective* (Honolulu: East-West Center, 1990).

12. Walter Nugent, *Crossings: The Great Transatlantic Migrations, 1870–1914* (Bloomington: Indiana University Press, 1992).

13. Paul Desruisseaux, "Foreign Enrollment Rises Slightly at College in the United States," *Chronicle of Higher Education* (December 12, 1997): A42.

14. Light and Bonacich, *Immigrant Entrepreneurs: Koreans in Los Angeles 1965–1982*, 152.

15. Abelmann and Lie also describe how American movies—mostly entertainment films and westerns—were powerful forces which influenced immigrants' longing for America. See Nancy Abelmann and John Lie, *Blue Dreams:*

Korean Americans and the Los Angeles Riots (Cambridge: Harvard University Press, 1995), 63.

16. Ronald Takaki, *Strangers from a Different Shore: A History of Asian Americans* (Boston: Little, Brown and Company, 1989), 437.

17. Abelmann and Lie, *Blue Dreams: Korean Immigrants and the Los Angeles Riots*, 69.

Chapter 3

THE LANGUAGE BARRIER

Even as the immigrants of the 1990s bring an ever greater variety of languages to America, technological change is boosting the economic and social importance of learning English. Language experts and economic researchers say that English skills—speaking, reading and writing—are worth more in the Information Age than in previous periods of high immigration. In the nineteenth century, it was not unheard of for an ethnic enclave to function in a foreign language, say German, right down to the schools. And as recently as the 1970s, many manufacturing jobs did not require much English. Not so anymore. Computers, automated phone systems, and E-mail are the standard tools of the modern American workplace and require English language skills. Cashiers at McDonald's used to have registers with pictures of menu items; now they ring up orders by touching a computerized screen with words on it.

Nobody knows better the value of English than Korean immigrants who struggle with it everyday in making their living. Although difficulties in surmounting the subtleties of language are not unique to Korean immigrants, the slipperiness of English is first among a broad range of difficulties most Korean immigrants cite frequently. As it happens, when one has difficulty in adapting to a new language—in particular one as different from one's native language as English is from Korean—the difficulty in finding a place in the dominant society for employment and social interaction increases many fold. In fact, the Korean immigrants' difficulty in finding employment often stems largely from their weak command of the English language, adding to their frustration because, while they are confident that they are quite capable of doing the work, their inability to communicate effectively in English forms an invisible cultural barrier that contributes to their social isolation. An immigrant mother who has three grown-up children regrets that she hadn't learned English when she came to the United States twenty-five years ago. She thought learning English was not imperative at the time. She was busy working as a factory worker at a sporting goods manufacturing company in Phoenix while taking care of her sick mother-in-law at the same time. Now, most of her activities, besides her work, center around watching Korean videos, attending Korean church, visiting Korean friends, visiting Korean relatives, and occasionally visiting Korea. She explains:

> When we came to America, my children were still in early teens. Since they spoke fluent Korean, I never thought I will have any communication problem with them. As my children grew up and were attending high school, they became more and more fluent in English and less and less fluent in Korean. Now, as adults, they feel much more comfortable speaking in English to me than in Korean. Although they left home a few years ago, when they come to see me, we become much more awkward in communicating with each other. I know they don't tell me many things because they think I don't understand English well enough to comprehend what they say. They used to tell me about their school activities, friends, summer jobs in Korean. Now telling me about what's going on in their lives in Korean seems a big chore to them. Two of my children are married to native-born Americans. It seems they easily get bored with me and my husband as we don't understand many things about what they say. Sometimes, I feel lonely. I used to look forward seeing them, but seeing them is no longer exciting event.

Although most immigrants know they have to learn English if they are to succeed, they are so absorbed in making a living that they have little time or energy left to do anything else, let alone doing anything as demanding as learning a new language. In addition, their everyday contact with other Korean immigrants at work, church, and social gatherings lessens the urgency for them to learn English. A woman factory worker in Dallas learned painfully that providing financial support for her children was not enough to create a closer relationship with her children. She learned that her ability to communicate in English with her children who speak only English was as important, if not more so, as providing financial support in creating a close bond between her and her children. She says:

> I am ashamed of my illiteracy of the English language. I used to say I came to the United States for my children's better education and their bright future. But frankly speaking, I have not spent enough time with them. I spend more time working. I thought it was best way for them. I mean, I thought financial support was a more important factor than anything else. I have a sixteen–year-old boy and a twelve–year-old-girl. I came to the United States in 1977, when my son was two years old. After my son entered junior high school, I realized we had some gap between us. The gap was getting wider and wider because of a lack of communication. I should have learned the English language or I should have taught Korean language to my children, but I did not do either. Now, I wonder why I came to the United States. For my children? Or for myself?[1]

DIFFICULTIES OF LEARNING ENGLISH

There are three complementary parts to the mastery of English. First is the ability to speak the language without too much of an accent. Then there is the ability to express one's ideas in writing, a matter that troubles even most native speakers of English more than they care to admit. Finally, there is the ability to read and understand the subtle nuances of written English. Of the three, the most problematic for the majority of Korean Americans concerns their inability to speak relatively accentless English, which often causes them to feel unintelligent or at least to make them think that is how they are being regarded.

Many Asian immigrants into the United States, especially those from Hong Kong, the Philippines, India, and Pakistan are in some measure familiar with the English language because most of these immigrants have had the experience of being raised in some state of Anglo-colonialism and thus are familiar with English as a second language. The Korean immigrants, on the other hand, have had little exposure to Westerners, their culture or their language. Exposure to Western culture, especially that of the United States, cannot be said to have been extensive, in spite of significant missionary presence, especially in the founding of schools and occasional contact with American soldiers during and after the Korean War.

As a result, the Koreans who come to the United States are largely ignorant of the English language at the most fundamental level. For example, immigrants from Western countries are less handicapped in learning English than are Korean immigrants because those of European origin usually share the Roman alphabet, speak languages that are derived from the Indo-European family of languages, speak languages that share similar grammatical structure, share a large body of cognate words, and express themselves with phonemes that are much closer to English than Korean. It seems that European immigrants, even adult immigrants, become more fluent in English in a much shorter time than do immigrants from Korea. Not only must Koreans, as well as other Asians, learn the Roman alphabet, they must learn to distinguish homonyms, synonyms, and antonyms. Korean grammar has little in common with English grammar.

Further, the Koreans' practice of never venturing too far from their ethnic enclave after their arrival in America has served in some measure to delay their mastery of English. Many adult Korean immigrants, even after living two or three decades in the United States, get their news from Korean-language newspapers, watch only Korean-language television programming, listen to Korean music, and prefer Korean-language radio broadcasts to anything available in English. In such a case, it is not surprising to learn that some Korean immigrants have difficulty in conversing in English. They excuse themselves by claiming the English language is too difficult, or else claim that English is useless to them because they earn their livelihood in the Korean community. This is particularly true of many adult Korean immigrants who are repeating a pattern fairly typical of most first-generation immigrants. Speaking and understanding English for the Korean merchants who work outside the Korean community often determine the success or failure of their businesses. It is clear that one of the major causes of conflict between black customers and Korean merchants in the black community is a lack of communication between the two groups in business transactions. To many black customers the Korean merchants seem aloof, distant, and discourteous. In fact, because of their limited command of English, many Korean merchants are unable to exchange pleasantries or engage in the kind of small talk with their customers that is so important in smooth business transactions. As the immigrants get older, it becomes more difficult to learn English and so more and more they depend on their American-educated children to help them with the oral and written aspects of their business transactions. Ironically, a teen-ager who helps his parents in a store on weekends says that his parents' lack of English knowledge is sometimes a blessing in disguise as it helps prevent serious conflict between the English-speaking customers and his parents when the dissatisfied English-speaking customers spit out cuss words at his parents who do not respond because they don't understand the meaning of the profanity

Although it is difficult to evaluate how well Korean immigrants speak English because they have subjectively assessed themselves, some students of the subject have estimated that only around 3 out of 10 of first-generation immigrants speak English well.[2] For example, 49.5 percent of Koreans who entered the United States between 1975 and 1980 spoke English poorly or not at all.[3] Also the 1990 census reported that 63.5 percent of Koreans in the United States did not speak English very well, and 41.1 percent were "linguistically isolated."[4] In their study of assimilation patterns of Korean immigrants in the Chicago area, Hurh et al., found that 59 percent of the Koreans rated their ability to speak English as less than adequate ("Fair," "Poor," and "Not at all" categories).[5] At the same time, Kim and Hurh found the chances that Korean immigrants' usage of English increased at home were proportional to the length of time they spent in the United States, and as their confidence in their ability to express themselves increased, the more willing they became to use English.[6]

CONSEQUENCES OF A LANGUAGE BARRIER

The consequence of being insufficiently fluent in English can be devastating as one might imagine. First, immigrants can be easily exploited by employers or underemployed in the sense that someone who is well educated often is forced to take low-paying jobs or perform menial tasks simply because he or she is not fluent in English. Second, there is the damage to their self-esteem, their self-image, as they realize they are treated as if they are less than intelligent human beings, or even "idiots" as some Koreans put it bluntly. An immigrant woman who came to America with her parents when she was ten recalls a humiliating experience that occurred because her parents couldn't speak English.

I used to go with my father to translate for him at the store or bank. Once a woman asked if my father was my husband, even though I was only twelve years old. They couldn't differentiate. It was so humiliating for my father to have his daughter mistaken for his wife. What was heartless was to tell the child to translate threats and insults to their own parents, like "Tell your father that if he does that next time, I'm going to sue him," or "Why can't he speak English? This is America." I would just translate the necessary facts. It's almost like people think they have a right to be inhuman to whoever can't speak English.[7]

A manager of a clothing manufacturing firm in Pennsylvania mentioned that he liked to hire as many Korean women as he could because they work hard and seldom engage in time-wasting conversation or in small talk with their English-speaking co-workers because they can't speak English very well. He said he alternated Korean women and native-born American workers on assembly lines because he discovered the English-speaking women would not waste time trying to chat with the Koreans while they worked.

Most Korean women who are employed as manual workers in factories and industries know they are being exploited by their employers, but this is the only kind of work available to them. In her study of Korean immigrant women in the Dallas apparel industry, Um concluded, among other things, that the industry takes advantage of the fact that immigrant women with children who lack skills in English are eager to take any kind of job by paying them minimum wage or on a piecework basis. The language barrier is one of the major reasons that prohibits Korean immigrant women from seeking other alternatives. In fact Um found—among seventy-four respondents whose average length of stay in the United States was 7.2 years—only one woman reported she was able to speak English fluently.[8]

In the past few decades, as manufacturing firms moved offshore, industries such as apparel and garment factories were still able to hire cheap female immigrant laborers, usually from Asia and South America, frequently without fringe benefits such as health insurance or pension plans. The immigrant laborers help these industries remain competitive. Many immigrant women have labored for years in factories merely because they never became sufficiently fluent in English to find a better job. In fact, lack of fluency in English and the absence of an American education make them almost unemployable in jobs requiring both some expertise in English and a high school diploma or GED. Hughey compared the incomes of females from fifty-nine countries who immigrated to the United States between 1970 and 1980 and found that English language ability and educational attainment are among the important determinants of women's income.[9] Using census data, University of Illinois economist Barry Chiswick estimated that immigrants who become proficient in English can expect to earn 15 percent to 19 percent more than those who don't. Chiswick's research separated the effect of English proficiency from other important factors that affect income, such as schooling, age, and homeland. Without such adjustments, the gap is even larger.[10] The Korean women tend to choose to work where there is little or no need for proficiency in English, or else they choose to work at almost any type of job within the Korean community where they do not have to speak English because their customers are mostly Koreans.

Many Korean immigrant entrepreneurs are unable to choose a business of their choice or foray into the American labor market as long as their command of the language effectively bars their employment. Korean immigrants who thought that getting licenses in semi-skilled or skilled occupations such as plumbing, welding, painting, and auto repair would pave their way to steady employment are surprised to find out later that having technical skills without some degree of fluency in English prohibits them from being gainfully employed. A Korean immigrant explains this particular dilemma: "As soon as we arrived in Los Angeles, I enrolled at a plumbing and welding school for six months, but I was not able to get a job, partly due to problems with English. Next, my wife and I enrolled in house-painting school and earned a state license, but we still had trouble getting work, so we had to do janitorial work for a while to get by."[11] Some Korean immigrants with limited skill in English who venture outside the Korean community frequently have to pay a heavy price. A Korean immigrant mechanic who owns a motorcycle repair shop in Phoenix, Arizona, laments:

I have been operating a motorcycle repair shop for almost fifteen years. It is becoming increasingly difficult to repair motorcycles because the mechanical aspects of the motorcycles are changing rapidly and new manuals and instructions are being published every week to explain these changes. In the era of high technology, not only do I have to keep up with changing mechanical aspects of motorcycles but also new ways of doing business. I can't read English, although I am able to converse with customers in simple matters. Therefore, I have to hire an American manager who can read manuals, order parts, and deal with sometimes difficult customers. Frankly, I can't afford to hire a manager because my business overhead is already too high.

The language barrier not only restricts the opportunities of small entrepreneurs but of professional people as well. For most Korean immigrants, past skills and education may not be as important as the immigrants' proficiency in the English language. Indeed, the language barrier is especially cruel to those who had professional careers in Korea. First, it is an obstacle to entering certain professions where one must pass detailed written exams that require an ability to understand complex technical terminology and which require a week or more to answer. Such exams intimidate native speakers of English. One of the Kennedy children, for example, failed the

New York state bar exam a number of times. Should it surprise anyone to learn that many Korean immigrants are unable to pass licensure examinations required of anyone who would practice law, medicine, accounting, and dozens of other professions not because they do not know the material but because of their lack of fluency in English? Furthermore, racism, the low repute of Korean college degrees among Americans, and a lack of understanding of American professional practice on the part of the Korean immigrants are other stumbling blocks the Korean immigrants have to overcome in order to obtain American licenses.

Most frequently, however, Korean professionals mention their lack of knowledge of the English language as the major impediment to their obtaining an American license. For example, in 1973 only a third of the South Korean-educated nurses in Los Angeles held state licenses, while six hundred Korean American physicians in Southern California could not practice medicine.[12] Meanwhile, Korean-educated doctors, engineers, and research professors were forced to take menial jobs as clerks, technicians, nurse's aids, and janitors in the hope of scrimping and saving enough to become small business entrepreneurs and perhaps buy a gas station, liquor store, convenience market, or Laundromat. As a result, many small business enterprises are run by immigrants with solid educational or professional backgrounds but whose difficulty with English have driven them to take a lower-status path because they were unable to obtain American licenses. In his study of small business owners—most of whom had college educations and white collar occupations in Korea—Min found one of the major reasons these store owners entered small businesses instead of white-collar occupations in the United States was their anticipated difficulties in gaining white-collar occupations because of their language barrier.[13] Ironically, the Korean professionals who pass the licensure examination after receiving additional training at American universities and acquiring English language proficiency still gravitate into the Korean community, such as Koreatown in Los Angeles and the borough of Queens. In such places one can see numerous signs displayed prominently advertising Korean accountants, lawyers, dentists, and physicians of all kinds. Predictably, professionals like these also advertise in Korean business directories and newspapers specifically targeted for Korean-speaking clients. The reasons they have for choosing to set up practice in Korean communities instead of nonethnic communities are probably many, although there is no doubt that their fear that they lacked fluency in English was a major factor in their decision to practice in the Korean community.

The effect of the language barrier can be felt by all adult Korean immigrants as it permeates every aspect of their life in America. It even affects their future in numerous, often subtle ways. As with many other Asian immigrants, the Korean immigrant professional aspirants frequently choose their career from the fields of engineering and the physical sciences, which emphasize mathematical exactness and technical expertise more than fluency in English. In a recent survey conducted by the University of California, a high proportion of Asian American college professors, 43 percent, worked in the physical sciences, mathematics, engineering, and other technical fields, while only 20 percent of white and 9 percent of black professors worked in those areas.[14] Although the survey does not indicate the separate percentage of Korean American professors who worked in these fields, it is probably true that a high proportion of Korean American professors in academia are also employed in these fields.

It is surely not coincidental that Korean American physicians tend to concentrate in the areas of radiology, anesthesiology, oncology, and various fields of medical research rather than in private practice where greater fluency in English is necessary. Some Korean immigrant scientists become eminent in research while many others hit the "glass ceiling" (that is, they find they can only rise so high in an organization) after ten or twenty years, even though they feel they are qualified for a more important, perhaps executive, policy-making position. Not long ago, almost one hundred Asian Americans (probably Korean immigrants were included in the suit although that was not made clear) with advanced degrees brought a class action suit for racial discrimination against one of the major telecommunication companies in Los Angeles. The plaintiffs argued that they were rarely if ever promoted or offered jobs outside the laboratory where they worked; they believed this neglect was racist. The company spokesman defended the company against the charge of racism by arguing that Asian Americans are not aggressive enough and have a serious communication (language) problem; therefore, it was not possible to give them serious consideration for managerial or executive positions.

When the immigrants realize their career advancement is slow or not forthcoming after many years of service, they sometimes blame themselves for poor communication skills or not knowing how to play politics, while others blame racism and insensitivity on the part of corporations. Probably a combination of weak communication skills, racism, and lack of political savvy may have affected the immigrants' chance of advancement. As Allen Lee Sessoms, a black college administrator who became President of Queens College in New York, puts it succinctly, "College administration, one has to be honest, isn't rocket science. It's politics, politics, politics, with a little good judgment thrown in."[15] In the case of the Korean immigrants, however, it takes more than just politics. A Korean chemical engineer in the Pittsburgh area, who is employed by a large engineering firm, comments:

> When I was hired by a firm after my graduate degree about twenty years ago, I was delighted at the prospect of working for the company. Unfortunately, my career advancement has been very slow. My white colleagues, who were hired at the same time with me, advanced their career ladder much more quickly than I did and even became my direct supervisors and were promoted into managerial and executive positions after a while. Much to my chagrin, some of my colleagues who were hired much later than I also surpassed me. I guess this can happen to anyone regardless of employees' racial and nativity background. That's why people move from one company to another for advancement and higher pay, if they feel they are going nowhere. In my case, going to another company would not help my career advancement. Joining a high level decision-making group, one has to have exceptional communication skills. On top of that, you have to play politics by mingling freely with people in top echelons, who are willing to accept you to their inner circle. Of course, if you are a native-born white, that would help you being accepted more readily. Since I am not all of these, my job will be confined more or less to the technical areas wherever I go.

FACING SUSPICION OF COLLEAGUES AND PATRONS

The Korean immigrant professionals who are thrust into careers where public speaking and writing are necessary, as in teaching, journalism, and law, encounter a form of double jeopardy. First, they may face the suspicion of their colleagues about whether they are qualified to take up these professions where the command of English is essential. Second, they must overcome the skepticism or distrust of clients or patrons whom they are supposed to serve. Native-born Americans prefer professionals in these types of profession who are accentless and skillful writers. Writing and speaking well at the level of native-born Americans require more than correct grammar. Foreign-born Korean adults are consistently handicapped in competition with native-born Americans, no matter how linguistically talented they may be. A couple of years ago, Larry King interviewed the former U.S. Joint-Chief-of Staff General John Shalikashvili who was born in Poland. Mr. King asked the general how many languages he speaks. The modest general, who has no problem expressing himself in English, answered, "I speak some Polish and English. If you ask me which language I speak 'fluently,' the answer is none!" Like the general, some Korean immigrants who came to America thirty or forty years ago as foreign students and then became professionals frequently acknowledge that they are fluent neither in Korean nor English. They know they are handicapped competing successfully at all professional levels with native-born Americans in the United States. Furthermore, writing skills of native-born Americans improve much more quickly than the foreign-born as time elapses. One can observe this phenomenon among college students and professionals in every field.

It appears that as years go by the gap between immigrant professionals and American-born professionals is becoming wider in terms of productivity and recognition. Although most professionals, particularly academics, don't want to admit that recognition by their colleagues and other professionals is important, there is constant competition for visibility, respect, and prestige. Undoubtedly, excellent communication skills, membership in the white race, male gender, and academic credentials help enhance the visibility of a professional. However, for immigrant professionals, gaining social support from native-born American professionals is not an easy matter as the latter have nothing to gain from supporting struggling immigrant professionals. In most professional fields, immigrant professionals tend to be isolated from the mainstream professional practice and often form their own social network to secure support and encouragement from other compatriot immigrant professionals. One can find Korean immigrant medical and dental associations in most large metropolitan areas, and these associations sponsor various professional conferences and social activities in the United States. In academia, for example, Korean sociologists and political scientists who teach at American universities and colleges have established their own associations and opened communication channels for themselves. Sometimes Koreans' intense involvement with their own ethnic professional associations further delays acceptance by native-born professionals and retard their communication skills at the same time.

In academia, particularly in the humanities and social sciences, American-born professors still dominate in the publication of both minor and major scholarly works and they are highly visible at the same time, not only through academic work but also through the social network. In the non-physical sciences, often how the fact is presented and packaged becomes as important as the fact itself. In the employment bulletin of *The*

Chronicle of Higher Education, employers in non-physical science fields frequently emphasize particular qualities of candidates, among other things, teaching ability and communication skills. Sometimes these latter two are inseparable as it is difficult to be a good teacher without having good communication skills, although one can be a poor teacher with excellent verbal communication skills. Immigrant professionals are not only disadvantaged in finding employment vis-à-vis native-born professionals, but also they have to overcome obstacles that most native professionals don't face. Particularly in teaching, immigrant professors frequently have to contend with a few students who blame their low grades on their immigrant instructor's accent. A Korean history professor who teaches at a highly selective liberal arts college in central Pennsylvania still hears complaints from his students about his accent after teaching there almost thirty years, even though his accent is scarcely noticeable. A Korean immigrant sociology professor in upstate New York, who has lived in America more than forty years and speaks fluent standard English, also gets complaints from his students about his accent. It seems that any speech pattern or sound which is not consonant with students' expectations becomes the target of complaint and criticism.

Even well-educated American-born adults exhibit suspicion of a foreign accent. I remember a comment made by an American-born colleague when German-born Henry Kissinger became Secretary of State: "How could a person who can't speak proper English become Secretary of State?" Still, however, certain European accents are much more readily accepted by the public, particularly the British accent. Many years ago a Korean immigrant professor was dismissed from a state college in New Jersey because of his accent. He sued the college for racial discrimination by claiming that German, French, and other European faculty members were not dismissed in spite of their strong accents. It is true that some students may have legitimate complaints about their immigrant instructor's accent, speech patterns, mannerisms, and other idiosyncrasies which the students find disconcerting and which may make their professor hard to understand. It is also true that most foreign-born instructors who received their advanced degrees in the United States and who were hired by a college after thoroughly checking their background can deliver an understandable lecture and students should be able to understand them if only they expend a little effort.

Unfortunately, in the era of declining enrollment and oversupply of college teachers, most colleges and universities are willing to pacify the complaining students, even if that means they have to dismiss foreign-born faculty members. As a result, getting tenure or promotion is becoming increasingly difficult for foreign-born instructors. According to a recent survey of faculty teaching and research activities by the University of California, 79 percent of Asian American faculty hold doctorates compared with 61 percent of the white faculty. Further, as percent of the faculty, Asian American faculty published more articles than their white counterparts. In spite of these apparent advantages, 60 percent of the Asian American faculty found the review-and-promotion process "worrisome" while only 44 percent of white professors did so.[16] Although their concern for tenure and promotion may have derived from many sources, such as campus politics, racism, popularity among students, language proficiency is still a major concern for foreign-born Asian faculty members because language proficiency is understood to affect the quality of their teaching more than the high caliber of their scholarly productivity. This is so because unless one is in a pure research field, proficiency in English is essential in teaching, and teaching is ordinarily the major criterion in determining tenure and promotion. Some Asian immigrant faculty, particularly in the areas of humanities and social sciences, specialize in fields dealing with Asian societies and Asian American issues where they are better equipped than American-born scholars. By concentrating in these specialized studies, they can find employment in flagship state or in elite private universities where such special areas are normally included in the academic discipline. Since research is emphasized in such institutions, contact between Asian-born faculty and students is limited to a few graduate seminars where their knowledge of non-Western societies is appreciated by their students and colleagues alike. Yet suspicion of the foreign-born faculty, particularly about their ability to express themselves clearly in English, is still wide spread. For instance, in 1992, I applied for a teaching position in the sociology department at a state university in the southwest. Almost immediately the chairperson asked one of my referees how well I spoke English. From my last name alone, the chairperson just assumed I would have a thick accent and would be difficult to understand.

The Korean immigrant professionals have yet to break into mass media such as newspapers, radio or television broadcasting, though occasionally second generation Korean Americans enter into fields once exclusively white. Although race and gender barriers have been breaking down in journalism and the entertainment industry, stringent requirements for proficiency in relatively accent-free English still present immigrants wishing to enter these professions with a major obstacle. Furthermore, they still have to overcome the suspicion the native-born Americans have of their ability to write well. A Korean political science professor, who teaches at a small college in the Midwest, relates his experience of encountering suspicion by a colleague. As chair of the political science department, he had to write a brief description of his department for the college catalogue. He wrote the description and showed it to American-born colleagues in his department. They read it and made it smooth reading. When he took it to the catalogue committee chair, the committee chair told him to rewrite the entire description because sentence structure and grammar in the description were awful and suggested that he consult with his department colleagues. Since there was no need to consult with his colleagues in the department because he had done so already, he resubmitted the same description to the catalogue chair after a few days and told the chair it had been carefully gone over by his colleagues in the department. The catalogue chair looked it over and commented that it was clear and well written.

Lawyering is also difficult for foreign-born Korean immigrants in spite of their law degrees from American universities. Again, they tend to be drawn to the Korean community where they often deal with cases involving immigration law. Some Korean lawyers specialize in defending Korean immigrants accused of criminal offenses while others specialize in real estate or corporate law, and occasionally one will take on a civil rights matter. The Korean immigrant lawyers who are hired by American firms usually handle cases concerning Asian matters related to trade with Asian countries. A Korean lawyer who is employed by an American firm mentioned that his firm assumes that he speaks or understands Korean, Japanese, and Chinese. His superiors think that if one speaks Korean, then he should be able to speak other Asian languages too. At least in this law firm, the assumption seems to be that not only do all Asians look alike but they all speak the same languages. In the early part of the twentieth century, lawyers who had Italian last names had difficulty attracting clients because their names were associated with the Mafia or Cosa Nostra, while Jewish lawyers were stereotyped as brilliant. In the case of foreign-born Asian Americans, no matter how well they speak and understand the English language, the suspicion remains that Asian immigrants cannot handle the English language well, and this is yet another factor driving them to practice their profession within their own ethnic community.

FACING NEGATIVE PUBLIC IMAGE

The public perception that all Asians in America are newly arrived immigrants and not conversant with English still plagues American-born Asians and immigrants alike. Native-born Americans are still surprised at hearing an Asian speak flawless English. A third generation Japanese American recounts his experience when he was working for the passage of the reparation bill to compensate Japanese Americans for their illegal internment during World War II; he frequently went to Capitol Hill to lobby for this particular cause. Making an appointment and talking to senators and congressmen proved to be extremely difficult. Finally seeing an influential senator who was about to enter an elevator, he rushed into the elevator and talked to him as fast as he could about the importance of the passage of the reparation bill until the elevator stopped. The senator listened to him without response and finally said, "You speak English very well. Where did you learn it?" Senator D'Amato from New York State, with a heavy stereotypical Asian-born accent, once mimicked the third generation Japanese American judge, Lance Ito, who presided over the O. J. Simpson case. A second generation Korean American engineer almost quit his job because his boss repeatedly asked him where he learned his English, while giving him entry-level assignments at the same time, even though he had worked for the firm for more than four years after graduating from one of the top universities in America.

But the typical American's negative image of Asians is based not just on the Asians' level of fluency but also on their race. Many Korean immigrants who speak and understand English well resent it when native-born Americans speak to them loudly and slowly, as if they are slow witted. There is anecdotal evidence concerning the American's perception of the Asian's mishandling of his adopted tongue. Here is one: An Oxford-educated Chinese went to Iowa to attend a dedication ceremony of some sort, at which he was one of the guest speakers. At the banquet a small town mayor in Iowa who was seated, slowly and loudly in English asked the Chinese, who was eating soup, "You likey soupy?" The Chinese nodded without speaking a word of English and thought he would impress this small town mayor with his speech. When his turn came, he delivered his speech in flawless English and returned to his seat thinking he probably shocked or at least impressed the mayor. The mayor smiled at the Chinese and said, "You likey your speechy?" The point is that many foreign-born English-speaking Asian Americans are offended when native-born Americans speak to them as if a father were speaking to his five year-old child ending the conversation with a question, "Do you understand?" The negative public image of inarticulate foreigners haunts anyone who doesn't have European characteristics. A foreign graduate student from India who had been speaking English all his life enrolled in one of the graduate schools in Tennessee. He was told he had a severe language problem by his graduate student advisor as soon as the advisor heard the Indian student speak with an accent. The incensed Indian student challenged his graduate student advisor to an English-writing contest. Many native-born Americans frequently assume that all foreign-born Asians with an accent are not fluent in English. Even if they know many foreign-born Asians are fluent in English, sometimes native-borns seem to not want to admit that some foreign-borns can speak English as well as they do.

About a year ago, a major TV network ran a program about how American college students are short changed because they are taught frequently by foreign-born graduate assistants whose thick accents make them difficult to understand. The narrator then introduced brief clips showing Asian graduate assistants lecturing. Selecting Asian graduate assistants as representative of poor English speakers reinforces the popular idea that all Asians, regardless of their educational level, speak poorly. A Korean immigrant, who happened to be a minister, thinks that the language behavior of American-born whites is a form of racism. Upon hearing someone speak with an accent and realizing the speaker was born in another country gives the native-born American a sense of superiority. They usually ask questions such as, "Where are you from?" and "What is your nationality?" Even though answers to these two questions may be Los Angeles and the United States (nationality is legal status, not where a person is from), they are not happy until you admit that you were born in Korea. The minister comments:

> In America, there is a kind of chauvinism about language; the way established Americans use language, as a leverage to put you down. . . . Language becomes status. Unless you become fluent, with no accent, you're nobody. America tends to make everyone nobody, before they can become somebody. If you don't speak English well, then you are stupid. I went through that in high school. So that what I said didn't count, because I didn't speak the language the way they did. . . . There's automatic marginalization in everything you do and everything you are. Especially in high school and college, when you're still trying to develop who you are, it's an incredibly depressing situation.[17]

The established standard of English language usage set by native-born whites may appear to mean status, power, control, and racism, particularly to those non-white immigrants who do not speak English the way the native English speakers expect. A Korean immigrant college professor is constantly amazed at native-born Americans who assume that all Asian Americans, regardless of their educational backgrounds, have a limited English vocabulary. In conversation with native-born white Americans, he noticed that whenever these native-borns use English words or phrases that are a little out of the ordinary, they stop and ask him whether he understood the meaning of the words or phrases, even though they are neither American slang words nor idioms. He is convinced, however, that most native-born Americans *know* he perfectly understood those words or phrases, knowing he is a college professor and lived in the United States more than thirty years. But asking him whether he understood a particular word or a phrase in the middle of conversation is not only extremely condescending on the part of native-born Americans but also a form of social control. There is a rather humorous story about an exchange between former Chancellor Chang-lin Tien of the University of California at Berkeley, a Chinese immigrant, and his secretary. Shortly after Dr. Tien became Chancellor, his secretary presumed to suggest that he needed to go to a speech therapist to rid himself of his Chinese accent. Dr. Tien retorted that she (his secretary) should see the speech therapist so that she could understand his Chinese accent.

It is probable that elements of power, control, and racism factor in to any consideration of language behavior. While many Korean Americans construe it as a form of institutionalized racism, particularly some Korean professionals who were unable to obtain employment commensurate with their educational background, most Korean immigrants are self-conscious about their command of English and thus attribute any social or other apparent rejection by the whites to their language problem. In fact, many Korean immigrant parents think that their children will not have difficulty in finding employment and be subject to racism as their children have no language barrier. They believe that their English-speaking children will be fully accepted by American society, although their children may encounter numerous barriers later on which have nothing to do with English skills. Abelmann and Lie note that quite often the boundary between racial discrimination and linguistic and institutional barriers is ambiguous. Even then, accented, albeit adequate, spoken English may contribute to examination failure, unsuccessful job interviews, and continual unemployment, or frustration of being condemned to low-paying, even menial, work.[18]

NOTES

1. Quoted in Shin Ja Um, *Korean Immigrant Women in the Dallas-Area Apparel Industry* (New York: University Press of America, 1996), 61.
2. Mangiafico estimated that only 3 percent of Koreans speak English fluently, while Kim approximated around 10 percent. See Luciano Mangiafico, *Contemporary American Immigrants: Patterns of Filipino, Korean, and Chinese Settlement in the United States* (New York: Praeger, 1988), 162; David S. Kim,

Korean Small Businesses in the Olympic Area (Los Angeles: School of Architecture and Urban Planning, University of California, Los Angeles, 1975), 52.

3. Herbert R. Barringer, Robert W. Gardner, and Michael J. Levin, *Asians and Pacific Islanders in the United States* (New York: Russell Sage Foundation, 1993), 185.

4. U.S. Department of Commerce, *Statistical Abstract of the United States: The National Data Book* (Washington, D.C.: U.S. Bureau of Census, 1990).

5. Won Moo Hurh, Hei Chu Kim, and Kwang Chung Kim, *Assimilation Patterns of Immigrants in the United States: A Case Study of Korean Immigrants in the Chicago Area* (Washington, D.C.: University Press of America, 1979), 25–26.

6. Kim and Hurh surveyed 622 adult Korean immigrants in Chicago area between the ages of thirty and fifty-nine and the average length of stay was eight years. The immigrants' English ability was tested through an objective vocabulary scale drawn from the Wechsler Adult Intelligence Test (WAIS) and through subjective self-reports. See Kwang Chung Kim and Won Moo Hurh, "Two Dimensions of Korean Immigrants' Sociocultural Adaptation: Americanization and Ethnic Attachment," Paper presented at the Annual Meeting of the American Sociological Association, Atlanta, Georgia, 1988.

7. Quoted in Elaine H. Kim and Eui-Young Yu, *East to America: Korean American Life Stories* (New York: The New Press, 1996), 188.

8. Shin Ja Um, *Korean Immigrant Women in the Dallas-Area Apparel Industry* (New York: University Press of America, 1996), 105.

9. A. M. Hughey, "The Incomes of Recent Female Immigrants to the United States," *Social Science Quarterly* 17 (1990):383–390.

10. Quoted in R. A. Zaldivar, "Immigrants Find English Skills Rising in Importance," *Albuquerque Journal* (June 8, 1997): B14.

11. Quoted in Kim and Yu, *East to America: Korean American Life Stories,* 182.

12. Bong-youn Choy, *Koreans in America* (Chicago: Nelson-Hall, 1979), 227, 250.

13. Pyong Gap Min, "From White-Collar Occupations to Small Businesses: Korean Immigrants Occupational Adjustment," *The Sociological Quarterly* 25 (1984), 344.

14. Higher Education Research Institute, Graduate School of Education and Information, *Race and Ethnicity in the American Professoriate, 1995–96* (Los Angeles: University of California Press, 1997).

15. Kim Strosnider, "N.Y. Public College Aims to Raise Funds from Public Sources," *The Chronicle of Higher Education* (March 14, 1997): A31.

16. Higher Education Research Institute, Graduate School of Education and Information Studies, *Race and Ethnicity in the American Professoriate, 1995–96* (Los Angeles: University of California Press, 1997).

17. Joann Faung Jean Lee, *Asian Americans* (New York: The New Press, 1992), 51.

18. Nancy Abelmann and John Lie, *Blue Dreams: Korean Americans and the Los Angeles Riots* (Cambridge: Harvard University Press, 1995), 126.

Chapter 4

MAKING A LIVING

In the United States, Koreans' struggle with the English language can be a formidable barrier to their success in any number of ways. When the language barrier is coupled with a lack of capital then the chances of achieving material success is made extremely difficult. Further limiting their choice of occupations is the need to carefully husband their meager financial resources. This was particularly true prior to the 1980s when the Korean government restricted the amount of money an emigrant could take from the country. This restriction meant that their available capital was in all probability too limited to start a business without some outside help, but once in the United States they found it next to impossible to get loans from banks or other lending institutions because few financial institutions were willing to lend money to people with no established credit history. The fact that they were resident aliens undoubtedly was a factor as well. As a result, Korean immigrants have learned to resort to unusual means to acquire start-up capital for their businesses. As one might expect, many Korean immigrants have supplemented their limited capital with loans from their friends and relatives. If these sources do not provide enough money, they sometimes borrow money from "money clubs."

"Money clubs," known as *kye* in Korea, were created by merchants who found the usual sources of capital unavailable to them for whatever reason. Briefly, "money clubs," in principle, are similar to credit unions but work this way: Individuals come together and form a combine, or "club," out of a common need for capital. The members operate the club themselves. Each member of the money club contributes to the fund, and each may, in turn, borrow from the fund. An established or a would-be entrepreneur can borrow from the pool of money in the club (typically the money is used to open new shops, or else to meet short-term expenses of restocking the inventory of an existing one, perhaps). The merchant can then repay the loan from his profits. Typically the sums of money borrowed are rather small (a few thousand dollars or less) because most money clubs are modestly funded; however, an ambitious merchant may be able to borrow larger amounts by buying into a well-funded club.

By the 1980s, Korean immigrants were somewhat better prepared to do business than were immigrants in the 1970s. In fact, a predeparture survey conducted among immigrants in Korea in 1986 indicated that 71 percent of male respondents intended to go into business once they arrived in the United States.[1] Many of these immigrants were well informed about opening and operating businesses in the United States. Much of what they knew they had learned from their relatives and friends who were already established businessmen and businesswomen in the States. Moreover, some of the immigrants already had experience in operating small businesses in Korea. Although most of those who immigrated from Korea in the 1980s and 1990s were less well educated and poorer in general than those who immigrated in the 1970s, a small number of them were comparatively wealthy and were able to leave Korea with their wealth because, in the 1980s, the Korean government eased its restrictions on the amount of money emigrants could take out of the country.

Korean immigrants who came to America in the 1970s or earlier were much less prepared to run small businesses. Many of those who came to the United States were educated professionals and their primary motive for immigration into the United States was to pursue a career in a white-collar profession or occupation, but most definitely not for the purpose of establishing a small business. The low status of such businesses in Korea at that time precluded that as an option. However, they soon discovered that their particular professional skills were not wanted by the host society. Further, they found it next to impossible to translate their Korean credentials into profitable American careers, and their inability to converse easily in English (essential for white-collar jobs), was a major obstacle. In spite of these and other obstructions, some, whether better prepared or else more determined, succeeded in securing white-collar or professional jobs in spite of the odds against them.

ATTRACTION TO SMALL BUSINESS

Many more early immigrants, though, were forced to abandon their original dream and thus gravitate into small business ventures—the only option available to them. Consequently, a large number of Korean immigrants, regardless of their background, found themselves gravitating toward similar low-status kinds of business and competing fiercely with each other, not because the entrepreneurial spirit ran strong among this particular wave of Korean immigrants, but because there were no other alternatives available to them. According to Min's survey of the Korean employment status in 1986 in the United States, 75 percent of Korean immigrant adults in Los Angeles and Orange Counties in California were either self-employed or else employed in Korean firms, and in New York City almost 86 percent were so situated.[2] In fact, Yoon, based on reports of U.S. Bureau of Census, found that Korean immigrants showed the highest rate of self-employment among seventeen groups who arrived in the United States between 1970 and 1980. The number of self-employed Korean immigrant entrepreneurs has grown steadily with each new wave of immigrants arriving in the United States. The number had reached 17 percent by 1990, whereas the corresponding rate for the general population increased moderately to 9.7 percent.[3]

What is revealed in Yoon's study, as well as the work of others, is that Korean immigrants are attracted to businesses which require limited start-up capital, little need for proficiency in English, or previous experience, and which require little interaction with customers. The irony in this last point is that, all too often, Korean immigrants try to establish small businesses in communities where interaction with their customers is not only necessary, but vital. Generally, they prefer to establish businesses which are not only easy for them to learn, but also which offer quick cash returns because they are operating on such a thin profit margin. Many of them plan to sell their businesses, at a profit, to other Korean immigrants when they decide to move on to something else. A Korean shopkeeper explains why so many Korean immigrants are attracted to small businesses.

> Koreans don't have much perseverance. They had experienced Japanese colonialism, Korean War, division of country, and now feel a perennial threat of war from North Korea. They feel everything has to be hurried instead of looking at things from a long-range perspective. This feeling is also applicable to making money. They want to make money as quickly as possible and as much as possible. They are willing to take a chance in black, Mexican communities, New York City streets, and any undesirable places as long as there is a chance to make money. They think that a small business is the only way and fastest way to accomplish their money-making objective.

Abelmann and Lie illustrate this point graphically when they quote the owner of a dry- cleaning store in Los Angeles. The owner claimed: "We [Koreans] are a nation that has lived through many hungry periods. So we have learned to work hard. We like doing everything quickly—quick, quick, quick—eat quickly, succeed quickly, get rich quickly."[4]

Others, such as Min, studying Koreans entering small businesses suggest their decision is a carefully thought out career choice, particularly for those who had managerial and professional occupations in Korea. Because of the language barrier, ignorance of American culture, as well as perceived racial prejudice, they feel they are disadvantaged in competing in the white-collar labor market, even if they could find such positions. Under the circumstances, the better course of action seems to be to start a business and through it attain economic mobility, which is not possible through white-collar occupations. Besides, operating business ensures personal autonomy, allowing one to become his or her own boss, no matter how small the business may be.[5] Although it may be a difficult transition for those who were former managers or white-collar workers, it has become routine to find Koreans who have immigrated to the United States in the 1980s who were small business owners in Korea and have brought with them some experience and knowledge of managing small businesses. They have found no difficulty opening small, family-operated shops with help from their friends in America. As Korea has become rapidly industrialized, the self-employment rate has increased proportionately. More than 40 percent of Koreans are engaged in small businesses in 1988, according to the Korean Ministry of Labor.[6] As more and more Koreans grow up in a society in which employment in a small mercantile enterprise is the norm, many recent Korean immigrants, regardless of their social background, no longer view operating a small business as contemptible. However, there are plenty of Korean immigrants, particularly those with a college education and with professional jobs, who still regard operating small businesses as a last resort. In fact, few store owners want their children to become shopkeepers.

Most businesses developed by Korean immigrants are small "mom and pop" retail stores that mostly offer fresh produce, groceries, or liquor. They may offer items of interest to Asian tastes, especially Korean, or else they may invest in general service businesses: dry cleaning or laundering, retail jewelry, gas stations, beauty salons, and numerous other such small businesses. Usually these businesses are labor intensive and of the sort that had also attracted recent immigrant groups from such regions as Southeast Asia or the Middle East. These newer immigrants frequently purchase businesses from aging members of earlier immigrant groups such as Jews, Italians, and Greeks. The result is that Korean immigrants' businesses vary widely. In addition to the usual retail outlets, they may operate modest import and export concerns, as well as manufacturing businesses. Of course, these tend to be larger in scale than what we think of when we think of small-scale businesses ordinarily operated by Korean immigrants. Then there are those who operate even smaller-scale businesses such as push carts, hawking wares along beaches or city streets, or else tiny hole-in-the-wall boutiques offering various clothing, jewelry, or small electronic items. Some enterprising Koreans set up stalls in malls or swap meets to attract the public—particularly on the West Coast.

Koreans also own semi-professional businesses, including travel agencies, insurance companies, real estate agencies, and martial arts studios. Although their numbers are small now, their numbers are increasing rapidly, especially in places such as New York City and in the Los Angeles area. Then there are those who have established professional practices in such white collar occupations as accounting, law, and medicine. These businesses are usually successful because they primarily serve Korean immigrants settled in Korean ethnic communities, or else, they are situated in large metropolitan areas or very near these communities. Most Korean immigrants still depend on other Koreans for help in understanding the different aspects of business transactions. Buying and selling businesses, houses, automobiles, and even insurance, are done through other Koreans, who either act in an intermediary or a professional capacity. While seeking the help of a fellow Korean may make the Korean immigrant feel more secure, there is no guarantee that their purchase through a Korean intermediary is, in fact, a better buy than one bought through any other broker. Indeed, there is evidence to suggest that Korean brokers buy businesses from white sellers at a discount and sell them to newly arrived Korean immigrants at an exorbitant price.

While most Korean stores are located in, or on the fringes of, the white neighborhoods, a significant number of Korean-owned businesses are found deep in minority neighborhoods. For example, 33 percent of businesses in Brooklyn and 22 percent of those in the Bronx owned by Koreans are located in neighborhoods where blacks and Haitians, Jamaicans, and other immigrants from other Caribbean islands reside. In South Central Los Angeles, which connects Inglewood and Compton, 80 percent of the businesses in the black neighborhood are owned by Koreans.[7] The reasons for their attention to fringe economic opportunities are many, but they ordinarily locate in these areas because of their difficulties with English and their limited start-up capital. Perhaps the most important reason has to do with the fact that they are drawn to large metropolitan areas where there is access to a relatively large Korean-speaking population and consequently they have greater opportunities to deal with their peers. As a result, the economic health of ethnic Korean businesses is not much affected by the ordinary fluctuations in state and national economies. The Korean immigrants' livelihood in Los Angeles, for example, which has the largest Korean economy in America, is little affected by fluctuations in the general economy of Los Angeles.[8]

KOREAN-BLACK CONFLICT

As anyone who has read a newspaper in the past fifteen years has noticed, where Koreans have opened businesses in black communities tension with the black residents has soon reached the flash point. Charges and counter-charges leveled by these two groups have caught the attention of official-dom at all levels, as well as that of civil rights workers. The friction between Koreans and the black residents has become so contentious that it has led to physical assaults, destruction of property, even murder and civil disturbances. This heightened strife has directed national attention to the conflict. During the Los Angeles riots in 1992, televised images of black men targeting Korean stores and of a Korean grocery store owner shooting a black girl suspected of shoplifting are still vivid in the minds of many people.

Sources of the conflict between these two groups are complex and deeply rooted. Basically, the black residents accuse the Korean business owners of overcharging them for goods and services, blatant price gouging, discourteous and rude behavior, taking over black businesses, taking dollars away from the black community, and giving little back to the black community. To all such charges Koreans have responded that the major cause of conflict is simply a misunderstanding caused primarily by the language barrier or a result of cultural differences. They also insist that they are not "taking over" black businesses in the community. They claim that they buy such properties only because of the availability of such properties at reasonable prices, an important factor for Korean immigrants with little capital.

Reasons for Koreans operating businesses in the black community are many. However, there are four basic social and economic reasons for Koreans establishing businesses in black neighborhoods. In the past few decades, the presence of Korean store owners in such large numbers in black neighborhoods across the nation is largely the result of social and economic changes in America that have brought about significant structural transformations in the black community. In the 1940s and 1950s, when racial segregation was strictly enforced in America, black entrepreneurs were able to maintain various businesses, such as small hotels, funeral parlors, beauty salons, grocery stores, and other small scale businesses because they had an essentially captive black customer base. On the surface, black entrepreneurs seemed to be doing well enough to form their own middle class. However, in his well known work, *Black Bourgeoisie: The Rise of a New Middle Class,* E. Franklin Frazier, after studying the emergence and success of black businesses in the black community, concluded that the existence of a black bourgeoisie is a myth. In fact, he discovered that most of the black businesses were barely subsisting in spite of the appearance of success.[9] In short, he pointed to the very real fact that most businesses located in black communities were economically marginal, capable of providing bare subsistence for their owners, if that. The least shift in blacks' buying patterns could prove disastrous to black small-business owners.

With racial integration becoming a reality in the 1970s and the 1980s, blacks who had been forced to patronize black businesses could now shop elsewhere. The growth of shopping malls undoubtedly had its impact, too, but whatever the reason many black entrepreneurs suddenly found themselves unable to sustain their marginal businesses. As a result, many black businesses closed, and their owners were forced to find other forms of employment. Although some remained in the community, many young black entrepreneurs were forced by economic necessity to leave their communities in order to seek professional or other economic opportunities elsewhere.

The gradual demise of black businesses created an opportunity for other risk-taking racial and ethnic groups. Korean entrepreneurs, in particular, under-capitalized and willing to work their entire families seventy hours or more a week, took advantage of the changing structure of the black neighborhood in the 1980s and started to provide services which once had been offered only by black entrepreneurs. Koreans quickly realized the cost of starting a business in a depressed neighborhood was much lower than in other, more thriving neighborhoods. They discovered that they could rent a store that had stood empty for months at a lower rate than they could in more economically healthy neighborhoods. They learned that they could buy run-down or dilapidated buildings for very little capital outlay and restore them for use in their businesses. At least, this was true in the early stages of Koreans' business incursion into the black community. However, a decade later, as has been the story for decades, the "gold rush" was over. Buying successful, established businesses in the black community cheaply was no longer possible, although some recently arrived Koreans still believed buying a business in the black neighborhood was a bargain when compared with the opportunities in other places.

Secondly, while the chances for making money in minority neighborhoods was greater than in other areas, the risk was great also, as too many headlines attested. For example, the fact that large, well-capitalized corporations are unwilling to invest in these neighborhoods would be regarded by most people as sufficient warning that there is little chance of profit making. However, Korean entrepreneurs have been willing to set up shop in black neighborhoods and offer goods at a very low profit margin to the black underclass. For example, Korean immigrant merchants offered Abelmann and Lie their reasons for doing business in the South Central Los Angeles black community. A female merchant comments: "The reason people go into South Central is because of money. You can make a lot of money there." Another interviewee expressed a similar view: "After Watts [the 1965 civil disturbance], desperate (Korean) immigrants went into those stores. They would sit in there all day long—click, clack, click, clack—at their cash registers, going absolutely bonkers. But they were making lots of money. This appealed to all sorts, but particularly to those who had failed once in Korea."[10]

In minority communities, such as that occupied by blacks in South Central Los Angeles, Korean merchants became intermediaries between minority customers and large corporations. Social scientists call these intermediaries "middlemen," and if the middlemen themselves belong to a minority, the social scientists refer to them as "middleman minorities." A generally accepted theory in sociological literature useful in explaining the role of middlemen minorities in the United States and other countries,[11] and which explains why intermediary minorities such as Jews, Italians and now Koreans are disliked, even hated, by minority residents, essentially says, minority residents who already harbor deep resentment toward the large corporations regard intermediaries as representatives, or agents, of the corporations and therefore are held largely responsible for the current underprivileged status of the minority residents. In short, the minority residents transfer their dislike of the corporation to the middlemen minority. Recently, Min analyzed the conflict between blacks and Koreans in minority neighborhoods based solely on the middleman minority theory and pointed out that the role played by Korean immigrants as the middlemen minority has brought some positive consequences for the Korean immigrant group. Although their middleman role was disliked by the minority residents, it has brought about ethnic solidarity among Korean merchants who face a similar economic predicament in all minority neighborhoods, which in turn, Min argues, has sharpened their political skills that protect their common interests.[12]

A third reason for Koreans' presence in minority neighborhoods is that their limited command of the language and lack of start-up capital forced them to choose from among many unattractive possibilities. Put simply, they couldn't afford the luxury of choosing better business locations. Then, they had to learn from bitter experience of the economic and physical risks and dangers involved in opening businesses in minority neighborhoods. Such neighborhoods have a notoriously high crime rate; moreover, the merchants had to learn to cope with shoplifting, vandalism, and occasional physical assaults. In spite of all the hazards and the potential for economic ruin, they were willing to take the risks because they believed they could realize a reasonable profit. Plenty of these shopkeepers have given up and left for better and safer neighborhoods, but many have stayed because their profit margin has borne out their decision to do business in the black neighborhoods. A Korean shopkeeper said it was worth taking a risk in a black neighborhood because business is so good.

The fourth reason given by Koreans for setting up businesses in the black community is to take advantage of black consumer habits. In interviews with Korean merchants in the black neighborhoods of Philadelphia, they frequently mentioned that blacks are less price conscious; that they are impulsive shoppers, and that they are fad conscious. This means that a shrewd beauty salon operator can make large profits selling beauty products such as wigs, shampoos, nail polish, and other high-profit items. And of course, styles change rapidly. Those selling clothing can make a tidy profit from fashion accessories such as belts, purses, and shoes where styles are ephemeral. While some black observers are critical of black women for throwing away their money on tacky and impractical fashions, and argue that marginalized and powerless black people are exploited and victimized by Korean merchants, other researchers report that the Korean store owners frequently mentioned that black shoppers were less choosy in selecting items, more often involved in "accidental [impulse] shopping," and were generally "less sensitive to prices" than white customers.[13]

It should be pointed out, however, that Korean merchants are not the only ones who take advantage of black consumers' behavior. Black store owners are doing the same thing. In fact, it has been found that the prices of goods in both Korean and black-owned stores are comparable, and that prices are generally higher in black neighborhoods than the prices of comparable merchandise in white neighborhoods. At one point, the A&P grocery chain used to be the target of very loud, even angry, complaints because the A&P

management would charge 10 to 20 percent more for food in the stores serving the minority neighborhoods than it would for the same food in white neighborhoods. A black store owner, moreover, complained that Korean store owners have an advantage over black store owners because, for whatever reasons, black consumers have come to believe that consumer goods offered by black merchants are inferior to similar goods in Koreans' stores, or any other non-black store. How widespread this notion is among blacks is difficult to judge as there has been no systematic study of this belief.

No particular inferences should be drawn from this black consumer behavior, rather, it may be nothing more than a reflection of typical consumer behavior among all low-income groups. The people who live in isolated pockets of poverty are seldom astute shoppers and are usually ignorant of the true value of goods and services. Even those who are alert to the costs of merchandise don't always have access to transportation that could take them to shops and stores that offer better values for their money.

The conflict between the Korean shoppers and their black customers will not subside, in spite of recent efforts to promote racial harmony, as long as the black residents remain in the underclass and the Korean store owners are regarded as "exploiters" or "interlopers," as had been the case with shopkeepers from earlier ethnic groups, such as the Jews, Italians, and other European immigrant groups. The resident minority had long since concluded that the Europeans were there solely for profit and contributed nothing to the welfare or betterment of their neighborhood. It is natural that the resident minority imputed the same motives to the Koreans. Furthermore, because the influx of Korean immigrants eager to set up stores in the black neighborhood continues apace, there is the strong suggestion that history is repeating itself. That, in turn, suggests the antagonism between these two racial groups will not subside unless both groups are deeply committed to resolving conflicts based on mutual understanding.

The more black residents understand Korean immigrants' experiences, motives, and intentions, the greater their awareness of why Korean merchants set up shop in their neighborhoods. A black merchant summed it up this way: "Korean merchants are hard working people, and black people can learn a lot from them. They are here just to make a living like anybody else. They must be desperate to take a chance and open a store in this neighborhood. I am concerned about their safety."

The black-Korean conflict has certainly aroused the interest of many social scientists. Their analyses of the causes of the conflict have led to some constructive proposals as possible solutions to resolve the tension between the two groups.[14] There are many signs of improvement in relationships between Korean shopkeepers and their black patrons. Recently, a black reporter was pleasantly surprised when she visited a Korean-operated beauty supply store in the black community. She found that conditions had improved to the point that good will was being expressed by both groups. For instance, Korean immigrants have learned that they must make a systematic effort to fit in with their surroundings. They have started to play music, such as rhythm and blues, that appeals to their largely black customers and have made efforts to hire black employees where once they would have employed only members of their family.[15] In many different ways, Koreans changed their ways in order to better serve their customers. Now, for instance, instead of following customers around as though they were trying to catch them in the act of shoplifting, they have tried to make sure their customers understand they are there to help.

COMPETITION AMONG COMPATRIOTS

As most Korean immigrant merchants operate on the margin, that is, they barely break even, the competition among them can sometimes become disastrous. For instance, where a single Korean grocery store or restaurant has become established, within a matter of months and in a few blocks radius, other Korean-owned businesses soon crowd in, effectively diluting the opportunities for all. A frustrated Korean produce-store owner aptly describes the competitive working conditions: "There is a proverb which says 'united we stand, divided we fall.' In the case of the Koreans, it is the opposite. The more we gather in one place and try to do the same thing, the more likely we all fail in our business." A Korean dry cleaning store owner in Virginia, located on the outskirts of Washington, D.C., describes his frustration with this practice:

When I bought a dry cleaning store, there was no other dry cleaner around mine. Now there are four dry cleaning stores near my store, all of which are operated by Koreans. For example, I used to charge $1.25 for washing and ironing a shirt. One of my competitors charges $1.00 and another even went down further to 95 cents! When I hire Korean helpers, they usually stay a short period of time until they become familiar with operating a dry cleaning business and they usually leave to open their own. I don't mind that. But what I do mind is that some of them open their stores not far from mine! The problem with Korean entrepreneurs is that they all want to do the same thing. They should do something else.

There are many other Korean entrepreneurs who are frustrated and angry with their compatriots who create cut-throat competitive working conditions. A successful California businesswoman deplored business practices of Korean entrepreneurs:

> Koreans are killing California's economy. They don't pay insurance and they cheat on taxes. . . . People compete until they kill each other. There used to be only a few *noraepang* [song rooms] in town, and now there are over forty. They used to charge $25 an hour, and now they charge $13. If you order *pulgogi* [barbecued beef] at a Korean restaurant, the dish is filled with water. The meat suppliers put water on the meat and freeze it so that it will weigh more. Koreans have to earn their living honestly. They have to pay taxes and vote.[16]

A California cab driver also describes how competition among Korean entrepreneurs eventually will result in a no-win situation for all.

> Of course, most of these Korean taxi companies aren't licensed or regulated, since they cater only to Koreans. People who can't speak English can't ride in American cabs, because they can't communicate. It's hard to say how many Korean-operated taxis there are altogether because the companies are all different sizes. Some of them are one-man companies, but they didn't necessarily start off that way. Maybe they started out with ten men, and each of them leaves to start his own company. There's a lot of competition. I'd say there are three hundred fifty or three hundred sixty taxi companies in downtown Los Angeles. There's a lot of turnover. Every day, you can see seven or eight taxi company ads for new drivers in the Korean newspaper. There will come a time when they will all kill each other off. That's inevitable, because in the end, the only way you can survive is to kill someone else.[17]

A Korean store owner in a major metropolitan area may receive many telephone calls from other potential Korean entrepreneurs about the possibility of opening businesses in his area. He says, "I like to help my compatriots, because I was helped by my Korean friends when I arrived in the United States. But I am hesitant to give them any advice about the business because eventually they will become my competitors. Sometimes, I have to say the business is so-so, even though the business is doing very well, and I feel guilty because I discouraged them. I am afraid to attend any kind of Korean gatherings, such as churches, picnics, and sport events because Koreans are constantly looking for new business ideas and new ways of making money. I have to be constantly on guard not to brag about my business lest I want to tangle with them."

Ironically, however, many Korean immigrants are hesitant to leave their familiar surroundings in spite of the threat to their livelihood posed by their compatriots. A Korean produce store owner considered leaving the suburb of Philadelphia where his business was well established because he felt battered by the fierce competitive practices of other Korean produce store owners. His brother-in-law, who lives in Albuquerque, New Mexico, suggested he should take a look at an ice cream parlor located about 100 miles outside Albuquerque that was for sale. However, the produce store owner decided against buying the ice cream parlor and he explained why:

My wife and I went to Albuquerque and met our broker and drove to the ice cream parlor, which was located on Highway 40 about 100 miles from Albuquerque. The ice cream parlor was located near a truck stop. We sat there and observed activities in the store for one hour and thought the store could generate a good income. All of sudden, the feeling of isolation and loneliness hit me. How could we live in such an isolated place with no friends! There are no Koreans, no Korean churches, and no Korean groceries, nothing except a money-making opportunity. Since my wife and I are not conversant in English, it is not easy to make friends other than with Koreans. We hated our Korean competitors so much that we thought we could go anywhere in the United States as long as there are no conniving Korean competitors. Now, we were faced with choosing between money making in a lonely place and hardship in a familiar place. We chose the latter.

LEARNING THE BUSINESS ROPES

The long hours of hard work, learning a new language, and dealing with hazards of life in the minority neighborhoods are not the only concerns for self-employed Korean immigrants. Understanding American capitalism with its corresponding subtleties of supply and demand, the ever-changing market system, American labor laws, as well as knowledge of local business are still beyond the level of Korean immigrants' comprehension. Newly arrived Korean immigrants who bought businesses in predominantly white neighborhoods are often surprised later to discover hitherto unnoticed clauses in contracts or changes taking place in the neighborhood of which they were unaware when they purchased the businesses. A dry cleaning store owner in Maryland laments:

> When I bought my dry cleaning store in the mini-shopping mall, I thought I bought a good business. I examined the previous owner's gross income and expenditures, and I thought I could do even better if all my family members jumped in to work and worked hard. Through my Korean lawyer, I signed a lease contract. Later I discovered my rent was going up every year, and I was told by the landlord that the rent increase was due to an increase in the cost of living. I didn't know my rent would be adjusted to the cost of living increase when I signed the lease. A couple years later I also learned a major supermarket, which is the center of economic activity in the mall where my dry cleaning store is located, was going to move out. I knew my business would be affected negatively when the supermarket moved out. Did the previous owner of the business know the supermarket was going to relocate? I could have sold my business to an unsuspecting, newly arrived Korean immigrant, but I couldn't do that. Finally, the supermarket moved out and a book store replaced it. As I predicted, my business began to slow down at the beginning and has almost come to a grinding halt. Now, I am in the process of renegotiating the lease with my landlord. If that falls through, I am thinking about moving out, leaving everything behind.

Lack of knowledge of business operation in America can be detrimental to launching a successful business by Korean immigrants. A daughter describes how her immigrant parents failed in their business because they were not familiar with American business practices.

> My parents got into the garment contracting business in 1983, when the woman my mother was working for became pregnant and had to unload her small garment factory. My parents didn't have any money, so the woman just let them take over and pay her back later. For three or four years, my parents made more money than they had ever seen. That was when they bought a house in Walnut and I started college. But they don't know how the system works or how to take care of a lot of important things. They didn't even know anything about taxes; they just thought that after paying their employees, they could keep what-

ever money was left. Ultimately they had to close the factory because they got into tax trouble.[18]

Most Korean entrepreneurs acknowledge that they are not familiar with the complexities of American business laws and practices and the unpredictable shifting of demographics which affect their businesses, as well as the ever-changing consumer tastes and habits. However, many observers have difficulty believing that some Korean store owners are so ignorant of certain basic obligations of all small or large entrepreneurs as to neglect to do such things as pay taxes on their earnings, establish social security accounts, provide for such fringe benefits as health insurance, and other amenities for their employees. A shop owner commented: "I can't believe they are ignorant about tax obligations. Like most Americans, they will do anything to minimize their tax burden. They hire part-timers and pay them hourly wages because most of their employees are not permanent. They come and go. Few employers are concerned about paying social security, health coverage, and unemployment compensation." A Korean-born Los Angeles police officer who has observed the Korean community in Los Angeles for many years lamented about how Korean business practices are destroying morale in the Korean community:

Many people think that all Koreans go to Harvard and get A-pluses; that all Koreans are rich. This is not so. This community has a lot of tragedies, a lot of stereotyping in reverse. We have a lot of poor and uneducated people. Their living conditions are terrible, one crowded room, everyone working two or three jobs, without life insurance, dental or medical benefits, pensions, or workmen's compensation. They think that they are helping each other by just passing cash back and forth: employers not paying benefits and employees not paying taxes, but in the long run, that's very destructive. People are really living an oppressed life, mainly because they limit themselves and because no one is really giving them any emotional support or encouragement.[19]

Korean shop owners are also learning the art of customer relations, something they had frequently ignored. For many years Korean shoppers complained about the somewhat brusque manner of Korean employees or store owners toward customers. In fact, this curt way of treating customers was one of the major complaints of black customers about the way Korean merchants conducted business in the black community. The blacks interpreted the gruff manner of Korean merchants as a form of racial prejudice. The fact is that Korean merchants treated everyone that way, including Korean customers. It is not unusual to see an expressionless waiter or a waitress in a Korean restaurant literally throw menus at customers without saying a word. Sometimes they neglect to return with the customers' change, apparently assuming that they are entitled to keep it. Store owners do not smile or welcome their customers, instead, they may maintain a stony silence. One may attribute such glum demeanor to the fact that many Korean store owners were former white-collar professionals experiencing downward social mobility. Their unhappiness about their present work sometimes shows when they deal with customers. Someone suggested to a Korean store owner that he should be more cheerful and courteous to customers. The store owner retorted: "Do you think I came to America to do this kind of work?" An educated Korean store owner, on the other hand, blamed the lack of courtesy on the declining quality of recent immigrants. He thought many of them "don't know any better" when it comes to dealing with people. In the recent past, however, thanks in part to the competitive nature of various store owners and in part to their gradual acculturation to American business manners, more and more store owners are cultivating attentive and friendly attitudes toward customers.

The early Korean immigrants still remember when they shopped in Korean supermarkets. Most items of Korean food and goods were not only expensive compared with similar items in Chinese and American supermarkets, but also there were no price tags attached to items. Customers never knew the price of items until they reached the checkout counter. Now, the prices of foodstuffs in most Korean grocery stores are not only comparable to those in any other ethnic supermarkets, the price of every item is clearly marked. As many recent Korean immigrants have already learned to run small businesses in Korea, their main purpose for coming to the United States is making money. They are much more savvy in operating businesses than white-collar professionals turned store owners and try anything to attract customers. Now, most Korean supermarkets in large metropolitan areas are almost indistinguishable from their American counterparts.

Most self-employed Koreans work late into the night every day of the week. Korean teen-agers have said that their happiest days of the week were weekdays, not weekends, because during the weekends they had to help their parents in their stores. Small children stay home and play by themselves until grown-ups return home late at night. All family members are involved in running a business; it is truly a family business. Even grandparents contribute by babysitting while the parents and older children are out in the store. When they are not working at their family's store, wives are frequently found working in factories. Um's study of Korean immigrant women in the Dallas area apparel industry indicates that the median working hours per week of Korean women factory workers were fifty-five in her sample of sixty-nine women, and more than 17 percent of the workers put in between sixty-one and eighty hours.[20] A 1.5 generation Korean immigrant observes how work consumes Korean immigrants: "They (Korean immigrants) have no family life. No recreation, no reflection on anything, no participation in the world, nothing outside of materialistic pursuit."[21] As with most early immigrants in America, the work ethic of Korean immigrants is strong. They believe in an ethic similar to the Protestant work ethic: hard work, frugality, and sacrifice, which will eventually lead them to achieve the American dream.

Unfortunately, however, in the late 20th century, with a knowledge-based economy, specifically an economy based on advanced technology, jobs based on physical endurance or manual labor, qualities of thrift and resourcefulness alone may not be enough for the Korean immigrant group or any contemporary immigrant group hoping to rise above a minimum level of subsistence. Although it is difficult to determine per capita income of a self-employed Korean immigrant because the entire family is usually involved in running a business, one survey indicates that the household income of the average self-employed Korean immigrant in Los Angeles is around $50,000 a year.[22] However, per capita income of each worker in the family may hardly amount to subsistence wages. When their children leave home and they have to hire outside helpers, most parents quickly feel the effect on their household income.

It would be a mistake, according to Abelmann and Lie, to compare the Korean self-employed on equal terms with American small business owners who are considered to be pillars of their community, the bedrock of small town life, and who not only provide goods and services but also contribute to the welfare of the community. They don't imagine self-made Korean entrepreneurs emerging as heroes of laissez-faire capitalism as did Henry Ford who was an innovator in the evolution of the automobile industry and John D. Rockefeller who amassed a fortune in oil and became something of a philanthropist. They note that Korean-American entrepreneurs are petty merchants who run small markets, dry cleaners, or liquor stores. Although these occupations are valuable, Abelmann and Lie say there should be no illusions about their grandeur. Korean-American entrepreneurs are not as yet innovators who will spur economic growth, nor do they, by and large, amass a fortune or make a major contribution to society. Abelmann and Lie ask whether a family with a shop of its own, working seven days a week and making $50,000 a year, has achieved the American dream. They question whether this is the entrepreneur celebrated by Schumpeter or American folklore. [23]

Korean immigrants may not realize their American dreams as have many early European immigrants. Availability of opportunities, demand for a wide range of labor, and social mobility which existed at the turn of the century may not exist in late 20th century America. On the other hand, it is premature to judge the prospects of Korean entrepreneurs at this juncture as most of them immigrated to America after the 1970s and are in the process of economic adaptation. It will probably take a much longer period of time for Korean immigrants than those of European descent to become innovators and pillars of the community considering their racial and cultural background. We still vividly remember how Chinese and Japanese immigrants were treated by American society not too many decades ago. Korean entrepreneurs are still learning how to run small-sized or medium-sized businesses, overcoming language and cultural barriers and racial prejudice.

INTRA-ETHNIC CONFLICT

Besides tension created by competition among Korean entrepreneurs for the limited available ethnic businesses, there are also many internal squabbles within the Korean community. Some of these disputes are business related and others are indirectly related to business practices. Some business-related disputes include charges made by employees that Korean employers don't pay taxes, social security, or health insurance premiums. The Korean employers respond by saying that most Korean employees don't want deductions for social security or health insurance taken from their pay. They claim that their employees would like to have as much cash as possible in preparation for the time when they can open their own stores. The employers also believe many of the Korean employees work in their stores just long enough to learn their "business secrets." Of the many sources of conflict between Korean employers and their employees, some are derived from a failure of understanding between the employers and the employees. Nevertheless, these misunderstandings have serious consequences. For example, a successful business woman in Los Angeles explains how difficult it is employing Koreans:

At the peak time for in the 1970s, my company was grossing $400,000. I didn't know much about taxes or licensing at that time. We had 120 employees, all of them Hispanic. At first we hired some Korean workers; once, we had thirty Ewha University [one of the elite women's universities in Korea] graduates in the shop, as well as many pastors' wives. On Fridays and Saturdays they would call members of their church all day long, using our company phone. If I said something, they would shout, "Don't you have a mother?" I couldn't make business calls because they were tying up the telephone. It was very difficult to handle those Koreans. Sometimes they would set up their own shops and take away twenty or thirty of my workers. Or else they wouldn't show up when the work was hard, only when it was easy. So I started to cut down on Korean workers. I haven't used any Korean workers since 1975. That's why I was able to last so long in business. I have contributed to a lot of Korean community causes, but I didn't employ Koreans in my shop.[24]

Although the racial and ethnic composition of the community where the store is located affects the store owner's choice of the make-up of the racial characteristics of his or her employees, more and more Korean employers are hiring non-Koreans. In his study of 960 Korean store owners, Yoon found 46 percent had Korean employees and 43 percent had Latino employees.[25] Korean employers frequently complained that Korean employees asked for raises after a very short period of employment and if they didn't get the raise, they wouldn't show up for work, especially during the busiest time, such as Christmas holiday seasons. The Korean employers also alleged that most Korean employees regard their employment as temporary. They don't show very much loyalty to their employers, either. As a result, the employers feel no compunction about hiring other racial groups, particularly Mexican Americans. Although the language and cultural barriers are pronounced, many Korean employers consider Mexican-American employees hard workers and very loyal to their employers. These qualities more than compensate, the employers feel, for the inconveniences in communication and cultural differences. Since many Mexican-American employees are themselves immigrants, Korean employers believe that their Latino employees understand them better because they have experienced prejudice and discrimination similar to that experienced by Koreans. Consequently, Koreans believe it is easier to establish an affinity with their Mexican-American employees, something they do not think possible with blacks. This is one of the major reasons why many Korean employers prefer hiring Mexican Americans. A store owner in Venice Beach, California, who employed a Mexican-American teen-aged girl said she regarded her Mexican-American employee as a daughter. Further-more, she said, Mexican-Americans' emphasis on strong family unity, re-specting the elderly, and caring for children are similar to Koreans' values. She also added that hiring a Korean is too much headache and besides, it is too expensive.

Charges and countercharges among Korean store owners about who is not paying taxes, who is exploiting Korean workers, and who is charging too much for their goods and services are normal by-products of competi-tion among Korean entrepreneurs. Even though Korean entrepreneurs are themselves in business to make money, they accuse other Korean entrepre-neurs of being too materialistic, too selfish, and unconcerned with other hu-man beings. There was a case where a Korean employee reported his employer for not paying his federal taxes. The employer was investigated by the IRS and eventually had to declare bankruptcy because he owed the government back taxes. In another case, according to one auto mechanic, there was a rumor that illegal Korean immigrants were arrested because a Korean turned them in to the Immigration and Naturalization Service Of-fice. Whether this type of snitch is intended to cut down on competition or grows out of some sort of vengeance is not clear. Store owners also accuse Korean landlords of charging exorbitant rent for their stores. Such charges became more frequent as more Korean store owners have Korean landlords. In fact, Yoon found that 38 percent of Korean store owners in Los Angeles had Korean landlords.[26] A hair dresser in Los Angeles mentioned that, when she had an American landlord, he treated her courteously. When he needed to raise the rent, he explained his reasons for such a raise. When a Korean bought the building, he immediately raised the rent without expla-nation and curtly told her to move out if she didn't like the rent hike. A Ko-rean store owner in Venice Beach, California, mentioned some Koreans rent stores then re-rent them to other Koreans at a higher price. He commented that he had dealt with many ethnic entrepreneurs, such as Jews, blacks, Mid-dle Easterners and found Korean entrepreneurs were the most difficult with which to deal. Another Korean store owner accused some Koreans of spe-cializing in buying businesses and selling them at an exorbitant price to other Korean immigrants. Still other Korean businessmen, sometimes re-ferred to as "hawks," have been accused of setting up new stores for the sole purpose of selling them to newcomers at a high margin of profit. Here is how hawks work, as reported in a Korean-language newspaper:

A [Korean] couple in Flushing worked sixteen hours a day for two years and accumulated some savings: the husband had labored in menial jobs and the wife had toiled at a garment factory. Their dream was simple: they wanted to have their own business rather than work for someone else. One day, a church member [in their Korean church] approached and asked them whether they wanted to buy a fruit and vegetable store, saying that the owner of the store was a conscientious Christian. He added that the business of the store was very good but that the store owner had to sell the store because of a lack of hands. When the couple heard this offer, they were very excited. In order to determine the volume of customer traffic, the couple loitered around the store for two weeks. Then they decided to pay $20,000 in "key money" for the store because it always bustled with customers coming and going all the time. Two or three weeks after they finally took over the store, they realized that they had been swindled. All of the customers suddenly disappeared. The unfortunate new owners finally realized the previous owner had cut his retail prices in half to attract customers while they watched his store.[27]

There is also tension between Korean immigrants who came to America with a substantial amount of money and those who came to America without much money and had to build up their businesses from scratch. The hard-pressed Korean store owners believe that Koreans who brought large sums of money to America were able to do so because they had worked for the Korean government or large Korean corporations and implied these people's monies were made illegally, perhaps by accepting bribes. A Korean store owner explained: "These people bring bundles of money from Korea after the Korean government relaxed the law on the amount of money an immigrant could take to the United States. In the States, they put their money to work buying buildings and renting them to Koreans. They have also bought gas stations, large grocery stores, and liquor stores and hired managers to run them. They have an easy life—playing golf, driving expensive cars, and living in luxurious homes while we work like the devil for ten and sometimes twelve hours a day." Sentiment toward the rich Korean immigrants among the Korean immigrants who had to work hard for their money include envy tinged with intense dislike. A middle-aged woman who regards herself as a hard-working and successful immigrant spoke about "the problem of new immigrants" in Los Angeles. "The new immigrants—the rich ones—drive around in [Mercedes] Benzes; earlier immigrants don't do this. Of course this angers the blacks; those people aren't contributing anything to the community. People like me, who have worked really hard to finally be able to afford a house and live somewhat well, hate people like that who are just capitalizing on the incredible strength of the *won* [South Korean currency]."[28]

Ironically, these hard-working store owners also wanted to differentiate themselves from those Koreans who didn't own stores but who sold their wares in swap-meets or along the California beaches. These store owners looked down on non-store owners as if they were wandering Gypsies. They claimed these vagabond-like people are uneducated, can't speak English well, and have no manners. Abelmann and Lie cite numerous cases of how these store owners deemed swap-meet stall owners as undesirable people. Statements like the following are uttered by these store owners:[29] "Only 10 percent of them [swap-meet stall owners] are OK. They don't behave well. I can't stand dealing with them so I don't go to swap meets"; "Swap-meet stall owners haven't been in the United States very long. They can't speak English. What they have lost [during the Los Angeles riot] didn't have so much value, so they can start up again. They are—well, I don't say this in the bad sense—low class"; "The lower-class immigrants really know how to work hard and make money, and since they are uneducated they are the ones who don't speak English."

Although there are Korean immigrants who operate swap-meet stalls, push carts through city streets hawking their wares, or else hold down menial jobs as, for instance, janitors and thus belong in a strictly technical sense to the lower class, many of them are, in fact, highly educated, formerly middle-class citizens in Korea. Largely because of difficulties mastering English, white-collar jobs are not readily available to them. A swap-meet stall owner in Phoenix, who was a former Korean Olympic volleyball coach, expressed his view of social class. "What does it make any difference whether you own a swap-meet stall, a dry cleaning shop, a small grocery store, or a fish market? In the eyes of outsiders, we are all in the same boat. We are not doctors, lawyers, or engineers. As a stall owner, I was told I was making more money than Korean doctors who can't practice medicine because they failed a medical license examination. It's ridiculous, store owners think that they are superior to swap-meet stall owners. In fact I was once a store owner and I became a stall owner because I do better as a stall owner." Another former stall owner, now a church minister, commented that he put his two children through college with the earnings from a stall. Ironically, in some cases, uneducated, lower-middle class Korean immigrants are usually successful at business in America because of their experience in Korea, unlike the well-educated, formerly white-collar professionals who have been forced to try to operate small businesses. Although social class distinctions in the Korean community based on the type or size of business, its degree of financial success, and the educational level of its owner may develop in the future; at present, it is still premature to attempt to delineate Korean immigrants' social class by any traditional measure of American success because most Korean immigrants, except for a small percentage of U.S.-trained professionals, are doing similar kinds of work regardless of their educational and occupational backgrounds. Of course, this will change. As we have seen, some Korean immigrants are already very much class conscious.

Moreover, there is a clear chasm developing between Korean professionals and shopkeepers. The latter sometimes refer to the former as an elite group or intellectual class who are concerned only with themselves and avoid getting involved with the problems of other immigrants. The established professionals (doctors, lawyers, engineers, accountants, and college professors, most of whom have obtained their degrees and certificates from U.S. colleges and universities) are frequent targets of disapproval expressed by nonprofessional Korean immigrants. A shopkeeper in Los Angeles remarked: "They don't involve themselves with Korean community matters at all. We seldom associate with them. They don't know anything about us. Yet a few professors commented about the Los Angeles riot on television as if they know everything what caused the riot." Choy, a frequent writer on Koreans in America, characterized the Korean intellectuals in America as a "do-nothing class" within the Korean community. He has observed: "Most Korean-American intellectuals isolate themselves from the community and live by themselves, looking only after their own interests. Their ambition is to be a part of an American establishment, to secure their position first and then to advance into the American circle. Some even forget that they are descendants of Koreans."[30] To such charges, Korean professionals and intellectuals respond by saying that they are not a bunch of snobs. However, they cannot seem to relate to recent Korean immigrants. A Korean college professor remarked: "My brother and my wife's relatives are store owners. At our family gathering, I pretend I am interested in their businesses, moneymaking plans, operating stores, Korean politics in Korea, Korean church activities. Frankly, none of these subjects is interesting to me."

In major metropolitan areas where a large number of Korean immigrants are concentrated, there is contention between those who promote close ties with the South Korean government and those who think Koreans should distance themselves from the Korean government. They say the immigrants should claim the privileges of American citizenship and try to fit in to American society. In the past, those who wished to maintain close ties with South Korea collected money and sent it to their homeland for the purpose of relieving various natural disasters or for other social causes. In turn, they always sought advice and counsel about how to deal with matters in the United States on various matters, such as immigration and naturalization, business, specifically import and export, and race matters such as the Korean-black conflict and the Los Angeles riot. Those who advocate cutting ties with the South Korean government view the desire of those trying to maintain close cultural and business ties with those in South Korea as an aberration. The "separatists" argue that immigrants must dismiss the notion that "Los Angeles is part of Seoul, Korea." They insist that Korean immigrants must give up the sojourner's mentality and get involved in the cultural, social, and political affairs of the United States.

Their demand for the Seoul government to adopt a "hands-off policy" is not completely without reason. According to Kim, since the beginning of mass immigration of Koreans to the United States, the South Korean government has regarded overseas Koreans as its subjects in need of its constant care and protection as well as its "corrective guidance and education." For example, in the case of New York, Kim argues, it is no exaggeration to say that the Korean Consulate General is the "de facto" mayor of New York's Korean community.[31] However, as Korean immigrants become acclimated to life in the United States, get involved with their children's adjustment problems in school, and watch with pride and concern their children's careers begin to take off, not to mention their own careers, they become more and more indifferent to the interests of a remote South Korean government.

COPING WITH DOWNWARD SOCIAL MOBILITY

Through trial and error, beginning Korean entrepreneurs eventually learn common business procedures. Their goal in business is clear cut: make a profit from their business and become self-sufficient. Some will succeed and some will fail. However, there is a less tangible area of difficulty with which many Korean immigrants always seem to struggle and that remains largely unresolved; that is, they have not yet learned to cope with downward occupational and social mobility. This is particularly true for those Korean immigrants who came to America in the 1970s with the dream of pursuing a professional career but who ended up as petty entrepreneurs. Abelmann and Lie illustrate how a Korean store owner felt about his downward social mobility:

After graduating from Seoul National University, Yun came to the United States in the late 1970s intending to earn higher degrees in mathematics. He abandoned his plan for graduate study, however, because he needed to earn a living to support his wife and child. "I'm a failure of sorts," he said as we talked in his living room in a posh suburb. He joined one of his relatives in running a small store selling trinkets. "It is very embarrassing but there is an expression here: 'what you do depends on who picks you up at the airport.' I, too, just followed my relative into the same business." Drawing on personal and family savings and encouraged by his friends, he opened his own store and was then able to sell it and become a wholesaler by the late 1980s.[32]

Occupational downward mobility is commonly experienced not just by Korean immigrants, but also by other immigrant groups. Because of their difficulty with the language, their inability to transfer their skills to their adopted country, and their difficulty with the cultural differences, frequently immigrants are underemployed in a peripheral labor market.[33] It is not unusual to find that the owner of a small store, a gardener, a cab driver, and a restaurant employee were all college graduates and had held middle-level or high-level managerial positions in Korea. A few surveys on the background of Korean immigrants since 1965 in Chicago and the Los Angeles-Orange County areas indicate that nearly half of the Korean respondents held professional, administrative, managerial, or technical positions.[34] In the survey of Korean immigrant women in the Dallas area apparel industry, Um found 68 percent of her sample respondents' husbands held blue-collar jobs in the Dallas area, but to the question of their husbands' jobs in Korea, 54 percent of her respondents said their husbands held white-collar jobs.[35] Even more surprising, in his study of occupational adjustment of Korean business families (husbands and wives were involved), Min interviewed 137 male and 22 female small business owners in Atlanta, Georgia in 1981 and found almost 70 percent of them completed four years or more of college and 75 percent had held white-collar positions or else pursued professional occupations in Korea prior to their immigration. Of those who had white-collar occupations, only five respondents were involved in sales or did clerical work while the rest of the white-collar workers were engaged in managerial, technical, and medical professional occupations which required expert knowledge and leadership abilities.[36]

Underemployment and downward social mobility are also common among Korean professionals who usually project an image of "success" in their chosen profession. For example, Shin and Chang found that Korean immigrant physicians carry on the same kind of marginal activities within the medical profession as unskilled immigrant workers do within the non-professional labor market. Significantly, a larger number of Korean immigrant physicians are concentrated in peripheral specialties than are their counterparts who remained in Korea. (Core and periphery specialties are determined based on reported median income of practitioners in each specialty.[37]) Occasionally, there are immigrants who have received degrees from U.S. universities, and although it would seem they should be able to secure white-collar jobs, they also end up as small-business entrepreneurs. Indeed, it is not uncommon to find Korean immigrants who received bachelor's degrees, even in a few cases with doctoral degrees, from U.S. colleges and universities but who are operating small stores. A Korean ethnic newspaper reported how both Korean-educated professionals and U.S.-educated Korean immigrants in New York experience downward mobility.

> Mr. Park, who was a college professor at a Korean university in Seoul, has grabbed a steering wheel and become a taxi driver in New York City. Shoe repairing is the first job for a Mr. Yang, who once aired his name as a radio announcer in Seoul. In a small shoe-repairing shop he stakes his future American life on the continuous sound of his nailing work. Mr. Lee, an American Ph.D. in engineering, peddled while driving him from village to village, wigs and clothing. He has just set up a wholesale company and thus has entered the ranks of the big Korean businessmen in New York City. All these episodes reveal a naked facade of the economic struggle of our fellow countrymen. . . .[38]

For many Korean immigrants, an education in the United States does not guarantee successful entrance into professional careers unless they have an understanding of American culture and proficiency in English concomitant with their education. A Korean immigrant with an MBA degree earned at an American university decided to open a bakery in a suburb of Washington. He viewed his chances for success in an American firm as rather slim because of his limited command of English and racism. He figured that, instead of wasting time working for an American firm, he ought to start his own business.

Although most Korean immigrants did not expect to occupy positions in America similar or equal to positions they held in Korea, it does take time for Korean immigrants to come to terms with their downward mobility in the United States. This period of adjustment can be very difficult when one considers these immigrants came from a country where merchants and trades people are not highly respected, even though Koreans' attitudes toward small entrepreneurs are more favorable now at the time of South Korea's industrial boom. Once they accept the fact that they are very unlikely to regain their previous status, coping with their downward occupational and social mobility is an enormous mental and emotional adjustment for Koreans to make. As a result, most of them have devised ways to compensate for their lost status. One of the means they have used is to rationalize their pursuit of a career in business as a smart choice. A corner-store owner pointed out that he is glad he was not working for a corporation because, if he did, he couldn't go anywhere in terms of mobility because of his poor command of English and race. He also mentioned that he often heard from Koreans who had worked for American firms but were stuck in lower-level positions too long because their mobility had been blocked by their superiors. Another store owner pointed out that there are many 1.5 generation young people who have no difficulty in English, but who have sought employment in the Korean community after working for American firms. If anything, according to the store owner, they become more Korean after their experience with American firms. Others have asserted that they can't afford to be white-collar workers simply because they can't afford to buy houses and educate their children on the small salary they could earn from white-collar jobs. Yet many of these same Korean entrepreneurs talk glowingly about their previous white-collar positions in Korea. Ex-politicians, former military officers, and retired government employees love to talk about how much authority they had in their previous positions in Korea. For instance, a fish-store owner in Baltimore loves to tell Korean and non-Korean customers alike that he has a doctoral degree in engineering and used to work for a large, important engineering firm in Korea. An owner of a chain of dry cleaning stores likes to discuss Korean politics, his role as a military officer, and his contribution to shaping the Hyundai automobile company in Korea. On the other hand, he seldom wants to talk about his successful dry cleaning business.

To many Korean immigrants, conspicuous consumption is another way of compensating for their lost status. Buying an expensive car and house, sending their children to private schools, taking vacations in exotic places, playing golf, and frequent visits to Korea are some of the symbols of their success in business. These evidences of material or financial success thus become important means of gaining respect, at least among Korean immigrants. In fact, in every city where a large number of Korean immigrants concentrate, one finds golf is their most popular recreational activity. No matter how tired they may be from their work, they still have the energy to play in a golf tournament. To them, playing golf is not just for fun or recreation, it is a status symbol because playing golf in Korea is expensive and available only to a few well-to-do people. A store owner in Chicago described why he desires material things. He said: "America is a capitalist country. The only thing that counts is money. Your former education, family connections, types of occupation you had in Korea don't mean a thing unless you have money. Few Americans know about Korea, let alone the immigrants' backgrounds. The only thing they know is what kind of car you drive, what kind of house you live in, and how much money you have in the bank." A former middle-level government employee in Korea, now a liquor store owner in New Jersey, gloats about how well he is doing by maintaining a lavish life style that is the envy of average Korean immigrants who know him. He says he works only weekdays; the weekends he reserves for golf. He entrusts his store to his employees during the weekends. He repeatedly mentions how often he travels to Korea for pleasure and how long he stays there while his store is being taken care of by his employees.

While some, such as the liquor store owner, are able to indulge themselves in conspicuous consumption, others are not. However, they do try to keep up with the Joneses, so to speak, even though it is beyond their ability to do so. A social worker in California complained that Korean Americans are superficial and materialistic and said: "Many people live in cheap apartments, but drive Mercedes, wear Rolex watches, and play golf even though they can't really afford it. If you go to Koreatown restaurants you'll see these middle-aged guys hanging out after golf, showing off to each other."[39] A produce-store owner in Alexandria, Virginia, who was once manager of a large dental-equipment company in Korea, painfully remembers spending beyond his means in the United States:

> I bought a half-million-dollar house, expensive furniture, and a Cadillac. My church colleagues used to come to my house and admire my house and furniture. We even hosted choir practice, New Year's parties, and occasional church buffets at my house. Also having a bigger house than my relatives, who are professionals, meant something to me. However, I soon realized that most of my earnings from my store went to make payments for my house and car. I finally sold my house at a loss and moved to a smaller house.

The desire to display one's status through material goods probably was derived from the immigrants' wish to compensate themselves for their lost identity. Or else, the immigrants, who were, perhaps, underprivileged in Korea, see such material possessions as houses, cars, memberships in golf clubs, and the schools their children attend, as a means by which they hope to erase the last vestiges of any perceived class differences between themselves and other Korean immigrants.

Not all Korean immigrants choose to indulge in conspicuous consumption to boost their egos, however. There are many other indirect, subtle ways that are used to reclaim or remind others of the status these people had in Korea. For instance, it is a common practice to address people who were important in the homeland with deferential titles to remind them that they are still respected by others in the Korean community. If an immigrant held a responsible position in Korea, then his or her friends and acquaintances invariably address him or her with the title he or she had in Korea. If Mr. Shin was a colonel in the Korean army, then he is addressed as Colonel Shin; if Mr. Park was director of an accounting firm in Korea, then he is addressed as Director Park. However, in some cases, there are store owners, as well as blue-collar workers, who would like to conceal their previous identities. Calling a Korean immigrant who was a colonel in the Korean army but who now works as a janitor in a laundry, Colonel Kim, may seem more sarcastic than respectful. To avoid such an embarrassment, the former colonel may try to conceal his previous position. However, in most cases, in the Korean community immigrants love to flaunt their titles as long as these titles are associated with high status. It seems that, in spite of living in a democracy, calling someone "Mr." is verboten because it is regarded as the title with the lowest degree of respect. In fact, the proliferation of honorifics is a fascinating footnote to the issue of achieving status. For example, Koreans may address Mr. Kim, who owns a nursery in the States, as President or Director Kim. Mr. Lee, who is a barber, may be addressed as Teacher Lee, while Mr. Cho, who is president of the local Korean Association, will be addressed as President Cho, and so on.

There are many titles derived from belonging to Korean churches, such as minister, deacon, accountant, director of youth group, etc. A Korean immigrant commented, "There are many Korean immigrants who would like to attend church and become a deacon, the director of a youth group, a choir director, a sports program director, a leader, or a manager of various programs in his or her church. These titles give a tremendous ego boost to store owners and blue-collar workers who have experienced downward or else no particular social mobility. In the church environment, becoming a deacon is perhaps the greatest honor a member can achieve." These titles, or honorifics, become a permanent mode of address among their friends and acquaintances. Even though one no longer occupies the position, he still retains the title. Thus, although Mr. Park is no longer the church's accountant, his loyal friends will still address him as Accountant Park. That one knows someone who was prominent in government, the private sector, or in academia in Korea is a significant way to gain respect (reflected glory, one might say). A favored device of many Korean immigrants is to casually drop the names of people who used to occupy illustrious positions into their conversations, while letting it slip that this esteemed person is either a close relative or friend. They may even suggest that, had they remained in Korea, they would be enjoying intimate business and social occasions with these people.

Other ways of enhancing one's status include directing people's attention to one's children's academic and career successes. It is generally known that most Koreans are infected with the "Ivy League disease." Greengrocers, dry cleaners, and other retail store owners know a surprising amount about the admission processes and costs of education at Ivy League universities and other prestigious colleges, more in fact than the average American college graduate knows. Once their children are admitted to a prestigious college, they will pay almost any price to keep their children enrolled. They believe the financial hardship they bear for sending their children to one of these prestigious universities is well worth it, considering that their children will receive not only an excellent education but will reward their parents with enormous pride, prestige, and status for having a bright child graduate from such a school. A store owner proudly says that summer times are easier for her and her husband because their child from Harvard will be home to help them in their store.

Korean immigrants draw tremendous pleasure and pride from their children's success in pursuing careers, such as medicine. Sometimes it appears that Korean entrepreneurs wish to fulfill the American dream through their children. Unfortunately, Korean immigrants' wishes frequently conflict with their children's wishes. Some children are unable to enter prestigious colleges because of their grades or for other reasons. Some are able but do not wish to attend one of these universities because they have dreams of their own. Then, there are children who want to pursue careers of their own rather than realizing their parents' dream for them. A high school senior whose father owns a small grocery store confessed that ever since he was a young boy his parents told him he should enter Harvard and become a doctor. He is concerned that he may not be able to fulfill the wishes of his parents; it seems he is very much interested in photography and in pursuing a career in photojournalism. Sometimes these children experience great stress or guilt when they realize that they cannot fulfill their parents' wishes, especially for the sake of promoting their parents' own status within the Korean community. They also know that they are constant objects of discussion when their parents gather with other Koreans. They know their success in school and in pursuing a prestigious career means a great deal to their parents, particularly to those parents who have experienced downward social mobility and need the vicarious boost in status offered by their children.

A person's status is not always determined by conspicuous consumption, the prestige of the university his or her children attend, his or her skill at golf, or honorific titles, although these are important criteria to some in determining their status in America. But among Korean immigrants, these are *desiderata* in determining one's standing in the community, just as other criteria, such as income, membership in an exclusive club, or a tradition of wealth are almost unattainable to most Korean immigrants, at least at the present. Amassing wealth and displaying it conspicuously may indicate one's social standing, but how money is made is an important criterion in many people's judgment of another's social status. Professionals in law and medicine, executives, and other high-ranking officials command a high degree of respect, not because their income is high, but because their source of income is respectable and their conduct is cultured.

For many years, Korean immigrants have maintained a closer relationship with their countrymen, regardless of their background, largely because they were all Koreans in a strange land. Such a feeling is dissipating gradually among the immigrants and is being replaced with class consciousness. As more and more members of the Korean community become secure in their place in the United States, simple class dichotomy may eventually develop, driving a wedge between early immigrants and new arrivals, successful entrepreneurs and unsuccessful ones, professionals and store owners, and store owners and laborers. The process of class polarization is expedited as an increasing number of less-educated, less financially-prepared Koreans have immigrated to the United States in the 1980s and 1990s. According to the 1990 U.S. Bureau of the Census figures, the percentage of Korean American families at the poverty level was second only to the rate for Vietnamese immigrants.[40] The early-arriving Korean immigrants who are established in their own social circle frequently refer to the recent arrivals as uneducated, failures, or as the desperate. They assume, in light of the arrival of economic prosperity in Korea, only failures and incompetent people who have no other alternatives are immigrating to the United States.

It appears that Korean ethnic solidarity based on a common language, race, and culture will not be sufficient to maintain their solidarity. For example, during the Los Angeles riots, Korean immigrants throughout Los Angeles displayed a surprising degree of unity and solidarity by offering financial and emotional support to Korean victims of the riots. Unfortunately, however, the togetherness and cooperation shown among Korean immigrants during and after the riots seem to be dissipating. There was contention in the Korean community as to how money collected for the riot victims should be used. Some argued the money should be used for the improvement of that part of the Korean community which was destroyed during the riot, while others contended it should be given directly to those who actually suffered a loss. In the meantime, the victims complained that the money is controlled by an elite group in the Korean community who were ignoring the poor victims who desperately needed financial help.

NOTES

1. Insook Han Park, James T. Fawcett, Fred Arnold, and Robert Gardner, *Korean Immigrants and U.S. Policy: A Predeparture Perspective* (Honolulu: East-West Population Institute, 1990), 86.

2. Pyoung Gap Min, *Caught in the Middle* (Berkeley: University of California Press, 1996), 48. Although the 1990 census reported that 34.5 percent of the Korean immigrants between 25–64 years of age are self-employed, Min's survey suggests that the self-employment rate was higher than that of the census report. Without including the percentage of Koreans employed in Korean firms, the self-employment rate of the Korean immigrants was 47.5 percent in Los Angeles and Orange Counties and 56 percent in New York City. It has been suggested that the lower rate reported in the census report is because the Korean immigrants frequently don't respond to the census because of their language barrier and the family members who work for the family business such as wives may not report as self-employed. Consequently, the census usually under enumerates the self-employment of the Korean immigrants.

3. In-Jin Yoon, *On My Own* (Chicago: The University of Chicago Press, 1997), 11–12.

4. Nancy Abelmann and John Lie, *Blue Dreams: Korean Americans and the Los Angeles Riots* (Cambridge: Harvard University Press, 1995), 21.

5. Pyong Gap Min, "From White-Collar Occupations to Small Business: Korean Immigrants' Occupational Adjustment," *The Sociological Quarterly* 25 (1984): 333–352.

6. Quoted in Yoon, *On My Own*, 28.

7. Min, *Caught in the Middle,* 66–67.

8. Ivan Light and Edna Bonacichi, *Immigrant Entrepreneurs* (Berkeley: University of California, 1988), 154.

9. E. Franklin Frazier, *Black Bourgeoisie: The Rise of a New Middle Class* (New York: Free Press, 1957).

10. Abelmann and Lie, *Blue Dreams: Korean and the Los Angeles Riots,* 139–40.

11. See Edna Bonacichi, "Theory of Middleman Minorities," *American Sociological Review* 38 (1973): 583–94; Jonathan Turner and Edna Bonacichi, "Toward a Composite Theory of Middleman Minorities," *Ethnicity* 7 (1980): 144–58; Walter Zenner, "Middleman Minority Theories: A Critical Review," in *Sourcebook on the New Immigration*, ed. Roy Simon Bryce-Laporte (New Brunswick, N.J.: Transaction, 1980), 413–25.

12. Min, *Caught in the Middle*, 15–17.

13. In his interview with Korean store owners in the black neighborhoods in Atlanta, Min reported that 90 percent of them indicated that the black shoppers were less choosy in selecting items, less sensitive to prices, and tended to be accidental shoppers. See Pyong Gap Min, *Ethnic Business Enterprises: Korean Small Business in Atlanta* (New York: Center for Migration Studies, 1988), 72–73.

14. See, for example, some of the studies dealing with Korean-black conflict. Moon H. Jo, "Korean Merchants in the Black Community: Prejudice Among the Victims of Prejudice," *Ethnic and Racial Studies* 15 (1992): 396–411; Edward T. Chang, "New Urban Crisis: Korean-Black Conflicts in Los Angeles." Ph.D. dissertation, University of California, Berkeley, 1991; Abelmann and Lie, *Blue Dreams: Korean Americans and the Los Angeles Riots*; Min, *Caught in the Middle*; Yoon, On My Own.

15. Debra Dickerson, "Racial Fingernail Politics," *U.S. News and World Report*, April 14, 1997, 33–34.

16. Quoted in Elaine H. Kim and Eui-Young Yu, *East to America: Korean American Life Stories* (New York: The New Press. 1996), 206.

17. Ibid., 323.

18. Ibid., 188.

19. Ibid., 210.

20. Shin Ja Um, *Korean Immigrant Women in the Dallas-Area Apparel Industry* (New York: University Press of America, 1996), 66.

21. Quoted in Kim and Yu, *East to America: Korean American Life Stories*, 210.

22. According to Yu's survey of Korean immigrants in Los Angeles in 1989, which was published in an ethnic English newspaper *Korea Times,* about 40 percent owned their own business and had an average household income of around $50,000. See Eui-Young Yu, "Korean Community Profile: Life and Consumer Patterns," *Korea Times,* 1990. Cited in Abelmann and Lie, *Blue Dreams: Korean Americans and the Los Angeles Riots,* 121.

23. Abelmann and Lie, *Blue Dreams: Korean Americans and the Los Angeles Riots*, 122–23.

24. Quoted in Kim and Yu, *East to America: Korean American Life Stories,* 201.

25. Yoon, *On My Own,* 209.

26. Ibid., 152.

27. *Joong Ang Ilbo*, August 4, 1977. Cited in Illsoo Kim, *The New Urban Immigrants: The Korean Community in New York* (Princeton, N.J.: Princeton University Press, 1981), 118.

28. Abelmann and Lie, *Blue Dreams: Korean Americans and the Los Angeles Riots*, 110.

29. Ibid., 110, 111, and 112.

30. Bong-youn Choy, *Koreans in America* (Chicago: Nelson-Hall), 224–225.

31. Kim, *New Urban Immigrants: The Korean Community in New York*, 228.

32. Abelmann and Lie, *Blue Dreams: Korean Americans and the Los Angeles Riots*, 120–121.

33. Leon F. Bouvier and Robert W. Gardner, "Immigration to the U.S.: The Unfinished Story," *Population Bulletin* 41 (1986); Robert L. Bach and J. B. Bach, "Employment Patterns of Southeast Asian Refugees," *Monthly Labor Review* (Oct. 1980): 31–38.

34. See Won Moo Hurh and Kwang Chung Kim, "Uprooting and Adjustment: A Sociological Study of Korean Immigrants' Mental Health." Final report submitted to the National Institute of Mental Health, 1988; Pyong Gap Min, "Some Positive Functions of Ethnic Business for an Immigrant Community: Koreans in Los Angeles." Final report submitted to the National Science Foundation. Department of Sociology, Queens College of CUNY, N.Y., 1989.

35. Um, *Korean Immigrant Women in the Dallas-Area Apparel Industry,* 50.

36. Min, "From White-Collar Occupations to Small Business: Korean Immigrants' Occupational Adjustment," 346.

37. Eui Hang Shin and Kyung-Sup Chang, "Peripherization of Immigrant Professionals: Korean Physicians in the United States," *International Migration Review* 22 (1988): 609–626.

38. *Hankook Ilbo*, December 28, 1976. Cited in Illsoo Kim, *New Urban Immigrants: The Korean Community in New York*, 102.

39. Quoted in Abelmann and Lie, *Blue Dreams: Korean Americans and the Los Angeles Riots*, 115.

40. U.S. Bureau of Census, *1990 Census of Population, Asians and Pacific Islanders in the United States* (Washington, D.C.: U.S. Government Printing Office, 1992).

Chapter 5

FAMILY ADJUSTMENT

The adjustments required of Korean immigrant families to make a life in the United States are complex and can be quite difficult because they involve more than adjusting to a new language, a new culture, and a new life style. The fact is that most Korean families have left a more traditional culture where gender roles, for instance, are sharply defined. In the United States they find a culture in a continual state of flux, gender roles in particular. The fact is Korean families fit the pattern known as the extended family, where parents share their home with their parents, their children, and various relatives. They find themselves in the United States where the nuclear family is the norm. Adaptation to this norm requires fundamental adjustments in the relationships between husbands and their wives, between parents and their children, adults and their elderly parents, and even their in-laws. Unlike the early Chinese and Japanese immigrants, mostly single men, who immigrated in the 19th century, most Korean immigrants have come to the United States as extensions of complex family units, but including initially a husband and wife and their children. Later, once they have become established in the United States, their elderly parents and other in-laws join them. Therefore, any discussion of adjustment to life in the United States by Korean immigrants must include consideration of the adjustments that affect the dynamics of traditional Korean families. For instance, whereas in Korea a wife may have never worked outside the home, in the United States the couple may find it economically necessary for her to work. Even though she may work in the family's store, her presence in the business may serve as a subtle reminder that the husband cannot operate the business alone and is, therefore, somehow less a breadwinner, perhaps even a failure. That, in turn, can create not-so-subtle strains in the relationship between the husband and his wife that leads to friction, arguments, and even fights or abuse. The stresses on the marital ties in turn have their subtle effect on their relationship with their children, their parents, and their in-laws. However, there are other changes making their presence felt within the traditional Korean immigrant family.

The knowledge that there are tensions and conflicts in immigrant families is not news. Many reporters have praised immigrants for their determination in overcoming the stresses resulting from adjusting to life in a new land. Korean immigrants have been extolled by the mass media and scholars for clinging to their virtues of hard work and strong family values, for their academically successful children, for their low divorce and delinquency rate, and so on. For all the kudos, however, the typical Korean family is often hiding terrible tensions and conflicts resulting from each member of the family trying to accommodate such things as a wife working outside the home, or children who are becoming too "American," not all of which are necessarily acceptable to every member of the household. Some of the potential sources of Korean family conflicts are common to most families and applicable to all nationalities. Business failure, personal financial problems, religious differences, drinking or drug problems, troublesome children, infidelity, the loss of a job by the breadwinner, and a host of other problems would strain any family relationship. In the United States and other Western societies, the personalities and other psychological dimensions of family members are also studied as potential sources of tension and conflict, although few studies have been done from these perspectives on the tensions within Korean immigrant families.

There are sources of family tension and conflict, however, more characteristic of immigrant groups than of American families. In Korean immigrant families, a primary source of tension occurs between "traditional" Korean immigrant men, reared in families whose values were founded on Confucian principles, and their wives and children, who may challenge, even reject, these values and who may be more willing to accept American egalitarian principles. As a result, tension increases as long as no satisfactory resolution can be found. In time, the husband may come to believe his very role as head of the household has been undermined with his consequent reaction. In short order, not only the values of the family are threatened , but the harmony and consensus in other areas at the family's core are at risk. Other underlying sources of tension and conflict in Korean immigrant families include downward social mobility, especially that of the husband and the importance of the wife's economic contribution to the family. Although not all Korean immigrant families experience tension for these reasons, most of them seem to experience one or more of these conflicts at some point. The result of the strain is frequently manifested first in verbal abuse, escalating to threats and insults, then physical abuse, or other types of destructive behavior, such as alcoholism, especially by the husbands. Such behavior is rarely reported outside Korean immigrant enclaves, however.

The backgrounds of the husband and wife are significant factors bearing on the degree of difficulty in their adjustment to life in the States. For instance, poorly educated Korean immigrants with large families but with little capital to start businesses encounter more difficulty in adjusting to their new surroundings than do the highly educated young couples with large sums of money to invest. Economic security obviously facilitates ready adjustment of immigrant families, but so does an understanding of American culture that comes with education. Family adjustment is also particularly difficult for the Korean immigrants whose language, customs, values, and ways of life are distinctly Korean and who are unwilling to change their values or compromise their ways of life after coming to America.

MAINTAINING THE KOREAN TRADITIONAL FAMILY VALUE SYSTEM AS A SOURCE OF TENSION AND CONFLICT

The Relationship Between Husband and Wife

In a traditional Korean family the male is superior in almost all spousal relationships. Moreover, a traditional Korean family expects absolute obedience of children to their parents. Respect for their elders, particularly their parents and grandparents is a fundamental underpinning of traditional Korean family values. These values were mostly derived from philosophical concepts imbedded in the teachings of Confucius and that formed the moral foundation which has prevailed in Korea from the fourteenth century until the early twentieth century of the Chosun Dynasty. Moreover, Korean culture is an eclectic confluence of many ideals and values taken from Buddhism, Taoism, and Christianity, as well as a host of other material and not so material factors. These values, despite sweeping economic, demographic, and social changes that have taken place in Korea in the past few decades, continue to be the dominant influence on Korean families. Reviewing changes in family values as a result of industrialization and urbanization, scholars such as Park and Cho concluded that these changes have had little or no effect on the social, political, and legal status of women.

Thus, the notion of male superiority still persists within the society and the family. The father is the head of the household which he rules with almost unquestioned authority and his wife is his dutiful, obedient assistant. In such a household, sons takes precedence over daughters and they also have greater privileges.[1] The hold of Confucianism is quite tenacious and dominates the very approach to life of modern Koreans.

For most Americans who have spent decades listening to the arguments of feminists, it may be rather hard to understand the role of women in Korea, their social position, and their exact function in marriage. The most important part of Confucian philosophy concerns the social position of women, who are taught that they are inferior and are expected to be submissive first to their parents, then to their husbands. Wives must never challenge or question their husbands and under no circumstances are they to act on their own. Nor are women to seek achievements in their own name. There is a Korean proverb which Korean men often cite with approval: "If a hen crows, the household crumbles."

The roles of sons, daughters, even daughters-in-laws are clearly delineated by the Confucian concept of family relationships. Dutiful sons discover themselves in their parents through devoting themselves to their parents selflessly. Dutiful daughters, while at home, learn from their mothers how to be submissive and obedient. After marriage, the dutiful bride transfers her obedience and loyalty to her husband and to her parents-in-law if her husband was the first son.[2]

Given the cultural conservatism of Koreans, is it surprising to learn that Korean immigrants, although they may have lived in America many decades, have largely maintained traditional Korean family values? Kinship relations are very important to most Korean immigrants because, among other reasons, their kinfolks are the main sources for financial assistance, but perhaps more importantly, they provide emotional and familial support in a time of turmoil, in a land of strangers. Family also provide all important social support.[3] If their kin are still in Korea, they may fly to Korea frequently to see them, or stay in touch by telephone, or find other means to maintain the all-important family ties. In the absence of family ties, as a substitute for family, they reach out to other members of the Korean-American community in their neighborhood, either by means of Korean social organizations, Korean churches, or even by men sharing in a common interest, such as a round of golf. The more Korean immigrants associate with their kin and other Korean acquaintances in America, the more they reinforce their traditional family values, although doing so may aggravate the tensions and conflicts with members of their family who are trying to fit in the larger community.

The Korean immigrants who have brought their traditional Korean family values to the United States face innumerable conflicts in their family relationships as they cling stubbornly to their beliefs in the traditional Korean authoritarian and male-dominated values so incongruent with current American egalitarian values. Although immigrant husbands' beliefs in rigid sex-role distinctions may yield in the face of the reality of their wives' earning power in jobs outside their homes slowly sinks in, Korean immigrant women can expect little support from their husbands in pitching in to shoulder some of the household tasks. According to Kim and Hurh, the financial contributions of Korean women, no matter how significant or time consuming, did not lessen the number of household tasks they were expected to perform. A high percentage of Korean immigrant wives not only worked but continued to perform such tasks as grocery shopping, housekeeping, and dishwashing. The presence of children in the home meant that the wives assumed yet another major responsibility. Only in the areas of garbage disposal and the management of the family budget did the men take responsibility.[4] Min also found that full-time Korean immigrant housewives spent 46.3 hours per week on housework compared to 5.2 hours for their husbands. Among dual-earner couples, the wives' time on housework was reduced to an average of 24.8 hours per week while the husbands' time increased only to 6.7 hours.[5]

Some wives have insisted that they are willing to perform the dual role of traditional wife and wage earner, but only if their husbands, in return, admit a willingness to compromise, occasionally express gratitude, and recognize the valuable contributions their wives make to their well-being and livelihood. The tensions that arise when husbands continue to behave as if they are the sole breadwinner and that what their wives are doing, both as wage earner and home-maker, is unimportant. That their contributions are largely unacknowledged rankles many women.[6] A full-time seamstress at her husband's dry cleaning store in Washington, D.C. area expresses her frustrations:

> Before we came to America, my husband was the breadwinner. He was a typical believer in the Korean traditional family. I stayed home and performed all a traditional wife's duties. Since we immigrated to the United States, we bought a dry cleaning shop, and we worked from early dawn to late in the evening. We are both always tired when we come home. As a typical Korean traditional husband, he still wants me

to listen to and understand his feelings about living in America, his difficulty in dealing with customers, his dealings with business in general, etc., and everything centers around his problems. He wants me to understand his difficulties and wants me to soothe him as if we are still living in Korea.

How about me? I also work as hard as he does. He seldom tries to understand what I am going through. I am playing a dual role—both homemaker and wage earner. He rarely shows any sign he appreciates what I am doing. How about saying, "Thank you," like many American husbands do? Instead, he always demands or orders that I should do this or do that. I try to understand where he came from. And yet it is difficult to be passive and subservient, particularly when he orders me around in front of customers or other employees at the store. Sometime my anger toward him accumulates and bursts out when we argue over some minor thing.

Although some immigrant wives are uneasy about their changing roles and still wish to be part of a family based on traditional Korean values, many find they enjoy American egalitarian family values which promise less narrow roles, equality, individualism, self-fulfillment, and informality. As an illustration of this point, a wife commented: "I will never go back to Korea and live there because I can't accept the subservient role most Korean women still play. One of the reasons why Korea has not been progressive is Confucius' influence on Korean society." Another wife in Los Angeles complains: "Every time I saw Korean wives pushing a luggage cart with one hand and holding a child with the other while their husbands followed behind carrying only a brief case, I became so perturbed that I felt I was going to tell these 'emperor' husbands off." The wife of a professional man says: "Korean males are too sensitive about losing their sense of control over their wives. The more they feel they are losing control over their wives, the more they keep on ordering their wives about. Why can't Korean men, like most Americans, accept the idea of a more open and romantic relationship between husbands and wives and share economic and social activities without the encumbrance of sex role differentiation?" Most Korean immigrant wives did not expect their husbands to give up their traditional role as head of the family; however, they do want their husbands to exercise their head-of-household role with moderation and treat their wives with greater respect, courtesy, and consideration.

The change of immigrant wives' role from passive subordinate to that of equal partner sharing in the financial and domestic decision-making with little or no regard for sex roles is not what most Korean immigrant husbands are accustomed to experiencing. Some are willing to accept their wives' changing roles but others are less willing. There is a large number (the precise number is hard to pin down) of immigrant husbands who resist any change in their wives' role and insist on maintaining their authoritarian role. Such husbands are very sensitive to any suggestion that their wives are achieving a degree of equality. For example, in a traditional Korean family, a husband is referred to by his wife as "an outside gentleman" or "a father of their first child's name." Under the influence of the American egalitarian impulse, an Americanized immigrant wife may refer to her husband by his first name. "Unreconstructed" husbands regard this change in address with dismay. To them, their wives are presuming too much; some regard it as a sign of disrespect. One husband said: "This cannot happen in Korea. No wives in Korea call their husbands by their first name." These husbands also complain that their wives are no longer paying attention to their cooking, that they fix food in a hurry. A husband said: "If my wife cooks like what she is cooking in America, the 'dining table would have flown in the air.' "[7]

Most Korean immigrant husbands faced with their eroding position in the family usually keep silent, but occasionally they yell at their wives or break things in an outburst of temper or frustration. They may begin drinking heavily; the drinking may lead to violence. The more Korean men want to live by cherished images of the traditional Korean family, the more they come into conflict with everyday household realities of living in America. In her study of wife abuse among Korean immigrants in the Chicago area, Song found that 60 percent of the 150 respondents reported having some experience of wife abuse, most of which consisted of wife battering, led by closed-fist assaults (57 percent) and slapping (42 percent). She found that salient factors which differentiated battered wives from non-battered wives were that battered wives came from the families which ranked "high" on traditional Korean family values in such matters as marital interaction, dating and marriage, child-rearing, and sex role performance.[8] The conflicts within the Korean immigrant families, even including the battering of wives, accelerated in families where husbands cherished the traditional Korean family values and tried to maintain them in America. Even a decade ago, Theresa Yun, director of a Korean counseling center in Queens, said her group handled about 1,000 cases of wife abuse each year. But the government has not granted money for a women's shelter. So she takes, on average, one battered woman into her own home each week.[9] Reports on marital conflicts in Korean families are being reported to the police with greater frequency. In Los Angeles' Koreatown, the police report that marital battles are on the rise as wives take on jobs and leave the home, thus undermining the traditional Korean husband's role as the sole breadwinner. "It's bad and it's getting worse everyday," says a police sergeant.[10]

Although many Korean wives insist that they are not concerned with who is gaining or losing authority or control in the family, they are fully aware that their relationships with their husbands are changing. Their husbands are no longer in the commanding positions, as managers or teachers, they once had in Korea; nor are they surrounded by an entourage of friends, relatives, or sycophants they had in Korea. When immigrating to America their husbands lost all their trappings of authority. That may in part account for the reasons they cling to the notion of the traditional Korean husband's supremacy over his wife. A wife expresses it this way: "In Korea, I looked up to my husband, who was an office manager, and regarded him as a leader and a decision maker in our household. Now he is an owner of a small grocery store and looks so vulnerable, wearing an apron all day. Now I regard him as a partner, a friend, and a confidant. He seems, however, to be having difficulty in accepting the changing definition of husband-wife relationship."

Many husbands also notice the change in dynamics between themselves and their wives, especially in the matter of the authority relationship. A husband, whose wife is employed at an insurance company as a secretary, comments: "Before my wife was employed, she was a 'typical' Korean woman. When I lighted a cigarette, she used to bring me an ashtray right away. Now when I ask for an ashtray, she will say 'why don't you get it by yourself?' I feel that I am losing much of my authority and control over my family these days. I feel that my wife thinks that I am simply a shoe repair man who doesn't deserve respect."

Tensions between husbands and wives are not limited to those at the lower end of the economic scale. In the cases of some professional families, the role reversal they experience may be much more dramatic than it is among non-professional Korean immigrant families. Not only are the chances much greater that wives of professional men will pursue their own professional careers, but they stand a very good chance of achieving financial independence. A college professor who teaches in a small college outside Baltimore, Maryland comments:

My wife, who has a degree in chemistry from Korea, supported me while I pursued my graduate school training in political science for seven years while she was working as a lab technician. We were very happy during these years, even though we didn't have much money.

After getting my Ph.D. degree, we settled in the outskirts of Baltimore. When my teaching career began, my wife decided to enroll in a dental school. I supported her dental education as she did my graduate school education. Upon completion of her education, she established her dental practice and became financially successful. She put in long hours of work every day, including Saturday. On Sunday, she did paper work. To save money, she did most of her own dental lab work instead of sending it to a dental lab.

Her most frequent remark was: "When I was in Korea, even though I was a college graduate, nobody gave me a job, no matter how much I looked for it. My family was always poor. I am not going to be poor again. Now, I have a chance to be financially successful and I am not going to lose it. Korea didn't do a damn thing for me." She seemed driven. She wouldn't dream of taking time off for a family vacation or anything else. Most of the housework, including cooking, grocery shopping, and looking after our two children gradually fell onto me. Although I have lived in America many decades and believe in some of the Western family values, it is not easy for me to play the dual role of a house-husband and a breadwinner. After all, I grew up in the traditional Korean household, where my mother was a housewife and my sisters took care of household chores. I am not used to this kind of role reversal. When my relatives and friends visited and saw me cooking and doing dishes, I always felt uneasy. My wife's minimal contributions to the housekeeping and other duties associated with mother and wife have caused tremendous tension in our family. I was particularly upset when she criticized my cooking! Everybody knows preparing Korean food is difficult and time consuming. I still wonder whether all women dentists in America put in such long hours at work everyday, whether they are always tired, with no time for anything else.

The Relationship Between Immigrants and Their Children

Relationships between parents and their children are frequently strained precisely where traditional Korean parents demand absolute obedience, excellence in academic work, and pursuit of professional careers by their children. Most Korean immigrant parents pin their hopes on their children becoming successes in some professional career; consequently, they put a great deal of pressure on their children to get a good education. These parents, in turn, devote a great deal of their own resources and money, often at great sacrifice on their part, to the children's achievement. Fathers, in particular, are demanding—get all As, attend an Ivy League school, enter a professional school, and be a successful career person. A second-generation Korean American attending Columbia University describes how difficult it is growing up in a household where he felt the weight of his parents' pressure and expectations: "Growing up, you know the air you breathe in your house is not free. When your parents come home at night, you know they weren't out at clubs. They come home and they can't put food in their mouths fast enough, and then they go to sleep so they can wake up six hours later to go back to work. They're not working sixteen hours a day to get a Mercedes. There are easier ways to get a Mercedes. Their blood, sweat, and tears fund the success of the next generation. It's not luxury they're looking for."[11]

As I indicated, the pressure on the children comes primarily from one parent, usually the father. This may be in part because he has lost so much status when he left Korea, but whatever the cause, it contributes to the friction between fathers and their children. An immigrant mother says: "I think my husband is demanding too much from our children. He seldom listens to our children's concerns or discusses their future plans. Everything which has to do with our children's future is based on his wishes. There is no compromise or give and take in any kind of discussion. That is why our children avoid talking to their father. My husband thinks that our children are undermining his authority when our children don't pay attention to his suggestions. When I suggest to him that he change his approach to our children, he attacks me for siding with my children and undermining his authority." Another mother adds: "My husband thinks that he is making a great sacrifice for our children. Therefore, our children should be quiet, obey, and listen to what he says without challenging his opinions. I don't think his approach will work." Goldberg comments that his interviews with many Koreans in New York City revealed that Korean immigrants made almost superhuman sacrifices to give their children the American Dream. They never expected them to become Americans in the process.[12]

Most immigrant children appreciate what their parents are trying to do for them. Indeed, most of them have worked very hard to help their parents at the family business after school and over week-ends. They help their parents with housekeeping tasks and with their English language problems, whenever possible. Some immigrant children want to be academically successful in order to please their hard-working parents, who, their children realize, are making significant sacrifices for them. There are even a few who want to find a job as soon as they can after they complete their college education in order to begin to repay their parents. Some American-born children even visit Korea in an effort to understand their parents better.

However, many children are bothered by the authoritarian demeanor of their parents, particularly their fathers. They say their parents are "too demanding," "very authoritarian," "uncompromising," "overprotective," "undemocratic," "one-track minded," "not interested in social and sport activities," and so on. They often depict their parents as people "who tell you what to do without giving you a chance to express your views." A teen-aged child of an immigrant comments: "Every time my father speaks to me, it sounds like he is yelling at me. When I ask him why he always yells at me when he asks me to do something, he says he is not yelling. It is very difficult to talk to him or discuss my personal problems with him because he is so authoritarian. I guess his way is the Korean way of dealing with children." A college student in Los Angeles criticizes parents' way of emphasizing family values:

> Koreans' emphasis on family values is not wrong. The problem is that Koreans are so much concerned with their own family's concerns, especially traditional ways of relating to their parents, their grandparents, their cousins, and other family members that they forget how to treat people who are not related to them. They don't reach out to people who are less fortunate than they, and they are not much interested in doing public service or in engaging in public charity. They have a dim view of community service. I would like to work with American Indians on a reservation. None of my parents thinks this is an admirable thing to do. Instead, they think I should be preparing for a law school entrance examination.

Other students have commented that it seems to them their parents are narrow-minded, prestige conscious, and intolerant of other races, particularly blacks.

A few immigrant children offered the observation that their parents are too materialistic and self-centered. They know that their parents work long hours to maintain a decent standard of living for the family and want to make sure that their children will never suffer from lack of material things. Sometimes, however, children think that their parents' making money is not simply a means to achieve a desirable end, it becomes a goal in itself, because in their eyes, their parents seldom show signs of any interest outside their work, or making money. To hear the children tell it, their parents seem to believe their children should have no interests except preparing themselves academically. A second-generation Korean medical doctor says: "When I was growing up, my immigrant parents showed little interest in my social activities, my participation in sports programs, or other various extra-curricular activities. The only thing they emphasized was: study, study, study—nothing else. Everything I had to do was *their* way not *my* way. Also they thought money would solve everything. As long as I live in a comfort-able house, drive a good car, and attend an expensive college everything will turn out all right." A 1.5 generation person who became a businessman commented: "All the while I was in college I felt everything I was doing was meant to fulfill my parents' dream, not mine."

When children ignore their parents' wishes, the parents understandably search for the reasons why they believe their children have refused to obey them. The traditionalists usually find ways to blame American culture and society. They believe most American families fail to discipline their chil-dren. They begin to believe the society is corrupt and argue that American children don't respect their parents, their elders, and other authority figures. One immigrant parent was shocked when she heard an American child call her parents by their first names, an unthinkable act in Korean culture largely because it acts to level parents and children. Moreover, many of the Korean immigrant parents believe that most American parents are too permissive: they allow their children too much personal freedom. They cite teenagers' smoking, illegal drug use, sexual promiscuity, including high teen-age pregnancy rates, suicide rates, and many other examples to bolster their point.

The behavioral problems of American children justify the traditionalists taking a strong line with their children. When they are accused of being too authoritarian, they have a rationale. For instance, an immigrant mother comments: "We live in an undesirable area because my husband's business is located in this area. My husband and I are very strict about everything that our children do in the community: ranging from their choice of friends, their study hours, to their part-time work at our store on week-ends. Our children criticize us for being old fashioned and they feel that they are stifled." In short, they are strict for their children's own good.

Not surprisingly, many immigrants believe that the relationships be-tween American parents and their children are very superficial and business-like. A professional Korean immigrant cites an example of such a case: "My American colleague, who is an engineer, sold his car for $8,000. The next day his son told him that he would have paid him $8,500 for the car. My colleague was upset because, had he waited one more day, he could have made $500 more. The difference between American parents and Korean parents is that the Korean parents would have given their son the car. A father receiving payment from his son is unthinkable." Some have noted that American parents sell their homes when their children grow up and leave home. They then move into a small apartment and live alone. An immigrant father who has lived in America for many years observes: "Interaction between American parents and their children is business-like. A father will say to his son, 'This is *my* hammer and don't use it without *my* permission.' 'This is *my* car and don't touch it.' 'This is *my* house and you must follow *my* house rules.' In the Korean family everything belongs to *us*." Another immigrant father was stunned when he asked his teen-age son to mow the lawn and his son replied: "It's *your* lawn; why don't you cut it?" He believes his son's attitude is the result of the influence of American family values.

Even as they deplore American family values and praise Korean family virtues, some Korean immigrants do complain of the lack of closeness between them and their children. They say they want to have much closer ties with their children than they have now. Many are puzzled as to why they have not formed closer bonds with their children. Some blame American culture which encourages individualism and independence; some blame themselves for not teaching their children Korean family virtues; others blame their lack of fluency of English; still others blame their demanding work schedule for not spending enough time with their children. The father of a young adult bluntly comments: "I feel my American-born son is very distant. If I had known the type of relationship I would have now with my son, my wife and I wouldn't have made those sacrifices for all those years to send him to an expensive private college. I should have heeded the advice of an immigrant friend who used to say, 'Don't sacrifice too much for American-born kids. They are useless once they grow up.' Indeed, he is right." Another Korean immigrant father who lives in central Pennsylvania laments: "When my wife and I go to New York City for shopping, we used to drop in at my daughter's place without announcing ourselves. Now my daughter tells us to call her first. Can you imagine; we have to make an appointment to see her!" A Korean immigrant father who runs a small clothing store with his wife in Venice Beach, California complains: "I sent my daughter to a dental school. It was not easy to dole out tens of thousands of dollars for her education. While she was practicing her dentistry in Los Angeles after her graduation, occasionally she came to see my wife and me. One day she called me and said she was moving to San Francisco to practice her dentistry. When I asked her when she was going to move to San Francisco, she said next week! She never discussed moving to San Francisco with me. I would have appreciated it if my daughter had discussed the move with me and asked my opinion about her move to another city. My wife and I are saddened by my daughter's indifference toward our opinion. Can you imagine if my wife and I have to depend on my daughter when we become really old and sick? I keep on forgetting that we are living in America not in Korea."

The apparent indifference of their children to how their parents will manage when they retire, as the last respondent revealed, may be a very important concern. Most of the recent Korean immigrants, although gainfully employed, are, for the most part, middle-aged and do not have many years to go before they will retire; consequently, they have not had a chance to build up much savings. They have had to work hard to meet family financial obligations (they may be caring for their parents and sending children to college) and know they can't keep up their demanding schedule for many more years. A 55–year-old auto mechanic in Los Angeles estimates that he can work no more than five years. He would like to work at least ten years longer because he doesn't have enough savings for retirement. But, he says, physically he can't handle it. A sixty-three-year-old take-out-restaurant owner in the Chicago area says ruefully: "By this time I was going to retire, but I can't do that now. I don't have much savings, and I don't think I can ask for any kind of financial help from my children, even though they are fairly well off." Others, however, will be eligible for social security and are delighted with their financial prospects upon retirement. A bakery-store owner in Washington, D.C. area comments: "My wife and I will receive $2,000 a month of social security when we retire two years from now. Together with our savings, we can manage well. Most of all, I am delighted that we don't have to depend on our children." An erosion of commitment to the cardinal Confucian norm of filial piety is felt by many Korean immigrants and many adult immigrants are beginning to acquiesce in the changing nature of children's commitment to some important aspects of filial obligation. In their study of 622 Korean adult immigrants (twenty years or older) who resided in the Chicago area, Kim and his associates revealed that the majority of the respondents no longer believed that the relationship between elderly parents and adult children was more important than the children's marital relationship, suggesting a gradual emergence of the dominance of conjugal ties over the consanguineous, ties in their family-kinship relations.[13]

The Relationship Between Immigrants and Their Parents

According to Confucian tradition, traditional Korean family values also demand that children respect and honor their parents as well as all elderly.

This value is strictly observed and any deviation is frowned upon. Korean culture has found many ways to chastise violators; someone who refuses to accede to the wishes of the family and the community may be shunned, or even ostracized. A person who is disrespectful of his or her parents or the elderly is referred to as *Sangnom* (a beast).

In Korean newspapers published in Los Angeles and New York City, one frequently sees pictures of sons and daughters bowing to their visiting elderly parents. No matter how long they have lived in the United States, most adult Korean immigrants are ever mindful of their duty to respect their parents and the elderly. However, the financial burden of taking care of elderly parents has become acute for dutiful Korean Americans, particularly when the elderly depend on them for such things as housing, food, clothing, and health care. One must remember that many of the elderly may have lived in Korea where there is little or no equivalent to social security, free or subsidized health care, or other benefits; in point of fact, the children, had they stayed in Korea, would have been expected to look after their parents. Thus, many of the elderly parents who are brought to the United States are not only in poor health, they may be indigent. Most elderly Koreans can't speak English, don't know their way around, cannot drive and must depend on their children, or grandchildren, to see to it that they are on time for doctor's appointments, and visits to their relatives and friends.

Fortunately, there are those elderly parents who are able to contribute money or some work to maintain the household of their children. For instance, they may be able to babysit, cook, and clean house among other chores. An immigrant factory worker in Phoenix comments: "Without my mother, I don't think my wife could have worked full time in a factory and raised our three children. My mother took care of everything, such as cooking, babysitting, cleaning, and even entertaining our family friends." Some elderly parents even help their adult children in their work places. They may work in the kitchen scrubbing dishes and pots, they may serve as janitors, *kimchi* (pickled cabbage) makers, laundry folders, seamstresses, or in a number of other capacities wherever they can be helpful. Most of the help, however, comes from the elderly mother rather than the father, as the latter is not accustomed to doing such work.

In Korea, when an elderly husband is retired, his wife, because she performs "only" household tasks, must not only continue to take care of the household, but provide care giving and support for her husband should he become disabled or ill. Should both the husband and the wife become disabled, they expect their son to take care of them. Daughters, after all, are now members of her husband's family and her duties are in his household.

One of the more interesting problems that might arise occurs when the elderly wife becomes ill. Then, a very serious question arises: what will the woman's husband do now that his wife is seriously ill or disabled? After all, the husband is almost "incapable" of providing caregiving for his wife. Then, there is the equally serious question of what the elderly are to do when they don't have a son. They can not consider living with a married daughter when they become old because that does not follow the tradition of the Korean patriarchal system. This is a serious dilemma which most elderly face in Korea.[14]

When elderly parents arrive in America expecting to be welcomed into their son's home, they may be confronted by somewhat "liberated" daughters-in-law who question why their loyalty should rest in the husband's family without proper consideration being given the wife's family. After all, the wife's family may be facing very difficult times, too. Such daughters-in-law may challenge their fathers-in-law's right to contribute little or nothing to household upkeep. Although many daughters-in-law appreciate the assistance offered by their mothers-in-law, many of them wonder whether their mother-in-law's assistance outweighs the burden she represents. An immigrant librarian who came to America when she was a small child and who now works in Washington, D.C. is not certain about living with her parents-in-law:

> My mother-in-law helps us a lot, particularly in the area of cooking. But my father-in-law is a strictly conservative Korean traditionalist. He likes to be served and can't think of doing dishes and vacuuming around the house. Most of the time he watches Korean videos and reads Korean newspapers. One time my two-year-old son dropped a drinking glass and broke it into many pieces. As he was crying, I picked him up with my left hand and tried to sweep up pieces of glass with my right hand. My father-in-law watched my struggle and disappeared into his room without offering any kind of help. My husband keeps on saying that most Korean fathers, particularly elderly fathers, can't think of doing anything associated with housework because it belongs to women. I am frustrated with my father-in-law. Without my mother-in-law, I don't think I could put up with him. I heard many immigrant elderly fathers do yard work, vacuum, do dishes, and help their adult children at stores, but not my father-in-law.

But the old tradition not only created stresses and friction in the family when confronted with a rebellious daughter-in-law. Conflict also arises when the elderly parents, having only a daughter, want to come to the United States and live with her and her family. Their daughter, on the other hand, already may be taking care of her husband's parents and unable to accommodate her parents, too. A wife in Chicago illustrates this point in stark terms:

> Currently, my husband and I are taking care of my husband's parents. They are not in good health. My own parents in Korea, who are in their 70s, also want to come to America and spend their final years with me. But it is very difficult to assist both sets of parents. We are not financially well-off and don't have a big house to accommodate four elderly parents. At the same time I feel guilty for not welcoming my own parents to this country.

Should Korean immigrant wives express their desire to accommodate their own parents, as well as those of their husband's, friction between husbands and wives quickly creates heat should husbands balk at such an arrangement. An immigrant wife in New York faced outright hostility from her husband when she took in her mother:

> My mother works hard every day for us, like a housemaid, babysitting and doing housework. Yet I often feel guilty as if I am putting my mother ahead of my mother-in-law and my husband's kin. When I argue with my husband, my mother's presence in the house puts me at a disadvantage. Therefore, I try to placate him as much as possible. My husband often takes advantage of my situation and screams at me.[15]

In spite of the desire of wives to treat their husbands and their elderly parents equally, there are many wives who still believe looking after their parents-in-law takes precedence over their own, even under unusual circumstances. A wife in Washington, D.C. comments: "I have been looking after my mother-in-law for twenty-five years—ten years in Korea and fifteen years in America. My husband died about five years ago. He was an ex-police officer, had a violent temper and our marriage was rocky. Even after his death, I am still looking after his mother. Sometimes I wonder why I am doing this. But it is very difficult to break away from the Korean family custom." Also the preference shown one set of parents or parents-in-law may depend upon need and circumstances. A husband in Los Angeles comments: "I run a catering service. My parents-in-law, who are healthy and in their late 50s help us a lot, either in our store or at home. I don't mind that they are staying with us. My sister, on the other hand, had been taking care of her frail mother-in-law in both Korea and America until she died. In fact, while my own mother was still in Korea, my sister neglected our own mother who also was in poor health."

As the immigrants have become more acculturated to life in the United States, the strict rules for taking care of their parents have relaxed somewhat. More and more one finds the elderly parents are being shuffled between the siblings. A source of stress among the siblings arises from the fact that each sibling wants one of the other siblings to assume the responsibility of caring for the elderly parents. An immigrant man in Philadelphia complains: "I have two older brothers in Los Angeles. None of them want to take care of our parents, although they send me some money to help care for our parents. According to Korean traditional custom, the eldest son is supposed to assume responsibility of taking care of the elderly parents."

Then, when the elderly are infirmed or ill a serious question arises as to which child should assume responsibility given that each child may have serious financial, marital, or other problems generally associated with first generation immigrants. Because few adult immigrants want to go so far as to place their non-English-speaking parents in nursing homes, they struggle to find ways to care for their parents as best they can. However, there have been extreme cases where the children abandoned their elderly parents. Rev. Dong Chung Kwak, who runs the House of Agape for Korean immigrants with drug and alcohol problems, is focusing on the Korean elderly who have been abandoned by their families. He says he is getting two or three calls a month from the elderly who have no place to go.[16]

Some elderly Koreans have mixed feelings about their decision to come to the United States. Although many have tried to adjust to their new circumstances, others are downright miserable. A former high-ranking government official in Korea, who lives in New York, regrets coming to the United States to stay with his son: "I didn't know my son very well in Korea. As a typical Korean father, I was aloof from my son as Korean custom dictates in the father-son relationship. The more I got to know my son and his wife in their small house here in America, I discovered how difficult it is to get along with them. Furthermore, they expect me to help them around the house by doing small chores. I am not used to doing any kind of housework and will do very poorly if I do. I think I will go back to Korea and open up my own construction company at age 65." Another elderly immigrant is somewhat upbeat. Well known as a minister in Korea, he now lives in a suburb of Washington, D.C., he comments: "I was a minister at one of the large churches in Seoul. After I came to America, I saw how my son and his wife were struggling with their families. My son goes to work as a cab driver and his wife, too, as a waitress. Both come home very late. My wife cooks dinner, I clean the house, my wife does the laundry, I grow vegetables in the backyard. In the evening we both go to English language class. I am thinking about getting a barber license. I don't think about my former profession or status. I try to adjust to the current situation as best as I can."

In spite of the fact that elderly women who live with their children are seemingly happy, with fewer problems than elderly men, in her detailed interviews with twenty Korean immigrant elderly women in the Washington area, Pang found that, generally, the elderly women feel strongly that their role and status in the family are markedly reduced after their immigration to America as they lack knowledge of the new culture, skills that can help them get jobs, and financial resources to fall back on. They feel they are burdens to their children because of their gradual physical deterioration brought on by old age. That most of the elderly women are concerned about becoming a burden to their children is particularly significant and a continuing source of emotional stress. In fact, their fervent wish was not to suffer a lingering death so that they do not create yet another burden for their children.[17] For all that, other forms of stress arise because they believe they are losing their children's respect and consequently the deference they think is due them. As evidence, they point to the fact that their adult children no longer seek their advice, that they have become peripheral when they should be at the center of family life. They note their grandchildren have become the center of attention in the family. Moreover, the fact that they have to shoulder the responsibility for child care and housework makes them feel that their traditional privilege to relax and enjoy the leisure their hard work has earned them has been curtailed.

In the midst of the dispute among sons and daughters with regard to whose responsibility it is to care for their elderly parents, some elderly prefer to live by themselves. According to Min's survey of living arrangements among Korean elderly in New York City, the majority of elderly (53 percent) and a higher proportion of married elderly lived independently of their children.[18] Although some elderly feel uneasy about living separately from their children, they say they are doing their children a favor by living apart. First, they do not have the stress of thinking of themselves as burdens. Second, many who live by themselves say they enjoy the freedom to do whatever they wish; for instance, they may participate in leisure activities with other seniors without worrying about adapting to life in their children's households. Others confess that it is difficult to live with their adult children. Most of the elderly frequently cited difficulties created by cultural and language barriers, personality conflicts—particularly with daughters-in-law—feelings of being burdens, a sense of losing control over their lives and dignity as they are made to feel dependent, and an awareness that they have become the source of strife among their children. Perhaps the most important factor influencing their decision to move out of their children's homes was their ability to get a degree of financial independence through such support as Social Security, food stamps, health care, and federally subsidized housing.

Immigrant children, on the other hand, have ambivalent feelings about their parents living separately. An adult immigrant in Philadelphia expresses it this way: "My father enjoys living in an apartment with other Korean elderly. There, he can talk about Korean politics, Korean history, the Korean War, and brag about his children and grandchildren. My mother travels to hot springs with her friends and visits the Grand Canyon in Arizona. But I am not sure putting my elderly parents in an apartment is the right thing to do." A working mother in a small town in Pennsylvania says: "Although my mother says she enjoys living by herself, she says she misses us, her grandchildren, and doing such things as grocery shopping, visiting friends and relatives together, and going out to dine in a Korean restaurant. Furthermore, my Korean immigrant friends, particularly those who take care of their elderly parents, frown upon me when I tell them my mother lives in an apartment. This is a small town. Every Korean knows whose parents live with whom and where. I guess in cities like Los Angeles nobody would care about where their parents live."

THE LANGUAGE BARRIER AS A SOURCE OF TENSION AND CONFLICT

Immigrants' limited facility with the English language is another barrier which causes stress and tension in the immigrants' families. As I have already pointed out, the lack of fluency in English not only limits their choice of occupation, it limits occupational mobility. Even obtaining semi-professional business licenses; such as in real estate, travel agencies, house painting, and plumbing require the immigrants have some degree of English language proficiency. Furthermore, the immigrants have to deal with a host of other service people and professionals; such as real estate and insurance agents, teachers, doctors, accountants, and others who may speak only English. As a consequence, their lack of fluency with English is bound to affect their self image. An immigrant confesses: "What good father am I? I can't go to see my daughter's teacher and discuss her academic progress. I have to ask my brother and children for help whenever I have to sign documents for buying and selling a house or a business, making a loan from a bank, and other government-related matters. I am getting tired of constantly asking someone for help. Also my entire family, including my wife, think that I am incapable of handling matters of significance. It is a constant embarrassment in front of my children and my wife when I can't understand exactly what a salesperson is saying in the department store, what a man is trying to say when I ask for directions, and what the mechanic is saying at the auto repair shop."

In some cases immigrant wives speak better English than their husbands. As a result, frequently they work as salespersons, become real estate agents, travel agents, and secretaries. In such cases husbands face the added realization that they are dependent on their wives when they encounter language problems and feel their authority is further eroded. A wife comments: "I don't understand why most Korean men can't take a semester of English language which is offered twice a week in the evening. They say they are too 'hot tempered' to learn a new language. Korean men somehow associate 'hot tempered' with masculinity. I think it is stupid on their part not trying to learn English. They will do much better in business if they speak good English." The language problem also affects white-collar professionals. A wife of a professional remarks: "When my husband sees others, who were hired later than he was, promoted over him, he becomes very depressed. He used to say 'so and so had made manager or so and so made vice-president.' Then he will say 'I wish I were born in America,' suggesting his language deficiency is the barrier to his promotion. He talks about finding employment some place else, but he usually stays in the same place and works without much enthusiasm which he used to have when he was hired. His stagnant professional career certainly has affected our marital relationship as he nears retirement age and gets closer to the end of his career."

The immigrants' limited ability to communicate effectively in English hinders them in joining various social and voluntary groups or organizations which exist in the community. Consequently, the immigrants' activities and interactions are confined to those involving their family members and ethnic community. Close, continued interaction within the confines of the family frequently heightens tension in family relationships, particularly in a small town where there are few other Korean Americans with whom to fraternize. A husband in a small town in Pennsylvania comments: "There are few non-Korean speaking people who visit our home. Once a year my relatives from Chicago and Denver visit us. Our son occasionally brings his

American friends to our home. I detect my wife's loneliness in her face. Although I know she can't make friends with Americans because of her language facility, sometimes I wish she would because confining social interaction to family members not only creates boredom and lack of excitement, but also loss of respect. Americans used to say 'too much familiarity breeds contempt.' In my case it leads to tension in the family." Some Korean social scientists recognize that immigrants' limited social contacts within their immediate family can lead to social stagnation and can become a major source of tension and disenchantment among the Korean immigrant families. Lee observes: "This restricted social network forces the Korean immigrants to overengage in leisure activities with their immediate family members, particularly their spouses; overengagement in turn causes stagnation in social experiences due to the lack of diversity and the paucity of new stimuli. The upshot of all these is marital dissatisfaction."[19] Some immigrants miss the close circle of friends and relatives they had in Korea. An immigrant man confesses: "When I visit Korea, I meet my high school and college classmates. We occasionally gather at a restaurant or a friend's house and we sing *karaoke* and exchange stories and reminisce about past events without any language barrier. I miss that when I am back in the United States. There is no comparison between our social life in America with what I would have in Korea. Limiting our social interaction to only family members and a few Korean families, whether you like them or not, is not healthy or exciting."

Some Korean immigrants try to overcome the social barrier caused by their language difficulty by taking the initiative. A husband says: "My wife likes to associate only with Koreans, and we drive hours to meet other Koreans. I suggested to her many times that we should join community activities and meet other Americans and learn English. PTA is a good start at least. I also suggested to her that she introduce Korean cooking to our neighbors. So far, none of my suggestions have been accepted by my wife. This disagreement has caused some tension in my family." Another husband complains: "For business reasons, some times we have American and Korean guests in our home. My wife always talks to our Korean guests in Korean, while ignoring American guests. I told her many times not to do that because it puts American guests in an awkward situation and also it is impolite. She says she is embarrassed speaking poor English in front of all others. Besides, she said, no American guest wants to talk to her. I told her to be courageous and take the initiative in talking to American guests. So far she hasn't taken my advice."

English language proficiency is not only associated with the choice of friends, but also with a preference in culture. A person who is not skilled in English is more likely to remain insular: that is, such a person continues to read Korean newspapers instead of English-language papers, listen to Korean radio instead of English-language radio, and celebrate Korean holidays instead of American holidays. A financial planner in a large accounting firm in New York expresses it this way: "After living in the United States for more than twenty-five years, my wife is not Americanized at all. She watches Korean videos, listens to Korean news (special channel), reads Korean novels, loves Korean food, and even furnishes our house with Korean furniture. Her English hasn't improved since she came to the United States. The problem is that I am much more inclined to embrace American culture. Sometimes, I feel we don't have much of anything in common to talk about. When we had small children, the topic of children consumed most of our conversation. Now that our children have left for college and employment, our personal differences are gradually driving us apart." Another professional, a chemical engineer, blames his wife for his lack of career advancement. He says: "I would like to invite my American colleagues to my house for drinks or dinner occasionally. Since my wife doesn't speak English well, she is very reticent and retiring when we have American guests. When we are invited to the homes of American colleagues, she is very quiet. She told me she is not comfortable with my American colleagues and their wives. I have an American boss and I am working for an American company, and yet my wife completely shut off the company's social activities. In the company of Koreans, though, she is very talkative and no one can even shut her off!"

Language problems of recent adult immigrants also create tensions between adult immigrants and their children. Children, more fluent in English than in Korean (sometimes they don't speak Korean at all), often don't understand what their parents are trying to say to them. The parents are also equally frustrated by their inability to inculcate their moral values, discuss their children's personal problems, or even help them with their homework. Many adults feel that they are not being adequate parents and thus get no respect from their children as long as the failure to communicate stands between them. Some immigrants feel that using their children as interpreters and translators undermines their authority and humiliates them when they believe they should be exercising total authority over their children. This perception appears to give children an advantage over their parents and makes family life seem topsy-turvy. A father said that often his child doesn't introduce him to his American friends when he brings them home.

He interprets his child's behavior as snobbish, or else that his son is ashamed of his father's broken English. A mother says: "When we have Korean company in our home, our children disappear to their rooms. They know they can't understand what we are saying to each other. When they do stay, they look so bored. You can't blame them."

Korean-American parents believe that as their children grow older they withdraw into their homes. They think that their children believe they don't understand them. This would be particularly true of more recent immigrants whose ability to speak English is limited. A father shrugs his shoulders and says: "Who knows why I don't have closer feelings toward my children. It may be cultural difference, age gap, or language gap. When my son visits me and my wife, he is awfully quiet. Frankly, he bores me, although my wife doesn't think so." Another immigrant couple confess that their children, who do not speak Korean, cramp their life style. A well-educated wife says: "As much as possible, my husband and I speak English in front of our children. Sometimes we feel like speaking Korean without worrying about the presence of our children. Why do we have to force ourselves to speak English?" From the children's point of view, their parents are not aware of the importance of learning English. A second-generation college student says: "My parents think that they don't have to learn English as they always interact with Koreans. Besides, they say they don't have time to learn English. I think these are all excuses. I think it's appalling after living in America for thirty years, my parents still speak English as if they just got off the boat."

The language barrier between grandparents and grandchildren is especially noticeable. Most adult immigrants are able to communicate with their children, although they may not be able to do so fluently. Some immigrants, who were educated in America, have little difficulty in communicating with their children. Most parents of immigrants are completely shut off from their grandchildren. The grandparents can't speak English, and the grandchildren can't speak Korean. Yet the grandparents must spend most of their time with their grandchildren as babysitters or caretakers. Generally, they communicate through gestures or signs. Because grandchildren usually act as chauffeurs for their grandparents, taking them to parks or shopping, to doctors' offices, to Korean senior centers, and to various Korean community activities, the grandchildren must act as interpreters. If the grandchildren are able to speak a little Korean, then the task of interpreting for their grandparents is relatively easy. If the grandchildren speak little or no Korean, then communication becomes a problem. A mother says: "When our son asks his grandmother to make Campbell's chicken soup, she makes beef. When his friends call and he is not home, his grandmother can't take a message. When he takes her to the optician for eyeglasses, she can't read the eye chart. The lack of communication between them is a serious problem. Yet my son knows he has to treat his grandmother with respect." Grandchildren getting along with their grandparents is one thing and communicating feelings and emotions is another matter.

In some cases, American-born grandchildren are often rude or even hostile, or else they completely ignore their grandparents. A father comments: "I know my children can't communicate effectively with their grandparents. But sometimes I feel they don't show enough respect for their grandparents. They conduct themselves as if their grandparents don't exist at home." A mother says: "Although grandmother doesn't speak English, her grandchildren know their grandmother loves them because she constantly smiles and shows her willingness to do anything for them, whether it is cooking, sewing, washing, making lunch, or in countless other little ways. They are getting along beautifully."

DOWNWARD SOCIAL MOBILITY AS A SOURCE OF TENSION AND CONFLICT

When immigrants decided to leave Korea, they probably never thought that they would experience downward social mobility, or if they did, they would never be able to rise to their previous status in America. As I have described in Chapter four, most Korean immigrants undergo downward occupational and social mobility. Some accept downward mobility as a price they paid to come to the United States; others have great difficulty in facing up to the reality of their current status. A high ranking auto company executive in Korea who now operates a take-out dry cleaning store on the West Coast remarks: "I used to brag to others about who I was in Korea. Now I don't say anything about my background. No matter how much I brag about my previous status, a laundryman is a laundryman." The more immigrants realize that their current occupational status as, for example, a shoe repairman, a green grocer, or a bakery store owner will not be changed drastically in the future, the more they focus on success in their new career. Their attitude becomes, "I don't care about what others think of me as long as I am financially successful and my children are successful in their professional careers." Their drive to achieve their financial goal at any price has driven them to operate their stores in minority residential areas, such as the Bronx, Harlem, and South Central Los Angeles, where financial risks, as well as physical risks are real. Furthermore, the Korean immigrants who experienced downward social mobility have tried to make up their lost status through conspicuous consumption.

The intensity with which they have concentrated on work has invariably taken a toll on their marriages and family life. An immigrant husband, who owns a vegetable store in Maryland, remarks: "We work from 7 A.M. to 7 P.M., six days a week. My wife, who was a high school math teacher, constantly complains that she is not used to doing laundry work and asked that we hire more helpers. I told her that, if we do, our profit margin will be too small, making it difficult to pay our high mortgage and expensive tuition for our children. Also she is afraid to work at the store because we were held up by robbers at gun point three times in the last two years." Others also complain that it is very difficult to do anything which involves all family members because they spend so much time at their stores. A mother says: "Because of our long hours at work, we don't even have time to eat dinner together. When our children were small, I tried to come home and cook dinner. Now our children have left home and my husband and I don't have to worry about taking care of our children. Many times we order take out food or eat at a restaurant after work instead of cooking. Sometimes, I feel I am missing the joys of family life."

Conspicuously flaunting the results of all the hard work (the cars, the houses, the clothing) may compensate for downward social mobility, but it also creates unspoken competition within the small, tight circle that makes up the Korean immigrant community. Although one might not realize it, it also creates marital tension as each member of the family vies with the other family members trying to win the recognition from others in the community. The only way to maintain the appearance of upward economic mobility is to flaunt things, creating envy in others about their sucess. In such a contest, even one's children become pawns, as when one brags about the college the children are attending and how well they are doing academically. A husband remarks: "Every time my wife goes to a Korean church, attends a Bible class in the evening, which is usually held at one of the homes of Korean church members, I am worried about what she might say when she returns. She will invariably recount in detail all about who bought what, who is going to open another store because his or her business is doing so well, who sent his son or daughter to what expensive private schools, whose sons or daughters are going to attend Ivy League universities, who is going to visit Korea again, whose daughter is going to marry a doctor or lawyer, and other gossip. Since all of these activities require a substantial amount of money and I can't afford these, I am worried what she might say about these things." Some immigrants jeer other immigrants for going overboard. An immigrant asks: "Do you know how so and so can afford such an expensive house? He works as a stock boy after his regular work. I know he is dead tired, and I don't think he will carry on like this too long. He will have to give up his house before too long, even though his wife brings in some income from her factory work." Such competition also inhibits those immigrants who have been less successful. The wife of an immigrant entrepreneur, who declared bankruptcy in Phoenix, Arizona comments: "After my husband declared bankruptcy, I rarely met other Korean families on a social basis. My husband suggests that we see our Korean friends as little as we can. I argue with my husband about his caution because I would like to socialize with other Koreans. But my husband is withdrawing more and more from other Koreans, except his relatives."

There are many stories about the well educated Korean immigrants who became store owners in America, effectively suffering a loss of status, and who cannot find a satisfactory accommodation with their new position. They do not fit into the social circle of those immigrants who were merchants in Korea because their interests and status are so different, nor do they fit into the social group of Korean Americans who are professionals because of their lessened status: they are "just merchants" now. Furthermore, when there is a disagreement between husbands and wives over who belongs in their choice social circle, another dilemma is added to the predicament. A former business manager in a large corporation in Korea, but who now works in a nail-care salon in a suburb of Philadelphia, complains that whenever he associates with immigrant professionals, he feels he is being slighted. But his wife thinks that they should associate with people in this group because she thinks they learn from these people. A husband who is caught in this dilemma has little recourse but to suffer the indignity. The wife of a Korean immigrant who has been running his deli store for ten years says:

> He has often expressed his bitterness about his position as a small store owner. And his frustration over his low status generally influences our relations. Five years ago, he left home after a little argument with me and came back two weeks later. He wanted to get respect from me. But a real source of his problem was not me, but his frustration over his low status.[20]

The sensitivity of Korean immigrant husbands about their social status is occasionally revealed when it comes to their wives' employment and their relationship with men in the workplace. Some Korean immigrants report

that many husbands are watchful, if not jealous, of their wives in such circumstances. Their envy of their wives' success may occasionally turn to
ugly suspicion. In a very revealing observation, a husband in Virginia says:
"These American guys are very glib. They say a lot of flattering things to the
girls. The wife of my friend was working at an insurance company as a secretary. A white American fellow became interested in her and brought flow-
ers and candies to her and showered her with all kinds of compliments
which few married and unmarried Korean males would do. She fell in love
with this white fellow and ran away with him leaving her husband and two
children!" As if to heighten the tensions between working husbands and
their wives, when the wife lands a good job in a lab or an office, she may acquire a higher status than that of her husband. Then, she may actually earn
more money than her husband. Her salary is a concrete reminder of the husband's "failure" and is a blow from which he may never recover.

To compensate for their downward social mobility, there are immigrant
fathers who push their children to succeed in some prestigious profession,
particularly in medicine and science.[21] In the process they unwittingly
come into conflict with their wives, who generally put the welfare of their
children ahead of achieving some goal designed to gratify the father's ego.
A wife in a small town in Pennsylvania commented: "Our son is not that
bright and I know he definitely is not doctor material. My husband thinks
our son could go to medical school if he tries hard enough, and he is saving
money for our son's medical school education. I am afraid that one of these
days my husband will be disappointed when our son isn't admitted to the
medical school. I also told my husband many times that our children should
decide what career they choose, not their father." Another wife offered:
"When our son came home for Christmas vacation, he told us that he is
dropping out of college and wants to join the army. My husband screamed at
him, saying things like, 'why were you born' and other remarks which are
not called for. My husband slammed the door in our son's face when he said
good-bye to us. I cried, and I still resent my husband for his behavior. My
husband was disappointed; he even stopped inviting Korean friends whose
sons entered medical school to our house."

Other immigrant men, who experience downward social mobility, take
out their frustration by abusing their wives. This is particularly true when
they feel that their career is going nowhere. The likelihood that they will resort to violence when they realize their careers are falling behind their
wives' is a growing phenomenon. As I indicated earlier, wife abuse by Korean immigrant husbands is becoming a serious problem. Some wives are
careful or sensitive not to hurt their husbands' feelings or kindle their wrath.

A wife who is a successful realtor in Los Angeles and whose husband is a door-to-door salesman comments: "When we were in Korea, I was a nurse and my husband was a hospital administrator. Now he is a salesman in America. When we are invited by some Korean friends, he used to say, 'Let's not talk about our jobs when we go there.' I usually do not talk about my job or my husband's at the gathering. When someone asks me about my work, he often tries to intervene or change the subject, sometimes without success."

Other men resort to heavy drinking, gambling, and excessive spending on cars and golf equipment. According to Min in his study of Korean immigrants in New York, status anxiety and frustration can lead Korean immigrant men to excessive drinking, golfing, and gambling which aggravate marital difficulties. He cites a case of potential serious marital conflict because of the husband's drinking. The wife of such a man comments:

When our discount store did well, my husband began to drink in Korean clubs regularly. Each night he paid over $300 for liquor and around $100 to the girls as tips. Sometimes, he drank until early morning and came back directly to the store. After sleeping in the store, he left for the club early in the evening with money [he took] from the cash register.[22]

ASCENDANCE OF WIVES' ECONOMIC ROLE AS A SOURCE OF TENSION AND CONFLICT

The fourth element which causes tension in Korean immigrant families is the gradual acquisition of economic power by wives. To many immigrant husbands, the fact that their wives are working outside their home is a troubling, if not baffling, experience. The immigrant husbands are largely unprepared to recognize their wives' earning power, but when their wives begin to demand a voice in the family decision-making processes, ordinarily reserved for husbands in traditional Korean families, they are stunned. In many cases, both husbands and wives work together in their family businesses and in doing so, wives become indispensable economic partners. The more wives participate in the family's economic activity, the more they expect to be treated as equals in not only the workplace, but in the family as well. While some immigrant husbands welcome their wives' contribution to their businesses and family finances, there are many immigrant husbands, already suffering from downward social mobility and sensitive about their current status, who resent the encroachment of the economic power and authority of their wives. A husband half in jest said: "My wife pays a few bills and now she thinks she is making 'a big noise' at home. One of these days, I am going to teach her a lesson about who is the boss." Invariably wives will say their demand for equality is not intended to undermine the traditional Korean husbands' role. A wife put it simply: "I am very sensitive not to hurt my husband's ego and pride. But I work very hard at a factory. Sometimes I must put in overtime and come home late and my husband has to cook. He always resents cooking, doing house chores, and grocery shopping by claiming these tasks are beneath his dignity. But he knows he has to do all of these things if we want to maintain our current economic status." Wives' newly acquired economic power and their assuming some of the traditional male responsibility can become a major source of friction, especially when the husbands feel they are losing their authority, power, and respect in their family.

Playing a dual role as both housewife and wage earner is not easy for Korean immigrant wives who never expected to play such a dual role because they were not accustomed to such a role in Korea. Once in the United States, many immigrant wives were thrust into the labor market out of economic necessity. Once in the work place, they tried their best to balance their obligations to their job with their family obligations. Once launched in the public sphere, at one time an exclusively men's preserve, they found their service was of value to their community. In a study of the activities of Korean immigrant women in the Korean community in southern California, Yu found Korean immigrant women's involvement in various community organizations was extensive. Yu reports they have been particularly active in church committees, education, youth services, literary circles, and journalism.[23] The more Korean immigrant wives gain earning power and assume some of the family responsibilities, the more they are likely to participate in community services, and the more their husbands find it necessary to adjust their thinking to accommodate the changing role of their wives, whether they like it or not.

Some immigrant wives early on have recognized that their newly gained economic power gives them a stronger voice in family decision-making. However, they insist that their reason for going to work was not intended to undermine their husbands' authority in the family, but to contribute to improving the family's financial condition, and perhaps increase their business capital. Furthermore, the influence of close relatives and friends who could give advice on financial matters dwindled once they immigrated to America. As a result, wives have had to become their husbands' advisers. It has been noted that one-third of working wives work in their husbands' stores. Consequently, the operation of the business becomes a joint venture, and it is almost logically inevitable that wives become involved in decisions affecting the business.[24] Some wives also claim that their reason for participating in business and family financial matters is because their husbands are not all that interested in financial matters. A wife in Los Angeles explains: "I run a small ice cream parlor and my husband is a shoe repairman right next to my store. I have a keen interest in running my business and have been doing very well. My husband, who was a school teacher in Korea, is not much interested in business matters or in family finances. Therefore, I make most of the decisions on matters having anything to do with money matters." Another wife, who is a nurse in the Washington, D.C. area, says: "My husband is working toward his doctoral degree in psychology. Although he received a small scholarship from the university, I have been supporting him for many years. I take care of everything ranging from our children's educational expenses, to insurance, home buying, and investments if we have some left over, and other financial matters. Sometimes I resent my husband for his lack of interest in the family finance matters."

Most Korean-American men still manage business and family finances, although their control over these matters has been weakened by their wives' involvement. However, some professional men such as doctors, engineers, college professors, and researchers, still regard showing any interest in running businesses and dealing with the details of money matters as undignified. Some of these professional people comment disdainfully about the merchants' drive to make a lot of money and show off their expensive houses and cars. An engineer in Albuquerque, New Mexico proudly comments: "I don't know anything about money. My wife takes care of everything about the family finances. She likes to do that, and she is very good at that." A sociology professor in central Pennsylvania says: "By nature of their discipline, most sociologists are not keen to make or manage money. My wife, who is a physician, makes three times as much as I do. Since my contribution to the family finances is limited, I don't have much to say about how our joint income should be used." A doctor in New York also comments: "My wife takes care of all taxes and investments. She is better [at managing our finances] than most accountants and financial planners. I trust what she is doing with our income."

Although some recent women immigrants may have had some experience running small businesses in Korea, most have had no experience before they came to America. For them running a dry cleaning business, a restaurant, a grocery store, or a fish market is a revelation. In some cases, wives discover their own business acumen when their husbands fumble. As a result, more and more husbands begin to rely on their wives, not only for their wives' labor, but for their advice on running the business itself. A wife in Philadelphia comments: "Running a clothing shop is not easy. My husband is bored working at the store, and he is simply not interested in matters such as overhead and earnings. Although my husband works hard, he should know hard work alone, without business savvy, will not lead to success." Some wives say that their husbands love showing off by buying expensive cars, houses, furniture, and memberships in golf clubs, without knowing too much about the source of their income. Wives believe they have to intervene in matters related to business and family finances because their husbands have a tendency to spend beyond their means.

The more wives step in to manage family finances, the more they influence decisions on expenditure for major purchases, such as houses, automobiles, children's education, vacation planning, and caregiving for their elderly parents. As a result, family financial planning has gradually ceased to be the exclusive domain of men. A working wife in a small town in Pennsylvania comments: "My husband would like to send our son to an Ivy League college, even going so far as to borrow money from a bank. I disagree with him because we simply can't afford such an expensive college. I told him Penn State University is good enough. This has been a constant source of argument between us. Furthermore, I don't believe in this business of sending kids to Ivy League colleges to enhance the status of Korean men." A few husbands observed that they used to make the final decisions with regard to their children's choice of school, buying automobiles, taking trips, and other costly undertakings. Now more and more, husbands wryly observe that their wives are taking the final, decision-making authority away from them. One husband says: "I am not going to fight with my wife over who has the decision-making authority in our family. To do so would give me *golchiapa* (headache)." Husbands also claim their children sense which parent has the authority in the family and often choose not to talk over their plans with their fathers. Women's role in the workplace does have an effect on the balance of authority between husbands and wives in Korean immigrant families, although many wives insist their earning power has nothing to do with the dwindling authority of their husbands.

Some wives, not in the labor market, dislike being completely dependent on their husbands. They would very much like a career and a chance to become more independent. The wife of a physician in a small town in upstate New York remarks:

Unlike in Korea, in America women who have careers are respected by others. Furthermore, when they become single mothers, they can take care of themselves. I came to America to become a pharmacist or a worker in a health field. That dream disappeared when I met my husband who is a physician from Korea. He has always practiced his profession in small towns where physicians are desperately needed. We moved many times but never to a large city where large universities and colleges are located. Now, we live in a town where a university is located fifty miles away from my place. But my husband doesn't like the idea that I go back to school to get a degree and pursue a career. He is very tradition-oriented. He wants me to stay home and take care of the children and "serve" him and his parents. I don't think he understands how I feel about foregoing my career for the sake his career. Furthermore, as I depend on my husband financially, I don't have much of a voice in deciding anything related to finance. My children's education, the mortgage for the house and car payments, insurance, and everything else is paid by him.

Another immigrant wife regrets the chance she lost to pursue her own career because she had to help her husband with his business while caring for her four children. Now she believes it is time to pursue her own career:

I decided to start a college degree program at this stage of my life to save myself, to save my career. For so many years I had been preoccupied with child care and family survival. But suddenly I realized that I had lost too much of myself. Of course, my study complicates my family life and marital relations. But I am now so determined that my husband cannot stop me.[25]

As Korean immigrant wives have gained more economic power, they have also shed the subservient role of traditional Korean wives. Although many wives still look after their husbands' parents, they are no longer blindly serving their parents-in-law as they once did in Korea. Furthermore, working wives have greater decision-making power on matters related to the welfare of their parents-in-law and their own parents. One example illustrates this situation perfectly. A man in New York comments: "My mother is being taken care of by my brother in California. I would like to send her some money, but it is difficult to do without consulting my wife as she controls all family financial matters. My wife keeps on saying that my mother is getting enough SSI (Supplementary Social Security) from the state of California.

When my mother had a stroke and became immobilized, I was going to buy a wheel chair for her. Again my wife objected, saying that the social welfare department will provide it for her. Sadly, the idea that daughters-in-law serve their mothers-in-law is no longer applicable in America."

As I have previously noted, the relationships between immigrant wives and their elderly parents have also changed as more wives control the purse strings. Particularly, the relationship between daughters-in-law and parents-in-law are no longer traditional. As their parents-in-law help their immigrant children at their workplace and at home, some daughters-in-law have begun paying them as if they were hired help. This has the effect of subtly changing the relationship between daughter-in-law and mother-in-law. A working mother in a suburb of Washington, D.C. says: "I pay my mother-in-law for her domestic help at the end of the month. She seems to enjoy having the extra money in addition to her SSI to spend on gifts for her grandchildren and for taking trips. However, I don't like creating a business-like relationship with my mother-in-law. Sometimes, I wonder whether I should raise her salary." Another successful woman realtor in suburban Philadelphia comments: "When my parents-in-law came to live with us, at the beginning they expected me to 'serve' them in the traditional Korean fashion. However, in a few years, they realized that our family budget was mostly managed by me instead of their son, who is a college professor, and consequently they knew that any activities involving monetary matters indirectly depended upon my approval. Once they recognized my authority in managing our family finances, they became meek in my presence. Sometimes, they act like guests, rather than family members."

While Korean immigrants have been extolled by the mass media and scholars for clinging to their virtues of hard work and strong families, the typical Korean family is often hiding terrible tensions and conflicts resulting from each member of the family trying to accommodate the strains of the transition to a nuclear family. They have left a culture where life has been governed for hundreds of years by Confucian philosophy with very strict definitions of gender roles and the family relationship based on a hierarchical system. In the United States they find new definitions of family beliefs, ideals, values, and norms which emphasize individualism, egalitarianism, and advantages of small families. Adaptation to these new meanings of family life require fundamental adjustments on the part of Korean immigrants in the relationship between husbands and wives, between parents and their children, adults and their elderly parents, and even their in-laws. That, in turn, can create misunderstanding, tension, and strain in the family relationship that often leads to friction, antagonism, and even abuse.

NOTES

1. Insook Han Park and Lee-Jay Cho, "Confucianism and the Korean Family," *Journal of Comparative Family Studies* 24 (1995): 117–134.

2. For an excellent article on status of women in Confucian society see Yunshik Chang, "Women in a Confucian Society: The Case of Chosun Dynasty Korea (1392–1910)," in *Traditional Thoughts and Practices in Korea*, eds. Eui-Young Yu and Earl H. Phillips. (Los Angeles: Center for Korean-Americans and Korean Studies, California State University, 1983), 67–93. See also Michael C. Kalton, *Korean Ideas and Values* (Elkins Park, Pa.: Phillip Jaison Memorial Foundation, Inc. 1979).

3. In his study of the level and kinds of kin involvement among Korean immigrant families in Atlanta, Min found that about 53 percent of those 70 respondents reported that they meet kin members once a week or more often. About 29 percent indicated that they meet kin members every month or more often but less often once a week. See Pyong Gap Min, "An Exploratory Study of Kin Ties Among Korean Immigrant Families in Atlanta," *Journal of Comparative Family Studies* 25 (1984): 59–75.

4. According to Kim and Hurh, in their sample of 70 families without children in the Los Angeles area, 78 percent of employed wives do grocery shopping while 71 percent of unemployed wives do so; 88.9 percent of employed wives do the housekeeping while 90.5 percent of unemployed wives do so; 82.6 percent of employed wives do laundry while 71.4 percent of unemployed wives do so; and 87 percent of employed wives wash dishes while 81 percent of unemployed wives do so. However, husbands outperformed their wives at such household tasks as garbage disposal and family budgeting. The burden of carrying out household tasks did not change for wives who have children. See Kwang Chung Kim and Won Moo Hurh, "Employment of Korean Immigrant Wives and the Division of Household Tasks," in *Korean Women in Transition: At Home and Abroad*, eds. Eui-Young Yu and Earl H. Phillips (Los Angeles: Center for Korean-Americans and Korean Studies, California State University, 1987), 199–252.

5. Pyong Gap Min, *Changes and Conflicts: Korean Immigrant Families in New York* (Boston: Allyn and Bacon, 1998), 43.

6. About two decades ago, Yu studied the working conditions of Korean immigrant women in Los Angeles. In his sample of the 63 percent of full-time married employed women, he found three quarters of them with dependent children managed without babysitters; 43 percent of them worked more than eight hours a day; 27 percent worked late evening and night shifts; and 48 percent worked on weekends. See Eui-Young Yu, "Occupation and Work Patterns of Korean Immigrants," in *Koreans in Los Angeles: Prospects and Promises*, eds. Eui-Young Yu, Earl H. Phillips, and Eun Sik Yang (Los Angeles: Koryo Research Institute and Center for Korean-American and Korean Studies, California State University, Los Angeles, 1982), 53–58.

7. There is a saying in Korea that when wives' cooking is unsatisfactory, the dining table flies. In other words, enraged by what he perceives as his wife's poor cooking, an angry husband will upset the table, spilling the food on the floor.

8. Young I. Song, *Silent Victims: Battered Women in Korean Immigrant Families* (San Francisco, Calif.:Oxford Press, 1987), 107–111. For another study of violence against Korean immigrant wives by their husbands see Sun Bin Yim, "Korean Battered Wives: A Sociological and Psychological Analysis of Conjugal Violence in Korean Immigrant Families," in *Korean Women in a Struggle for Humanization*, eds. Harold Hakwon Sunwoo and Dong Soo Kim (Memphis, Tenn.: Association of Korean Christian Scholars in North America, 1978): 171–199.

9. John Mints and Peter Pae, "The High Price of Success," *Washington Post*, September 7, 1988, A1–4.

10. Philip Taft, Jr, "Policing the New," *Police Magazine*, July 1982, 11–26.

11. Quoted in Jeffrey Goldberg, "The Overachievers," *New York Times*, April 10, 1995, 50.

12. Goldberg, "The Overachievers," 43.

13. Kwang Chung Kim, Won Moo Hurh, and Shin Kim, "Generational Differences in Korean Immigrants' Life Conditions in the United States," *Sociological Perspectives* 36 (1993):258–270.

14. Gender-role differences in caregiving and the performance of household chores among the elderly population and the persistence of the patriarchal family system are some of the major hinderances in providing adequate living arrangements for the elderly in Korea. See Hongsook Eu, "Health Status and Social and Demographic Determinants of Living Arrangements Among the Korean Elderly," *Korea Journal of Population and Development* 21 (1992): 197–223.

15. Quoted in Min, *Changes and Conflicts: Korean Immigrant Families in New York,* 62–63.

16. Dong Chung Kwak, "Mending Broken Immigrant Lives," *Los Angeles Times*, June 24, 1995, B7.

17. Keum-Young Chung Pang, *Korean Elderly Women in America: Everyday Life, Health, and Illness* (New York: AMS Press, 1991), 316–320.

18. Min, *Changes and Conflicts: Korean Immigrant Families in New York,* 86; Pang also found that only seven of twenty women in the sample of elderly Korean women in her study in Washington, D.C. area lived independently. See Pang, *Korean Elderly Women in America: Everyday Life, Health, and Illness,* 317.

19. Don Chang Lee, *Acculturation of Korean Residents in Georgia* (San Francisco: R and E Research Associates, 1975), 40–41.

20. Quoted in Min, *Changes and Conflicts: Korean Immigrant Families in New York,* 54.

21. According to the 1987–88 Korean Student Directory at the University of California at Berkeley, almost 50 percent of Korean students declared their majors in chemistry, biological sciences, natural resources, and engineering. See Eun-Young Kim, "Career Choice Among Second-Generation Korean Americans:

Reflections of Cultural Model of Success," *Anthropology and Education Quarterly* 24 (1993): 224–248.

22. Quoted in Min, *Changes and Conflicts: Korean Immigrant Families in New York*, 55.

23. Eui-Young Yu, "The Activities of Women in Southern California Korean Community Organizations," in *Korean Women in Transition: At Home and Abroad*, eds. Eui-Young Yu and Earl H. Phillips (Los Angeles: Center for Korean-American and Korean Studies, California State University, 1987), 275–299.

24. According to Kim and Hurh's study of household tasks peformed by husbands and wives in Los Angeles, when wives are not employed, 52 percent of husbands dealt with the family budget. On the other hand, when both husbands and wives are employed, 61 percent of wives tended to the family budget. See Kim and Hurh, "Employment of Korean Immigrant Wives and the Division of Household Tasks," 207.

25. Quoted in Min, *Changes and Conflicts: Korean Immigrant Families in New York*, 54.

Chapter 6

PREJUDICE AND DISCRIMINATION

Asian immigrants, whether Chinese, Vietnamese, Korean, or Southeast Asians, encounter few legal, discriminatory sanctions by the United States. Legislation such as the Chinese Exclusion Act of 1882, the Gentlemen's Agreement of 1907, and other legislation, including laws passed by various states designed to exclude or to restrict the civil and legal rights of all Asians, had originally been passed in response to the appeals of various white pressure groups. At first, only the Chinese and the Japanese immigrant laborers suffered from such restrictive legislations. After the passage of the Immigration Act of 1965, Asian immigrants have faced less open hostility from the American public. In fact, the mass media and even some scholars have praised the recent Asian newcomers for their hard work, emphasis on their children's education, their lower crime rate, and above all, for not "rocking the boat."[1] The mass media, in particular, singled out Asians' culture, especially those things that seemed to place great emphasis on hard work, perseverance, and strong family ties. Thomas Sowell, a black conservative scholar, observed that Asians have an advantage over blacks because of their culture that he believed put stress on such values as frugality, hard work, and enterprise. For Sowell, these values paved the way for Asians' economic success in America.[2] Many Asian Americans may recall more than one occasion when they were told by their American friends and acquaintances how much Americans admire them for their cooking skills, excellent automobiles, their perseverance and intelligence, their spirit of independence, and above all, their diligence, all of which, many Americans believe, separate them from other minority groups, particularly blacks.

Some Americans adroitly hide their racial prejudice by making pointed remarks about blacks and hinting that Asians are different; the suggestion is that Asian Americans are admirable because they do not ask for hand-outs from the government. A Korean immigrant remarks: "I used to feel good when Asians were looked upon more favorably than other minority groups by listening to whites' admiration of Asians. I don't fall into that trap of pitting one minority group against another by the dominant group any more."

Yet most Asians in America are very cautious about becoming complacent with how well they are fitting into American society because of all the positive images of Asian Americans that flood the news media and popular outlets such as television and movies. Not only do such images fluctuate with sociopolitical and economic conditions, but these positive images of Asian Americans seem to appear only when they benefit the dominant group. In fact, some students of Asian Americans have begun debunking positive images of Asian Americans and are studying the process that gives rise to periodic surges of such positive images.[3]

How thinly rooted the adulation of Asian Americans is became obvious, at least to Asian Americans, when Senator Daniel Inouye, a Japanese American and decorated war veteran, received hundreds of racially motivated hate letters when he chaired the Iran-Contra hearings in 1987. These hateful letters told him he had no right to question an American marine, Colonel Oliver North, who was alleged to have arranged for the illegal shipment of military hardware to foreign countries. In the 1970s and 1980s, when the Japanese economy seemed to be outpacing the U.S. economy in terms of productivity, Japan-bashing became very popular in America. Some Americans argued that restrictive Japanese trade policies limiting or banning the importation of American products into Japan while dumping Japanese products on the U.S. market was similar to the attack on Pearl Harbor. When some Japanese seemed bent on buying up American landmarks such as the Rockefeller Center, or famous golf courses in Hawaii and California, as well as luxury hotels and movie studios, newspapers and magazines carried breathless stories with scary headlines such as, "Japan Invades Hollywood," "The Danger from Japan," "Dismantling American Industry," "Containing Japan." These and similar dire headlines stirred once dormant American anti-Asian sentiment. Even a community such as Torrance, California, with a large Asian population, did not remain unaffected. The local newspaper headlined an "Asian Invasion."

The propensity of the media to alert the public to an "Asian Invasion" not only contributes to a climate of resentment, hatred, and fear of Japanese, as well as other Asian ethnic groups, but also contributes to a climate of hostility toward the growing Asian American community. A well known, third-generation Asian American professor at the University of California at Berkeley told an audience at a conference that, during the Vietnamese War, he found scrawled across his office window, "gook go home." The most infamous manifestation of this antipathy for Asians is the death of Vincent Chin, a Chinese American brutally beaten to death in 1992 by two men who assumed he was Japanese and therefore somehow responsible for unemployment in the American auto industry . In some places it reached the point where Asian Americans, who are not Japanese, have taken to specifically saying they are not Japanese when they encounter the American public. During the Los Angeles riot in April 1992, Korean shop owners in Koreatown were stunned when the police completely withdrew its protection of their shops. They were forced to arm themselves in order to protect their property from looters. Recognizing so many incidents of prejudice and discrimination which seemed to be deliberately aimed at Asian immigrants, whether long-time residents or recent arrivals, Asian Americans are not easily persuaded by all the praise of Asians as model citizens to be emulated by all other minority groups.

Although the actual experiences of prejudice and discrimination may differ among Asian Americans, all Asians, including Korean Americans, must confront the fact that they have been, are, or will be victimized by stereotyping, bigotry, and violence because these problems are common to all Asian groups. Incidents of hate crimes against recent Asian immigrants and Asian Americans are good for headlines in all major newspapers and they are a surprise to many Americans, including civil rights workers. The problems were serious enough to attract the attention of the U.S. Commission on Civil Rights in the 1980s and its investigation has continued into the 1990s.[4] Some of the newspaper headlines are reminiscent of the negative stories published when native-born whites felt their economic security was threatened in the mid-nineteenth century.[5]

- Shots fired into homes of Southeast Asian refugees in Seattle

- The words 'Nips Go Home' were spray painted on the home of a Korean family in Davis, California

- A 19–year-old pregnant Chinese woman was decapitated by a train when she was pushed in front of it at a New York subway stop by a man whose lawyer says the murderer was 'overcome by a fear of Asians'

- Bumper stickers reading: 'Toyota-Datsun . . . Pearl Harbor and Unemployment in Los Angeles'

- Death of a white crab fisherman in a conflict between Vietnamese and local fishermen

- Several youths taunted a Korean American employee, using ethnic slurs, at the Laurel Liquors store in Castro Valley, California

To most Asian Americans, racism in America is still very much present in the fabric of American society ready to surface when the occasion calls for it. The United States has a long history of prejudice and discrimination against Asians. In recent years, underlying anti-Asian sentiments have been aggravated by the increased visibility of Asian Americans due to the influx of large numbers of immigrants and refugees from Asia. Since Asians, regardless of their nationalities, are lumped together by most Americans, any Asians, whether Chinese, Japanese, Korean, or Vietnamese, who were mistreated or attacked by someone for racial reasons, served as an early-warning sign to all other Asians. This was true of Vincent Chin who, although he was Chinese American, was mistaken for a Japanese. Also, this was true of three Vietnamese youths severely beaten by a large group of black youths who mistook them for Koreans after an altercation between a Haitian woman and a Korean store owner of the Family Red Apple Market in Brooklyn, New York.

If one wishes to separate Korean immigrants' experience with prejudice and discrimination, it is purely for the purpose of limiting the scope of the analyst's study and not because their experience is necessarily different from that of other Asian groups. However, historical circumstances which encouraged Koreans to immigrate to America differ from factors that have influenced other Asian immigrants. In the case of Koreans, the Korean War was the triggering event for Korean immigration to the United States, although the liberalized immigration policy put in place in 1965 certainly encouraged mass immigration of Koreans, as it did other groups of Asian immigrants. As a result Asian immigrants, no matter what their nationality, who came to America after 1965 have related similar adjustment problems. Many Korean scholars have studied almost all Korean immigrants' adjustment problems, ranging from the education of their children, conflicts with other races, especially blacks, to difficulties in economic survival. Surprisingly few studies have dealt with Korean immigrant experiences with prejudice and discrimination in America. One of the reasons may stem from the scholars' belief that most recent Korean entrepreneurs are independent store owners with shops in neighborhoods largely populated with Koreans, and therefore they have assumed the shop owners have not experienced racism personally. Another reason, perhaps, is an assumption by scholars that

Korean immigrants' experiences with prejudice and discrimination would not be all that different from those of other Asian immigrant groups and about which much has been written. Yet it is enlightening to hear directly from Korean immigrants their experience of racial injustice in America and to compare their experiences with those of other Asian immigrants.

Most students of race and ethnic relations have known how Korean immigrants will be received by the American public based on the experiences of earlier Asian immigrants and periodic public surveys of the American public attitude toward Asian groups. Sociologist Emory Bogardus constructed a social distance scale to measure social distance between specific American ethnic groups and the American public.[6] This social distance scale has been used frequently as a means of measuring ethnic prejudice by Bogardus and other social scientists. From among thirty ethnic groups Bogardus measured for social distance in 1926, 1946, 1956, and 1966. Koreans were located at or near the bottom in terms of preference of closeness. Together with Chinese, Asian Indians, Blacks, Japanese, and Mexicans, the American public look upon Koreans as one of least preferred groups of people with which to be close, while English, Germans, and Swedes were found to be the most preferred groups.[7] In 1977, Owen, Eisner, and McFaul measured social distance of the same ethnic groups by using Bogardus' scale. This time Koreans ranked at the bottom in terms of Americans' feeling of closeness among the thirty ethnic groups.[8] The National Opinion Research Center and other small research organizations have continued to conduct surveys of the public's attitudes toward various ethnic groups. Invariably, Koreans were always one of least preferred groups, ranking only slightly above blacks. Although the public prejudice expressed in social distance does not always measure accurately how individuals act or think in real situations, Koreans and certain other Asians are definitely not people to whom most Americans feel close, or with whom they wish to be close.

FEELING LIKE PERPETUAL GUESTS

A Korean immigrant who came to America in 1955 still remembers vividly how he felt when he visited a southern state in 1958. He recalls, "When I visited Knoxville, Tennessee to see my older brother, who was attending the University of Tennessee, Jim Crow laws were still in practice. In the downtown area, there were many signs of 'colored only' and 'whites only.' When my brother and I entered a dime store to have a cup of coffee and sandwich, again I saw signs of a division into 'colored' and 'whites' in the store. Since we are Asian and colored, I asked my brother whether we should sit in the 'colored section.' He said they wouldn't mind if we sat in the 'whites only' section as long as we were quiet. I felt so uncomfortable asking the waitress for what I wanted for fear I might offend her even by my tone of voice." Although such racially discriminatory signs are no longer posted in southern states, many Koreans and other Asian Americans, perhaps remembering the color lines, are somewhat timid when dealing with white Americans by being extra nice to them lest they might awaken whites' dormant antipathy toward Asians. In many cases, Asians may feel they have to "behave" like model "guests" because of the label they have borne for so long. It is a commonplace among Korean Americans that whites dislike blacks, but tolerate Asians.

Some Koreans say that, even though whites in general are kind to them, they never feel close enough with whites to become intimate, no matter how long they have known them. Some people reason that language and cultural differences probably put distance between Asians and Americans, while others believe that whites don't regard Koreans, or other Asians, as their equals, or else feel uncomfortable in their presence. Describing his puzzlement with how Americans behave toward Koreans, a Korean American professor, who taught engineering for almost three decades at a medium- size private university in central Pennsylvania, says: "I have lived in America for almost forty years. I understand American jokes; I swear occasionally; I consider myself fairly Americanized. But yet our dean's secretary, who has been working for us for almost twenty-five years, always calls me Dr. (So and So), although she calls all my other colleagues by their first names. I told her many times to call me by my first name, yet she doesn't. Strangely enough, there are a few faculty members I have known for twenty years who always say 'hello' to me stiffly or formally in hallways or at the library and seldom greet me by my first name, even though I address them by their first names. On the other hand, some of these same people always call their other colleagues by their first names. I feel, somehow, I am not one of them."

Many of the earliest Korean students to arrive in the United States recall how formal their hosts and hostesses were with them and always called them by their last names, even though they quickly became more informal when addressing European students and seemed more at ease around them. A Korean professional remembers:

When I was graduate student, frequently Korean and European students were invited by American families to Thanksgiving or Christmas dinners. An American hostess invariably asked me how long I was going to stay in America, but she would encourage European students to find nice American girls, marry, and stay in America permanently. Now, even though I am an American citizen, I still feel I am not fully welcomed by Americans and deep inside my heart, I feel I am still a "guest. "

In fact, many Korean students think that most Americans believe they are not interested in sex, dating, or partying. They think Americans regard them as sober, serious students who are quiet, courteous, and only interested in studying and who will eventually go back to their country and marry Koreans. A Korean American professor ponders what the response would have been had Korean students informed their American hosts or friends that they had absolutely no intention of returning to Korea; instead, they intended to become American citizens, and marry Americans. He speculates that the hosts' reaction would not have been positive.

The Immigration and Naturalization Service is the agency many Korean immigrants recall bitterly as the place where they were first made to feel unwelcome. Many Korean students who came to the States in the later 1950s and the early 1960s remember vividly the unpleasantness of interviews with INS officers when they sought permission to work for a short time. They interpreted the immigration officers' unfriendly, even rude, behavior as gestures meant to warn them that they were not welcomed. They had, of course, heard all the rumors floating around that European and Canadian students had no problems with getting temporary work permits. They had all heard stories of immigration officers who coached European students on ways to become permanent residents. A recent Korean immigrant still thinks of INS as a gigantic, scary organization, where Asians were summoned to be interviewed. He remembers it as an unfriendly place. He still believes he would have been deported had he made any mistakes in speaking English with which he was still struggling at that time.

The degree to which Korean immigrants and other Asians feel that they are "guests," or are not fully part of American society varies from region to region. In cities like Los Angeles, Chicago, and New York City, where a large number of Asians are concentrated, Asians are very much a part of the mosaic that makes up America and probably their feeling of "foreignness" is substantially less than that of those of Asian descent who live in areas where there are few Asians. Perhaps some of the reasons why Asians continue to congregate in large metropolitan areas such as New York City and Los Angeles are because these cities not only offer diverse economic opportunities for Asians but also make them feel more secure. The reception with which Asian immigrants are greeted by Americans who live in small towns and medium-sized cities and in rural areas is quite different from that of large cities. Frequently, citizens in these towns and cities approach Asian Americans courteously, as if they are dealing with foreign guests. For example, an American-born Korean recalls an incident at a restaurant where he stopped for dinner on his way to Philadelphia. As he waited in line to pay for his meal, the man in front of him turned around and said, "You must be very lonely away from your home (in Asia)." No matter how long Koreans or other Asians have lived in America, no matter what generation of native-born American they may be, most white Americans assume the Korean American has recently arrived in the United States. A Korean businessman, who came to America when he was very young and who now lives in the Pittsburgh area, is puzzled by Americans' concentration on the subject of Korea. He says: "Whenever I talk to someone at a ski resort, a conference, or in an airplane, Americans usually turn the conversation to the subject of Asia and the Asian peoples, even though they quickly reveal they have little knowledge about these subjects, and in spite of my informing them that I know little about Korea and other Asian countries. When I try to turn the subject to American domestic issues, sports, or politics, invariably they show little interest in talking about these subjects. Their assumption is that, as a 'foreigner,' I don't know too much about these subjects; therefore, I am not worth talking to about these subjects." Another Korean immigrant, who lived in Philadelphia for thirty years (most of his adult life), explains why he feels he is still a foreigner: "When I travel to New York and California, occasionally I meet someone who is also from the Philadelphia area. I am always happy to see a fellow Philadelphian. Much to my surprise, the American-born Philadelphian could care less that I am from Philadelphia and went to school and work there. He is more interested in my nationality. When I tell him I was born in Korea and came to America when I was thirteen, he perks up and starts to tell me about a few Koreans he knows and begins to praise Koreans, saying how hard working they are. In spite of everything I have told him, I am a 'foreigner,' not a Philadelphian. After a number of these experiences, when someone asks me where I am from, I am not sure whether to answer Korea or Philadelphia."

Koreans and other Asian immigrants are made to feel that they are "outsiders" or "temporary guests" by their American colleagues and co-workers in their work places. Their American co-workers, who are usually friendly, are reluctant to discuss important matters such as company policies and their future plans. A Korean computer programmer, who works in a large corporation in New York, complains: "Every time, when the subject of the operation of the company, whether dealing with matters of personnel, finance, future strategy, etc., my American co-workers turn to other native-born white co-workers, and I am completely ignored, even though I try to contribute to the discussion." A Korean-American professor who teaches political science at a small Protestant college in central Pennsylvania had a similar experience. He explains: "My colleagues are friendly. We talk about our students' lack of preparation, salary, fringe benefits, office space, secretarial help, sports, etc. However, when it comes to the subject of reorganizing the curriculum or the selection of a new dean or president, all of sudden I am excluded from these discussions." Perhaps Americans' reluctance to include Korean Americans in the discussion of significant issues involving company operations partly stems from their view of Koreans as "outsiders" who are assumed to be unfamiliar with the complexity of the problems involved in running an American organization and only partly from prejudice, but it is very difficult to say for sure.

By viewing Asians, whether they are native-born or immigrants, as guests, visitors, or sojourners, Americans are short-sighted in focussing on Asians' ethnicity. In doing so, they are making their Asian compatriots feel they do not belong, that they are not Americans. Korean Americans are very quick to detect when they are not regarded as fellow Americans when they are bombarded with such questions as these:

- You speak English well, and how long have you lived here?
- You are more American than I am; I know Kim and his wife, and they are very nice people and do you know them?
- Is Korean food different from Chinese?
- Are you Chinese or Korean? Can you tell the difference between Koreans and the Japanese?
- My son has a Korean friend who is very bright.
- Do you intend to go back to Korea?
- Our church is very active in collecting clothes and sending them to Korea.

Sometimes these questions are posed to American-born Koreans, regardless of whether Koreans speak without an accent. Ethnicity or race is the most significant aspect in the mind of Americans when they meet Koreans. Of course, some of these questions stem from genuine curiosity on the part of Americans; however, most of these questions are viewed by Koreans as condescending and part of an effort by Americans to make them feel they are not "Americans." Americans' perception of Asian Americans as "foreigners," or "guests," may also impede the Asians' full participation in educational, economic, and political institutions. A Korean sociologist comments: "One of the reasons why Korean immigrants are active in Korean churches, interested in Korean politics, and are attracted to ethnic politics is because they don't feel they are yet American enough or comfortable enough to attend American churches, participate in American town meetings, and cast votes on election days. Sadly, voter turn-out of Korean immigrants on election days is extremely low. Consequently, Korean immigrants don't have leverage with American politicians."

Korean immigrants and even second-generation Korean Americans frequently mention their feeling of being guests, unwanted, disenfranchised, and discouraged. The result is that they do not feel that they are regarded as loyal and devoted company employees. A Korean immigrant, who had worked for a food company more than ten years as an assistant manager in the Washington, D.C. area says: "Most of my co-workers and my boss are very uneasy in interacting with me. People around me are more formal toward me than toward the white employees. Sometimes, I feel very isolated in the company. I work here to make a living. Otherwise, I don't have very positive feelings about the company. I feel I am not a part of the company. I haven't had a promotion for a long time." Under these circumstances, it is difficult for Asian employees to cultivate mentors, to understand corporate culture, and to "network" with their fellow employees which is essential for their promotion and other perks. Building social networks with fellow employees always has been problematic for Asians and other minorities. Even at medical schools, Asian and other minority medical professors face uphill battles in forming social networks with their peers which are necessary for promotion. For example, based on 1,807 U.S. medical professors for the study, Palepu found 58. 3 percent white faculty members had senior academic status. By comparison, only 30.5 percent of black, 43.4 percent of Asian American, and 40.8 percent of Hispanic faculty members held similar positions. She pointed out that some reasons for minority faculty members' slow promotions were related to their weak negotiation skills and inability to network with their peers.[9]

Asians always feel there is an aloofness on the part of their co-workers behind their outwardly friendly manner. A Korean engineer near Philadelphia comments: "I have worked for my company almost twenty years. I have always felt that my American colleagues, whom I have known for many years, are not as open with me as they would be with other whites, even though we play sports together and visit each other. Although they swear and exchange jokes with each other, they are very cautious in doing the same things in front of me as if I am still their 'guest.' " Although Koreans describe Americans as *sumuk sumuk* (feeling awkward) toward them, uneasy and hesitant interacting with them, some Koreans believe that Americans' uneasiness may mask prejudice rather than ignorance or na-iveté. A Korean immigrant college professor, who has lived in America for almost four decades, also acknowledges the problem: "Perhaps their [whites'] attitude toward recent immigrants will be different from that of professional Koreans who have lived in America for many decades. But there are always some Americans who make you feel that you are not one of them no matter how long you have lived in America and whether you are professionals or non-professionals. There were many instances when I felt that way. I felt that there was nothing I could do about people like that. So I swallowed my pride and moved on."

It is when Asian "guests" criticize some of the wrongdoings of the host society that they immediately notice what the American public really thinks of their Asian "guests." The usual rejoinder is, "Go back where you came from." Elaine H. Kim, a professor of Asian American studies (and who is of Korean descent) at the University of California, Berkeley, was quoted in *Newsweek* on the Los Angeles riot in April 1992 as saying that Korean shopkeepers, who were not protected by the police, must have felt they were betrayed by the trusted government and realized that the American Dream is only an empty promise.[10] In the following month, a reader of *Newsweek* responded to her article by saying that: "It's certainly ironic that Kim pro-claims the American Dream 'an empty promise,' given that she, the daugh-ter of immigrants, has become a university professor here. . . . America's doors swing both ways, Ms. Kim. If Korea is where your heart is, maybe you should follow your heart." This is another way of saying, "If you don't like it here, why don't you go back to Korea?" Invariably, when Asian mi-nority immigrants exercise their freedom of speech, a fundamental right, they are met with such rebuttals as quoted above. Naturalized European im-migrants have seldom been targets of such reprisal, at least in recent history. A Korean store owner in Los Angeles says: "I am getting tired of people telling me to go back to Korea. Whites are telling me to go back, blacks are telling me to go back, and now even illegal Mexican immigrants are telling me to go back to Korea!" Some Americans are puzzled why Asians are im-migrating to the United States. There is no potato famine, nor is some czar conducting a pogrom in Korea or China, and Asians are not hungry as were the European immigrants who arrived at Ellis Island early in the century. To some Americans, it is a mystery why Asians keep on coming to America and complain when they are mistreated. If they wish to stay in America, they should "behave" like "guests." A prominent sociologist, W. I. Thomas, said: "If men define situations as real, they are real in their consequences." If

Asians are treated by Americans as "guests," the Asians may have no choice
but behave like "guests." By doing so, they may become more and more
strangers in America as Ronald Takaki eloquently described in his book,
Strangers From a Different Shore.[11]

BECOMING QUIET ASIANS

For many decades, Asians in America were regarded by Americans as
quiet and scientifically minded, as if they were born that way. Nothing
could be further from the truth. Had Americans spent any time in Korea or
Japan, they would have found Koreans and Japanese males to be raucous
and quite unrestrained. In those countries, college students specialize in all
subjects and pursue their careers in all fields, unlike Asians in America who
tend to restrict themselves to careers in biological and natural science fields.
Such seemingly contradictory behavior does not emerge by chance alone, if
one examines circumstances giving rise to such contrasting behavioral patterns. For more than a century, Asian immigrants have been the target of bitter prejudice and persecution, not to mention physical attacks. Although
institutional discrimination at the societal level supported by laws and customs has subsided in the last half of the century, Asians are still the targets of
subtle and sometimes overt hostility from certain segments of the white majority. In the process, Asians in America have learned to adjust to or accommodate the white majority by becoming ostensibly passive. They have
made a living by operating small businesses and farming in some cases, and
carving out careers in the sciences, all of which minimize social interaction
with the public. Therefore, they are often labeled the "quiet," or the "model"
Americans.

Over one hundred years of experience have taught Asians to be reserved,
even obsequious, with the dominant group. Asian immigrants are fully
aware that they are living in a country that has a long history of oppressing
Asians, where all offices of authority are controlled by whites, where the
Asians have no political clout, and where as a consequence they feel powerless and isolated. In 1984 Hurh and Kim found that 47 percent of Koreans
stated they felt powerless and lonely, and 84 percent encountered serious
language problems.[12] Adult Korean immigrants, therefore, seek social security within their own ethnic community and by limiting their social interaction to kinship groups and a limited, carefully selected circle of friends.
However, their children must go to school and interact with non-Korean
children. Sometimes these children find themselves in a clique of Asian students. In a small town the child may be the only Asian student. Conse-

quently, they may be ridiculed because their "food is smelly"; or they "speak funny"; or they look like "Chinks"—a derogatory reference to Chinese, but one which may well include Japanese, or Korean children. The son of Korean immigrants, who came to America when he was eleven and who is now a physician, remembers how difficult it was adjusting to a new school environment. Because he was one of two Asian students in junior high and high school, he always stood out. Although his classmates were generally kind to him, occasionally they called him derogatory names when he played or quarreled with them. He recalls: "One time, I was very hurt when a kid, a classmate, who lived in my neighborhood, called me all kinds of names, and I went home and cried for more than an hour. My parents were surprised by what had happened, but I didn't tell them why I was crying. I didn't want to hurt them. Many unpleasant things happened to me because I was an Asian kid. But I kept everything to myself. Yes, I was quiet, but I studied hard to get into a good college." Some immigrant parents became concerned when their normally outgoing children became quiet and withdrawn. They conjectured that their children had been subjected to racial taunts, or else that they had encountered some sort of unpleasantness at school. But they never inquired too closely.

Even Asian college students are often quiet in the face of taunts or name calling. A Korean college student who came to America when she was eight, who now attends a medium-sized university in Pennsylvania, recalls how she coped with sometimes being excluded from activities by her American friends and acquaintances. When she arrived at the university, she observed that dozens of Asian students were very much isolated. They usually ate alone in the dining room, studied alone at the library, sat alone in the back of classrooms, and rarely participated in class discussions. She found that she was behaving just like the other Asian students and determined to do something about it. She explains:

When I was in high school in Philadelphia, I didn't have much time left for anything else after my studies because I had to help my parents in the store whenever I had time. When I entered college, I was assigned to a dorm with a white roommate. Although my roommate was as studious as I was, she liked to go to parties on weekends. One time she asked me to come along. There were many boys and girls at the party. During the entire party, few boys asked me to dance, nor did students talk to me or try to get to know me. When I tried to talk to them, it seemed their minds were on other white boys and girls. I had a few more similar experiences at other parties, with the same result. I always felt like I was a wall flower at these parties. After a few of these experiences, I stopped going to these gatherings altogether, offering as an excuse my need to study, or else I claimed I was going home for the weekend. At the same time, I began to realize I was becoming a loner. Finally, I talked with other Asian students and found that they, too, had similar feelings of social isolation. In an attempt to remedy this matter, we formed our own Asian American student association. The membership grew from ten to thirty-five, and included almost all Asian students on campus. Now, once or twice a month, we all get together, cook international foods, celebrate holidays together, and sponsor many "Asian nights" social events. I am having an enjoyable, active social life on campus, while I am studying hard as a pre-med student. Now, we are demanding that our university should increase its efforts to recruit Asian Americans, perhaps by creating an Asian-American studies program.

At large state universities in the west, such as the University of California at Los Angeles or Berkeley, Asian students are numerous and seldom have the sense that they are alone or cut off socially. Moreover, there are many Asian support groups which would stand up for Asian students at these universities. But this is not the case in most colleges and universities located in the east or mid-west. In these areas, Asian students are still a small minority within the student body. As a result their comparative isolation means they tend to be the least vocal and probably the least active minority on campus.

Isolation from the mainstream is not limited to students, it extends to Asians in the workplace. Those Korean immigrants who work as semi-professionals and professionals in private companies quickly realize they will never reach the top administrative level, and they frequently say, "If I become a manager, that is as high as I can expect to reach, but I doubt I will ever reach that position." Many feel they are "out of the loop," so to speak, as they are seldom included in the inner circle of decision makers. They are rarely among the friends of those who are decision makers in the company. Therefore, when the company starts to retrench or reorganize they feel especially vulnerable. They know the company may easily dismiss them by using such excuses as: the language barrier, the lack of leadership, the lack of assertiveness, and other subjective pretexts. As a result, they feel they have to be constantly on guard. A Korean working as a processor in an insurance company in Washington, D.C. comments: "I don't participate in company gossip; I don't complain; I just do what I am supposed to do. Although I am unhappy with the slowness of promotions, it's all right. With my limited

English speaking ability, I am lucky I still have a job." Under these circumstances, it is difficult for immigrants to ask for and get salary increases or play office politics in order to buck for promotion.

Unlike the black minority, Asians have not established strong protective organizations such as the NAACP or the Urban League; their church groups have not turned their attention to concerted political action; and they have yet to form vocal state and federal support organizations to promote their own interests. Although there are a few Asian organizations, they are usually located in a few major metropolitan areas, but have not yet injected themselves into the political arena. Since Asians rarely sue for racial discrimination, Asian legal aid agencies and other support organizations are often underutilized. State and federal agencies have been reluctant to intervene on behalf of Asian minorities because of their reputation as the "model minority," and whatever problems they may have encountered are assumed not to be significant. Recently, however, the Federal Commission on Civil Rights began paying more attention to civil rights issues involving Asians. But the agency is still in the information-gathering stage. Even in President Clinton's initiative on "Race Dialogue," among the committee members appointed by the President, Asian-American issues are on the back burner. When Asians feel they are discriminated against by their employers, landlords, school teachers, social workers, or police officers, they know they are very much alone: few allies will offer support. Therefore, Asians probably will continue to believe the best policy is for them to maintain low profiles and exercise great care and think twice before airing their grievances for fear of risking their job security or their social status. As an illustration of this point, take the case of a retired Korean immigrant college professor who taught in a small Protestant college in New York state. He says, "Since I was the only minority faculty member in the entire college, I knew I had to be extra careful for I had no one to count on in case I ran into problems with my students, other faculty members, or administrators. I didn't have any confidence in the local Equal Employment Office and other government agencies, as they don't seem to believe Asians are targets of prejudice and discrimination. You have this sense of loneliness and isolation. Since teaching jobs were scarce, I had to stay on by doing my job quietly without voicing criticism of the administration and provoking senior faculty members until I received tenure. Even then, I found it difficult to express my own opinion where it might do the most good because I felt I didn't have other faculty members' support. I was always treated as a foreign-born faculty member no matter how long I had taught there."

Feelings of powerlessness are felt among most professional and non-professional Korean immigrants. As a result, they are unlikely to be brave enough to challenge authority when they are discriminated against or passed over for promotion. One often hears of immigrant engineers and doctors, many of whom are educated or trained in the United States, who have moved from one position to another because they had "difficulty in getting along" with their American superiors. If one asks them what they mean by "difficulty in getting along," they will cite such things as low salary and lack of respect. Korean immigrant doctors, who are not independent practitioners, are often employed at church-run hospitals, county and state hospitals, community-run hospitals of all sorts, and state prisons located in sparsely populated areas: the sort of positions American-born doctors avoid. Hospital administrators know FMGs (Foreign Medical School Graduates) don't have much choice in their choice of hospitals and localities. A radiologist who used to work at a Catholic-run hospital in New York state remembers that, in the early 1970s, "I had so much difficulty in getting along with administrators. The head administrator of the hospital was a Sister who was very condescending to all foreigners, not just Koreans. She seldom responded to my greeting in the morning. Somehow you feel you are not that welcomed. It was as if she was saying, 'We are not going to hold you if you have someplace to go.' There was nothing I could do under these circumstances except work quietly without complaint. I guess we foreign doctors were expendable as so many doctors wanted to come to the hospital from foreign countries in the latter part of the 1970s. Sometimes it is more difficult to bear the coldness and indifference of your colleagues and administrators than to end overt discrimination. I resigned from the hospital and joined another Korean radiologist as an associate." A Korean professor who teaches at a small college in Maryland laments: "I admire black workers. When they are discriminated against, they sue establishments and bring in outside government agents to investigate the cause of complaints. That is why the white establishment thinks twice before they fire or discriminate against black employees. Koreans and other Asians would rather move on to something else when they are unhappy with their employers, instead of openly complaining about their treatment."

For all the pessimism about their treatment on the job, some Korean immigrants are optimistic about their future in America. They equate their experiences as immigrants with the experience of Jews. They say that Koreans, like Jews, now devote themselves to achieving economic security rather than social or political equality. They believe they will eventually assert themselves politically once their economic position is secure. They have high hopes for their American-born children, who are bright and capable of moving successfully into the American mainstream. Others, however, are not that optimistic. A Korean immigrant social scientist offers this rather stark assessment: "Right now most Korean immigrants seem satisfied with their economic success by engaging in traditional ethnic businesses. Also their children are doing very well in school and go to highly selective colleges and universities. But it is a mistaken notion that they will be like American Jews. First Asians are not white, few Asians control major banks, few Asians are mass media moguls, few Asians are Hollywood giants, few Asians are major players on Wall Street, and few Asians are major political contributors. If we are going to be like Jews, we have a long, long way to go, particularly for recently arrived Koreans. Once they try to move beyond the confines of their ethnic wall and seek to join the American mainstream, they will soon discover how racism against non-whites is deeply entrenched in American society. Then they will gradually *mekki upta* [to literally lose one's pulse][13] and become quiet. Look at those early Asian immigrants who are still struggling at the fringes of mainstream organizations. They are much more conciliatory, quiet, deferential than those recently arrived Korean immigrants. The Japanese Americans were not foolish or gutless when they went to relocation camps quietly during World War II."

EXPERIENCING SUBTLE DISCRIMINATION

Asians in America are able to sit anywhere in the bus, eat at any restaurant, vote on election days, attend school with whites, and live in most white neighborhoods, at least in the recent past. But many Asians feel that their acceptance by whites, even at this level, has not been wholehearted. Asians are very sensitive to subtle nuances of behavior that suggest discrimination. The following examples illustrate how Korean immigrants notice subtle discrimination at various public facilities. A Korean immigrant, who lives in a small town in New York, says frequently he felt he was discriminated against in subtle ways when he dined at a restaurant. For instance, the hostess or host would invariably seat him at an undesirable table near the kitchen, at a heavy traffic area near the buffet, or near the restrooms. Another Korean immigrant in Pennsylvania relates similar experiences. He and his family members were seated at tables in unpleasant or uncomfortable locations, sometimes right next to coat racks, even though there were empty tables in more pleasant places, near windows, for example. He is getting tired of constantly asking to be given different tables. Furthermore, when he pays for the meals, cashiers rarely thank him, even though they automatically thank all the other customers. At the very least, he feels he is not welcome in that restaurant. When well-to-do Korean immigrant women shop at upscale department stores, they are angered when they are steered to moderately priced goods by clerks who assume that they can't afford more expensive items.

It is very common to find underemployment among doctors, pharmacists, nurses, and other skilled Korean professionals educated in Korea but who were unable to obtain licenses often because of their difficulty with English rather than because they lacked the qualifications to pursue the discipline, or because they lacked the necessary skill. Because they have had to find employment in fields often far removed from the professions they left behind, these otherwise qualified professionals blame Americans for discrimination. Moreover, those doctors who have managed to secure licenses to practice medicine frequently find their competency is called into question by American-trained doctors . Even American-trained Korean American doctors have been challenged by their patients. An anesthesiologist in a well-known hospital in Boston explains, "It upsets me when patients ask me where I was born, which medical school I graduated from, how old I am, etc. I don't think they would ask me these questions if I were a white woman. I usually politely ask these doubters whether they want another anesthesiologist." Dentists are apprehensive about becoming periodontists, endodontists, or oral surgeons for fear that few white American general dentists will refer their patients to them. A Korean immigrant ear, nose, and throat specialist in central Pennsylvania observes that he gave up on the referral service in his town a long time ago and now depends on his patients to refer people to him by word of mouth. He says American-born physicians seldom refer their patients to him. They seem to prefer to send their patients to ENT doctors up to a hundred miles away. A Korean gynecologist, one of the few gynecologists in a medium-sized city in upstate New York, had a thriving practice until a few white gynecologists opened their practice in the same city. The number of his patients dwindled until he had to close his office and move to a small town in Pennsylvania where there were few gynecologists.

Most Korean ministers, largely because of their language difficulties, can't function effectively in American churches. They are very much dependent upon first-generation Korean churchgoers, whose numbers are declining as age takes its toll. Non-Korean-speaking, second-generation Korean Americans are less likely to attend Korean churches. Even though these Korean churches are affiliated with the major denominations in America, they receive fewer directives from the bishoprics. They are pretty much left to their own devices to do whatever they desire in their churches. As a result, they are left to struggle for their salaries, health insurance, housing, automobile expenses, and other compensations which most American ministers receive as a matter of course.

The degree of discrimination against Asian Americans depends upon how Asians make inferences from white Americans' behavior toward them. Clearly, some Asians are inferring too much—and some too little—from white people's behavior. Whatever inferences Asians may draw from their interaction with whites, in their minds, the white's behavior is real. For example, Korean store owners in Koreatown in Los Angeles have no doubt that when they call the police to report robberies or thefts the police are slow to respond and are too often rude. An immigrant who operates a dry cleaning store in the Washington, D.C. area complains that every time he visits the police station to file an armed robbery report, he feels he is ignored because of the inattentiveness of the police. Naturally, a store owner who has been victimized a number of times is going to want the police to drop everything and deal with his complaint. To the police, on the other hand, he is just one of many victims of rampant crime and is therefore no big deal. Obviously, the police need to reinvigorate their efforts at improving community relations.

Then, there is the matter of perception. Some Korean immigrants mentioned that one of the reasons why many Koreans drive expensive cars is that the police treat them with more respect. A Korean cab driver put it this way, "I think of Koreans as Rodney Dangerfield's: 'We get no respect.' This lack of respect gradually builds resentment toward whites." In another, rather comic case, a Korean physician traded his Chevrolet for a Mercedes Benz thinking he would get more respect. Now, however, he is getting more traffic tickets. He interprets this upsurge in traffic tickets as police resentment of Asians driving expensive cars.

A Korean immigrant who came to America in the early 1950s remembers how he was treated when he was a busboy. In one memorable case, he recalls entering a hotel room with drinks, only to discover a couple having intercourse. Shocked and mortified, he quickly tried to back out of the room. But the woman said it was all right and told him to put the drinks on the table. After recovering from his shock, he reasoned that the couple was not embarrassed to be caught having sex in front of him because, to them, he was not a human being, he was just a Chinese houseboy.[14]

George Bernard Shaw once said he didn't mind someone hating him, but he hated it when they ignored him. Most Asians may feel the same way about whites; however, they have become accustomed to being ignored by whites. Psychologist Dovidio, in his discussion of what he calls "aversive" racism, says limiting or avoiding interaction with minorities is not unintentional. It is well intended in the minds of aversive racists, Dovidio argues. As he explains it, aversive racists don't express negative stereotyping or resist racial equality. They do not show prejudice in situations where discrimination would be obvious to themselves or to others. As Dovidio explains it, they frequently express their biases indirectly by avoiding all interracial interaction and favor whites rather than discriminate against members of minority groups.[15] Avoiding interaction can take many forms, sometimes in the street, sometimes in the office, or other workplace. For example, when a white driver needs to ask for directions and sees an Asian and a white walking together in the street, he will direct his questions to the white, even though the Asian might be the obvious one to ask because of his proximity to the driver. When a salesperson walks into an office where there are both Asians and whites, he will skip over the Asian, even though he is obviously the office manager, and single out a Caucasian, even one in a junior position in the office. In other places such as colleges, conferences, parties, and even on golf courses, Asians have to make an extra effort to be included in conversations among whites. Otherwise, they will be ignored by the whites.

Although it is difficult to demonstrate that when whites avoid interacting with Asians it is a form of deliberate discrimination, yet many Asian immigrants interpret such avoidance this way. The fact is that being snubbed or ignored is not only perceived as rejection, it can be interpreted as hostile. A Korean college professor in Los Angeles recalls: "When I took my daughter to an elementary school for her first day in school, a teacher was there greeting all the children and engaging in small talk with the parents. But when I introduced my daughter to her, the teacher's face suddenly became expressionless and she turned away. On my way home, I kept thinking about what kind of experience my daughter would have in that teacher's class." Korean immigrant parents are always concerned that their children will be made fun of by the other children and will be shunned or ridiculed by these children. This father was troubled by the teacher's apparent rebuff of his daughter. In a not-unrelated situation, a Korean employee of a small engineering firm said that he hated company picnics. He said he and his wife never enjoyed the outings because they always felt so out of place even in the company of his colleagues and their wives. He thinks that even colleagues who are usually friendly at work ignore them. A Korean history professor in Pennsylvania describes an experience similar to that of the engineer in the previous example. He says:

After teaching more than twenty years, I can usually handle the subtle discrimination I receive from other faculty members and students. However one thing I dislike most and have difficulty in handling are the faculty receptions at the dean's or the president's house. At such receptions, my wife and I would be more or less isolated unless I tried very hard to talk to someone. Christmas dinner for the faculty and their wives in the college dining room is even worse. At one Christmas dinner reception, my wife and I sat at a table set for six all alone, although all the other tables were full. Supposedly friendly faculty members just passed us by with a "hi" and a smile. Finally, my Chinese colleague and his wife joined us. After I had a few more of these experiences, I decided to avoid as much as possible participating in these faculty social functions. Now I think I understand why I see Asian students eating alone in the cafeteria.

A Korean college student in a large university in a midwestern state said that when she takes a bus, she always sits in the aisle seat. She says that, if she sits in the window seat, the seat next to her is always empty until all other seats in the bus have been taken. She has always felt a little embarrassed when this happens. A Korean physician in a small town in Pennsylvania observes that when he and his family attend an American church, no one else offers to sit in the pew they have chosen, although all other pews are crowded with people. Eventually, he stopped going to the church, even though his wife and teen-aged daughter continued to attend. A number of Koreans say they believe some Americans feel self-conscious to be seen with Asians in public, whether simply talking with them, participating in sports with them, or eating with them.

If whites feel uneasy in fraternizing with Asians in public, the fact is that Asians also feel the same way. A few Korean immigrants say they prefer to associate with blacks, because they don't make them feel as uncomfortable as whites would. In their study of instances of discrimination responded to by blacks, Hispanics, and Asians, Cain and Kiewiet found that Asians experienced the highest percentage of social discrimination and the lowest percentage of economic discrimination.[16] The fact is that perceived social discrimination—the avoidance of contact with Asians, feeling awkward in the presence of Asians, and ignoring Asians—has apparently contributed to Asians' suspicions of white Americans, no matter however subtle, unarticulated, or unconscious it may be.

EXPERIENCING OVERT DISCRIMINATION

Some Koreans feel discrimination indirectly, some encounter it in subtle ways, and still others experience it overtly in the form of physical assaults or in the vandalization of their stores, a frequent occurrence in major cities such as Los Angeles, New York, and Philadelphia. Most Koreans who have lived in America for a long period of time have experienced some form of overt discrimination at one time or another. The early Korean immigrants in Hawaii and the West Coast at the turn of the century have recounted innumerable incidents of hostility. Even in the 1950s, open hostility against Korean Americans and Korean immigrants was very much in vogue. For example, an American-born Korean American gained national fame when he won the Olympic gold medal for diving in 1948 and again in 1952. He served in the U.S. Army Medical Corps during the Korean War. In 1955 he retired from the army and tried to buy a home in Garden Grove, California. Realtors in that city refused to show him houses because they claimed the presence of Orientals drove down property values.[17]

Those Koreans who experienced discrimination in the form of physical assaults or other overt forms of hostility know, in no uncertain terms, how upsetting and terrifying such discrimination can be. For instance, Korean immigrants who have visited Canada frequently find, on their return to the United States, that they are invariably pulled over at the U.S. border for a check of their credentials, while Caucasian drivers are allowed to enter with little or no formality by immigration officers. A Korean mother was upset when children from her neighborhood threw stones at her house and broke her window while screaming racial epithets. A Korean professor walked into a cafeteria at a conference. Finding no empty seat except at a table where a white person sat alone, the professor politely asked if he could sit at his table, assuming he was a conference attendant. Whereupon, the white person immediately stood up and without responding took his tray and moved someplace else. A Korean metallurgist in Pennsylvania became very angry with his neighbor who always knocked on his door to ask if he had seen his dog every time it strayed. The metallurgist was convinced his neighbor always knocked on his door because the man had heard Koreans ate dogs; therefore, whenever his pet went missing, the metallurgist became the prime suspect. A Korean proprietor of a small clothing store complained that Jewish wholesalers seldom gave him a chance to purchase "hot items" (popular items) from which he could make a quick profit. He assumed that the wholesalers reserved these items for Jewish retail merchants.

All Korean immigrants remember various incidents, some of which were serious and some of which were not. Korean swap-meet merchants report that American swap-meet merchants block the aisles to their stalls and show their displeasure in other unpleasant ways. A Korean couple from New York stopped to eat at a restaurant in upstate New York. While they were waiting for their food, they noticed two white men were reading a newspaper after eating. After the men left, the husband, noticing that the men had left the newspaper behind, picked up the paper, but one of the white men returned and snatched the paper from his hand and stuffed it into the waste can and left. The couple was flabbergasted and embarrassed by the man's behavior. A waitress who witnessed the man's rudeness quickly bought a fresh newspaper and gave it to the couple. In yet another example of a crude rebuff, another Korean couple stopped at a restaurant for coffee. When the wife asked for cream for her coffee, the waitress said there was no cream. But the wife had seen the waitress bring cream to people at another table. Whereupon, she and her husband left the restaurant greatly disappointed. Although Koreans and other Asians don't often experience blatant discrimination at restaurants of the sort experienced by blacks at a Denny's in Maryland, they do, from time to time, report occasional experiences with unpleasant or rude treatment by personnel at restaurants, stores, hotels, airports, and even at churches.[18]

Although many Koreans claim that they are private people and would like to keep their embarrassing experiences of discrimination to themselves, they do share their experiences with their Korean friends. A store manager in Virginia, outside of Washington, D.C., related an incident in which he felt he was discriminated against and was very disappointed by a white police officer's response:

Since I don't interact with whites except at my store, I didn't know whether Korean immigrants actually experience discrimination until I experienced it myself. Once I was in a car accident caused by a white fellow who banged into my car from behind. I was hurt and became immobilized. A white police officer came and talked with the other driver for a while, even though he was not hurt and his car was not much damaged. The officer came back to me and checked my driver's license and other documents without asking me any questions about the accident or my physical condition. Then he gave me a traffic citation and told me that, if I disagreed with the citation, I could go to court and appeal the citation. I asked the officer whether he could at least call an ambulance for my injury. He agreed to do so, but without much enthusiasm. One hour later, the ambulance came and took me to an emergency hospital. I will never forget this incident.

Highly educated Korean immigrants tell stories about some of their friends who have Ph.D. degrees in engineering but now drive cabs and others who received M.B.A. degrees from elite universities in America but who now run stores. The reasons they gave for driving cabs or operating small businesses primarily focused on the unsatisfactory environment for them in typical American companies. For instance, they experienced stagnation in the work place. Their contribution to the companies was either not appreciated or else ignored. As a result, they did not get the usual benefits one would expect. They were either passed over for promotion or else the promotions came very slowly, and they discovered they were not paid the same as their white co-workers. Sometimes they anticipate limited career opportunities based not only on their own experiences working in such companies, but also from observing how other Asian minority group members are treated. Yun Pang, a Korean American with a graduate business degree, quit a New York insurance company to open a retail store after seeing how an Asian-American colleague was bypassed by white supervisors. He remarked: "I thought, 'This guy is good, but if he's not making it, neither will I' "[19] In his study of Koreans in New York, Kim cited a case of a Korean, who came to the United States in 1970 and received an M.B.A. from a university in New York City, and who is now working for R company:

At his entry into the American white-collar job market, Mr. Lee was somewhat frustrated. He received only two job offers while he saw native-born American students receiving "a lot of job offers from famous corporations." He chose the R Company because the other company offering him a job intended to send him to its overseas branch in South Korea. He rationalized this discrepancy in job opportunities, saying to himself that "I am an immigrant with poor English." But when he started to work for the company, he met a Chinese worker who was born in the United States and had no foreign accent. The Chinese had worked in the same section for several years but received few promotions. "Many new American graduates bypassed him. One American guy, who started at the same time as the Chinese, reached the level of supervisor." The report of this experience caused Mr. Lee to strengthen his sense of the career limitations in the company, and so he decided to leave.[20]

Based on their previous experiences interacting with whites in social settings, most Korean immigrants, who have lived in America for many years, know what discriminatory hurdles lie in wait for them once they are employed at American firms. For example, a Korean, who came to America with his family when he was fifteen and who is now a police lieutenant in Los Angeles, recounts his experience of discrimination while he was in the U.S. Marine corps. After a year and half of college, he joined the U.S. Marine Corps. After his basic training, he was given an opportunity to become a Marine Corps officer when there was a shortage of junior grade officers during the Vietnam War. He was surprised and confused about becoming a Marine Corps officer:

> That was a very radical thing. Even I wondered how it would look to have a Korean immigrant serving as a lieutenant in the U.S. Marine Corps. You can't even picture that! It was just not acceptable; it wasn't done. It was like a female going out for NFL football. And at that time, the Vietnam War was going hot and heavy. All the instructors were Vietnam vets. I can't repeat the words they called me—every degrading thing you can ever imagine. They called me "gook" and "Mongolian fuck." They didn't want me around. They thought I didn't really care, but I did.[21]

Once I asked a Korean immigrant lawyer in Los Angeles, who worked with troubled Korean kids in Los Angeles, whether he had encountered prejudice and discrimination in pursuing his legal career. He said he thought that was a silly question because all Asians in this country experience prejudice and discrimination. Any Asian lawyer, he said, whether American-born or immigrant, will have much difficulty in becoming a partner in any white law firm, or else there will be fewer opportunities for advancement or choice of assignments. His observation is borne out by various studies of Asian-American lawyers. Citing various studies and reports, the U.S. Commission on Civil Rights points out that Asian Americans were only 0.7 percent of lawyers nationwide, although they constituted 2.9 percent of the U.S. population (1980 Census of Population). A 1989 survey of forty-nine New York law firms reflects that Asian Americans still make up only 2.1 percent of lawyers. Of these lawyers, only 0.8 percent, or thirty-one Asian Americans, were partners.[22] Discrimination against Asian employees is not limited to those with legal careers. The *New York Times* reported in January 1992 that, while Asian Americans comprised 26 percent of the engineers at the Hewlett Packard plant in Silicon Valley, there was not a single senior executive among them. Jim Tso, a spokesman for the Organization of Chinese Americans, has put it this way: "In the past, we had the coolie who slaved. Today we have the high-tech coolie." [23] In a survey of 308 Asian American professionals and managers in the San Francisco Bay area, Cabezas and others found that over two-thirds of the Chinese Americans, one-half of the Japanese Americans, and three-quarters of the Filipino-Americans felt that racism was a very significant factor limiting their upward mobility.[24] Supporting their feeling about being discriminated against, Tang found that Asians were significantly less likely to be in managerial positions or to be promoted to managerial positions than white engineers with the same measured qualifications, such as educational attainment, years of experience, and other characteristics, such as their field within engineering, region of residence, and other demographic factors.[25]

Sometimes, it is difficult to investigate how Asian Americans have been discriminated against at work because few Asians seek legal remedies for discrimination by their employers. Various organizations designed to promote the interests of Asian Americans, such as Japanese American Citizens League, Asian Pacific American Legal Center, Chinese for Affirmative Action, and others have been active in trying to help Asian employees redress their grievances. They frequently work with state and federal civil rights divisions to search for the causes and possible solutions to the patterns of discrimination against Asians in America. Recently, the U.S. Commission on Civil Rights reported frequently mentioned reasons why employers are reluctant to promote Asians in their companies. The Commission reported employers claimed Asians are unassertive; they are difficult to understand because of their accents, they have communication problems; they lack aggressiveness needed to lead; and, they are too technical.[26] Some of these reasons are based on employers' perception of facts through their experience with Asians; however, most of these reasons are based on rationalizations stemming from stereotypes employers hold about Asians. For example, second-generation and third-generation Asian Americans, who have no accent or communication problems, find their employment prospects or chances of promotion are substantially diminished because of their ancestry. When native-born Americans are too technical, they are welcomed, but when Asians are "technical," they are considered unfit to be managers. When Asians are aggressive, white employers are often offended because they expect Asians to be subservient. For instance, Jimmy Breslin, popular and sometimes abrasive columnist for *Newsday* on Long Island, was angered at criticism of one of his columns by a female colleague who is Korean American, and he publicly referred to her as a "yellow cur" and "slant-eyed." [27] Another example further illustrates the kind of reaction an Asian employee may expect to receive from her American superior when she becomes assertive in her work place:

When the Korean American programmer asked her new supervisor informational questions regarding new office policies or practices being instituted, she was rarely given straight explanations or answers. She was made to feel as if she was asking something she was not supposed to. While the supervisor treated questions from her co-workers with courtesy and professionalism, she felt that her questions were handled in an unfriendly way, sometimes with hostility. At one of the office meetings, the division chief pointedly said her behavior of questioning office policies was out of line. She soon began to feel that she was being singled out and that she was a target of harassment and disparate treatment.[28]

Employers have tremendous latitude in defining what is meant by "lacking leadership," "communication problems," and "unassertiveness." Whatever criteria employers use to define employability or promotion, these criteria are subjective. Employers continually review old criteria and contrive new criteria for hiring, firing, and promoting which would primarily benefit them. Recently, for example, many companies and organizations have advanced a new criterion. The result is that Asians are found wanting because they lack interpersonal skills and do not socialize well with their fellow workers. Thus, despite their technical talents, their reluctance to socialize with their co-workers is viewed as incompatible with American corporate culture.

The case of professor Chua illustrates this matter clearly. When professor Chua, a Chinese immigrant civil engineering professor at the University of New Mexico, was denied tenure, he launched his legal fight in 1994 claiming that such denial was based on his Chinese origin. Finally, four years later, the Federal Equal Employment Opportunity Commission of the U.S. Department of Justice eventually sided with professor Chua and ordered the university to grant him tenure together with back pay. Now that the case is settled, professor Chua's supporters have begun talking about the reasons for denying tenure. The reasons had little or nothing to do with his teaching or research, but with such vague reasons as "personal characteristics" and not fitting into the department "Country Club" ambiance. They say the discrimination in his case represented a fear of the unknown.[29] Employment discrimination, to varying degrees, is a problem facing all Asians in America regardless of whether they are native-born or naturalized citizens. A Korean immigrant says: "This is a white world; they can give whatever reasons they want for not hiring or not promoting Asians. They can promote us to the managerial level or even to a vice-presidency, if they see an advantage in doing so. For example, if they see us as people who are capable of increasing corporate profitability through Pacific-Rim-related activities, they can send us to South Korea to staff branch offices and even put us in charge of the offices. If they see us as useful in areas where Korean ethnic groups are highly concentrated, they can make us managers of that region. These are the only avenues we have to move up the ladder. Otherwise, we are stuck at the same level for a long time."

Reaction among those victimized by prejudice and racism varies from individual to individual. Some avoid contact with whites as much as possible; some avoid working for white-owned firms by opening their own stores; some hope to minimize the effect of racial discrimination by ignoring it, by hoping it will go away, or by focusing their energy in another direction. At the extremes some have refused to become American citizens even though they have lived here many decades; others are thinking of retaliating against the dominant group. A sociology professor in the Midwest comments: "I have always been extra nice to my white colleagues in order to be liked or accepted. I have only a few years left before my retirement. I no longer act like a nice, quiet Asian fellow. Much to my colleagues' chagrin, I am now aggressive and blunt in dealing with them, because I feel I have paid enough dues. If they don't like my "new" personality, I don't care at this point in my career." Others, recognizing any improvement in their status is unlikely because of their language difficulties and cultural barriers, still hope that their children will not be subjected to prejudice and discrimination. However, they are disappointed when they see their 1.5-generation and second-generation children coming back to the Korean community to do business after hitting the glass ceiling at white-owned companies. There are Korean immigrants who are bitter over the discriminatory treatment they have received at the hands of Americans. An owner of a small sundries store in California says: "When I finish paying off my debts, I hope I can go back to Korea. People are always saying that anyway: 'Fucking Chinese, go home!' It is very hard to live as an immigrant here. Race discrimination is far too strong. It's impossible to overcome the limitations first-generation immigrants face. There is a real limit to how far a person can go." [30] It has been reported that some recent Korean immigrants, disenchanted with the antagonistic racial climate in Los Angeles, particularly after the Los Angeles riots, are going to "pack up and go back home," while others have already left. There are even clubs in Seoul for returnees from Los Angeles. [31] A Korean doctor even blames Americans for Korean immigrants' high blood pressure. He says: "Korean immigrants have much higher blood pressure than Koreans in Korea. You know why? Korean immigrants have to endure everyday insults, prejudice, and discrimination exhibited by Americans everyday."

Some Korean immigrants urge other immigrants, old-timers and recent ones alike, to examine themselves before they start to blame others for their difficulty with finding acceptance by the dominant group, as well as other minority groups. Many Korean immigrants, who felt that they have become marginalized in American society, have blamed whites for creating such a condition, but at the same time they are not particularly interested in working with other minority groups, particularly blacks, to correct racial injustices. As a result, many of them have isolated themselves from both the dominant group and minority groups. How risky this self-isolation is can be seen in the film, *Do The Right Thing*, which was directed by the black movie director, Spike Lee. In the film, when a Korean grocer, fearful of rioting blacks, desperately shouts at them, "I not white! I black! Like you! Same!" The point is that they waited until their stores were being looted to identify with other minorities. Had Koreans engaged in meaningful dialogue with blacks and Latinos, they could have possibly averted the worst of the tragedy of the 1992 Los Angeles riots. Such voluntary self-isolation, according to some immigrants, not only saps Koreans' strength as a minority group, but also delays the time when they recognize the importance of their public contribution to the economic and social climate in their community. A social scientist in California says:

There are hundreds and hundreds of Korea associations and clubs, such as Korean churches, Korean soccer game associations, Korean youth organizations, Korean high school and college alumni clubs, Korean summer camps, Korean martial arts clubs, and others. Most Korean immigrants' activities revolve around these organizations. They spend large sums of money to be elected as leaders of these organizations. They also spend large sums of money to send their children to name-brand universities and colleges and boast about their children to other Koreans. After Los Angeles in 1992, then police chief Williams, although he was not police chief during the riot, came to the Korean community to find out specifically what happened during the riot and why Koreans feel discriminated against, specifically by the police. Only a few showed up to listen to the police chief. Ironically, however, when a South Korean politician shows up in the Korean community, the auditorium is packed. I am concerned about when Korean immigrants will come out from their self-imposed isolation and work at acculturation, integration, and assimilation, instead of complaining that they are neglected or discriminated against by the dominant group.

Reaching out to other minority groups, such as Hispanics and blacks, and joining coalition groups, for example, the Pan-Asian movement, the Rainbow Coalition, or the NAACP, has been problematic for Korean immigrants because of their language difficulties and cultural gap. Even at Asian American conferences, Koreans, Filipinos, Chinese, and other Asian conferees rarely mingle, although they all present papers which focus on the importance of forming coalitions. Because of the language barrier, some Korean immigrants cannot find common ground with Chinese, Vietnamese, and other recent Asian immigrants. Many believe whites can easily co-opt Asians and non-Asian minority group coalitions by making the coalition advocates cat's-paws for their own agenda. A Korean immigrant says: "Many times, I have worked with minority members. The results of my experience are the same. Minority workers are particularly kind to me as co-workers and show some empathy toward me, as I do toward them. Usually they are the ones who ask me to go out for lunch and to have drinks after work. But in the presence of our white boss and other white colleagues, our minority colleagues are too busy winning favor by flattery; they forget completely their other minority co-workers. Most Koreans don't know how to be sycophantic to anyone. I am always suspicious of minorities who say we should all unite and fight for minorities' rights. At this stage, we are still too insecure to do that." A Korean dentist who works at a community dental clinic in the southwest agrees with this view: "In our dental clinic many Hispanics, American Indians, and blacks work as secretaries, lab technicians, and chair assistants. However, dentists are mostly white. I am the only Asian dentist. These minority dental assistants and secretaries are courteous and prompt when they assist me. However, when a white dentist comes in, all my assistants' attention is directed toward him, regardless of whether the white dentist is a newcomer or an old timer, and I become a second-class citizen. White superiority is felt everywhere. Joining a coalition force? I don't think so. At least not yet."

NOTES

1. Jo and Mast trace how images of Asian Americans have fluctuated from the turn of the century to the present. See Moon H. Jo and Daniel Mast, "Changing Images of Asian Americans," *International Journal of Politics, Culture and Society* 6 (1993): 417–441.

2. Thomas Sowell, *Race and Culture* (New York: Basic Books, 1994).

3. In my earlier writing, I postulated a theory that the dominant group has manipulated Asian Americans by developing positive images of Asian Americans to suit its political, economic, and social needs. See Moon H. Jo, "The Puta-

tive Political Complacency of Asian Americans," *Political Psychology* 6 (1984): 583–605.

4. For more on the rise in hate crimes against Asian immigrants and Asian Americans, see U.S. Commission on Civil Rights, *Recent Activities against Citizens and Residents of Asian Descent* (Washington, D.C.: Government Printing Office, 1986); U.S. Commision on Civil Rights, *Civil Rights Issues Facing Asian Americans in the 1990s* (Washington, D.C.: Government Printing Office, 1992).

5. Some of the headlines are quoted from publications issued by the U.S. Commission of Civil Rights and some are from various newspapers the author collected in the 1980s and 1990s.

6. Bogardus asked his respondents to indicate whether they would accept a member of an ethnic out-group in varying social contexts, ranging from very close encounters to very remote ones. For example, he asked his respondents to indicate their willingness to interact with members of particular groups in the following circumstances: (a) as close kin by marriage; (b) as fellow club members; (c) as neighbors; (d) as workers in my occupation; (e) as citizens of my country; (f) as visitors to my country; (g) as persons to be excluded from my country. See Emory S. Bogardus, *Social Distance* (Yellow Spring, Ohio: Antioch Press, 1959).

7. Emory Bogardus, "Comparing Racial Distance in Ethiopia, South Africa, and the United States," *Sociology and Social Research* 52 (1968): 149–156.

8. Carolyn A. Owen, Howard C. Eisner, and Thomas R. McFaul, "A Half-Century of Social Distance Research: National Replication of the Bogardus Studies," *Sociology and Social Research* 66 (1981): 80–99.

9. Cited in Fred Woodhams, "Minority Medical Professors Are Less Likely to Hold Senior Posts, Study Finds," *The Chronicle of Higher Education*, September 18, 1998, A15.

10. Elaine H. Kim, "They Armed in Self-Defense," *Newsweek*, May 18, 1992, 10.

11. Ronald Takaki, *Strangers From a Different Shore* (Boston: Little, Brown and Company, 1989).

12. Won Moo Hurh and Kwang Chung Kim, *Korean Immigrants in America* (Cranberg, N.J.: Associated University Press, 1984).

13. *Mekki upta* is a Korean idiomatic expression which describes a person who loses heart.

14. Elaine H. Kim and Eui-Young Yu, *East to America: Korean American Life Stories* (New York: The New Press), 11–12.

15. John Dovidio, "Aversive Racism and the Need for Affirmative Action," *The Chronicle of Higher Education,* July 25, 1997, A60.

16. Cain and Kiewiet found 30 percent of Asians reported having experiences of social discrimination, whereas 19 percent of blacks and 16 percent of Hispanics reported having such experiences. In economic discrimination, 15 percent of Asians, 42 percent of blacks, and 19 percent of Hispanics reported having such

experiences. See Bruce E. Cain and D. Roderick Kiewiet, *Minorities in California* (Pasadena: California Institute of Technology, 1986), 111–115.

17. Brett Melendy, *Asians in America: Filipino, Koreans, and East Indians* (Boston: Twayne Publishers, 1977), 168.

18. In fact, sometime in 1997, two Syracuse University Asian students were physically assaulted by whites in a parking lot outside a Denny's restaurant in Syracuse, New York when they came out of the restaurant. The reason for the assault was never made clear.

19. Stanley Karnow and Nancy Yoshihara, *Asian Americans in Transition* (New York: The Asia Society, 1992), 45.

20. Quoted in Kim, *New Urban Immigrants: The Korean Community in New York*, 103–104.

21. Quoted in Kim and Yu, *East to America: Korean American Life Stories*, 214.

22. U.S. Commission on Civil Rights, *Civil Rights Issues Facing Asian Americans in the 1990s*, 174.

23. Karnow and Yoshihara, *Asian Americans in Transition*, 45.

24. Amado Cabezas, Tse Ming Tam, Brenda M. Lowe, Anna Wong, and Kathy Owyang Turner, "Empirical Study of Barriers to Upward Mobility of Asian Americans in the San Francisco Bay Area," in *Frontiers of Asian American Studies: Writing, Research and Commentary*, eds. Gail M. Nomura, Russell Endo, Stephen H. Sumida, and Russel C. Leong (Pullman, Wash.: Washington State University Press, 1989), 93.

25. Joyce Tang, "Asian American Engineers: Earnings, Occupational Status, and Promotions," Paper presented at the Annual Meeting of the American Sociological Association, Cincinnati, Ohio, August 1991.

26. U.S. Commission on Civil Rights, *Civil Rights Issues Facing Asian Americans in the 1990s*, 131–156.

27. Constance Hays, "Asian-American Groups Call for Breslin's Ouster Over Racial Slurs," *New York Times*, (May 7, 1990), 14.

28. U.S. Commission on Civil Rights, *Civil Right Issues Facing Asian Americans in the 1990s*, 154.

29. Juan A. Lozano, "Professor's Win Could Spur Change," *Albuquerque Journal*, April 12, 1998, A11.

30. Quoted in Kim and Yu, *East to America: Korean Americans Life Stories*, 40.

31. Miles Corwin, "Packing Up and Going Back Home," *Los Angeles Times*, March 4, 1993, 8.

PROSPECTS

The adjustment of Korean immigrants to life in American society varies according to the individual. Those who were struggling to make ends meet in Korea are more likely to be happy with their newly found financial security in America than those who were professionals in Korea. Those who had been someone prominent or important in Korea, and who found themselves reduced to operating businesses that did not confer the status they once enjoyed, long for their lost status. To them, financial success does not compensate for their former status. Another group enjoying its new social and economic freedom in America are Korean immigrant women. The patriarchal structure of society in Korea did not afford them the freedom as they possess in America. On the other hand, men have discovered they are losing their authority as heads of households. As a result, it is difficult to generalize about how Korean immigrants view their lives in America and whether their decision to immigrate is a wise choice.

To some extent, Korean immigrants' satisfaction with their decision to come to America depends on economic and social stability in Korea. The economic boom in Korea, and a demand for U.S. educated scientists and educators in Korea, lured many Korean immigrants back to Korea in the early 1990s, but the boom is beginning to wane as Korea's economic policies and financial system have proved to be inefficient as revealed by the fact that the country with a Gross Domestic Product of $508 billion dollars (1996 est.) owes $50 billion dollars to the International Monetary Fund.

It appears that there are three main categories of Korean Americans. There are those who wish to stay in the United States regardless of personal or familial ties to the homeland, or the social and economic enticements of the familiar surroundings of Korea. There are those Korean immigrants who will stay in America even though they think they will return to Korea when they accumulate enough wealth and reach retirement age. Finally, there is a third group of immigrants who are very unhappy with their lives in America and who are always looking for reasons to return to Korea. However, none of these groups is clear cut or predictable for all their complaints about their lives in the United States. For instance, many of these immigrants clearly mean it when they say they intend to return to Korea; however, their future plans depend upon many circumstances, such as economic opportunities, educational opportunities for their children, the slowness of social adjustment, the ready availability of health care, and many other factors, some of which are intangible. Then, there are the many recent Korean immigrants who are only concerned with the routine of day-to-day living and haven't thought too much about planning for the future. They have adopted a wait-and-see attitude.

Korean immigrants, particularly those nearing retirement, who choose to stay in America often cite financial or economic factors as their reasons. First, they say, it is much cheaper to live in America than in Korea, particularly in Seoul. The cost of food, housing, health care, the cost of their children's education, transportation, and other costs of living are much higher in Korea than in the United States. Even the cost of funerals is higher in Korea. Not only is it difficult to find rewarding employment in Korea, but some express doubts about whether they can maintain their standard of living in Korea. In particular, the elderly have no real choice but to remain in America. They have become dependent, not only on their children, but on federal and state governments for health care, food, housing, and other essentials. The elderly also find that, because their families are settled in the United States, they cannot readily go back to Korea for an elementary reason: they wish to remain close to their relatives. An immigrant says: "All my relatives, parents, brothers, and even cousins, are living in America. What am I doing if I return to Korea?" Another immigrant says: "Home is where my son and daughter live." The third reason is that they are not certain whether they will be able to readjust successfully when they return to Korea. This is a particular concern for those immigrants who have lived in America for a long period of time. Their adjustment is not necessarily limited to adapting to changes in Korean culture, but to the fact that they have grown accustomed to day-to-day conveniences of life in the United States, including reliable plumbing, shopping malls, public transportation, a lower population density, and a more open society.

Korean immigrants who have decided to stay put in the United States after their retirement face difficult decisions. Unlike other American retirees, who either retire to some place near where their relatives live or else join a planned retirement community, the choice is not as clear for the average Korean retiree. For instance, there are those immigrants who don't have relatives in America and who do not feel free to join a typical American retirement community. This is particularly true for the Korean retirees who came to America following the Korean War and who have worked all their lives in small-town America. After retirement some have moved to major metropolitan areas where they hope to meet and make friends among the large numbers of Korean immigrants who live there. All too often, though, they discover they have nothing in common with these immigrants because of the differences in their backgrounds and their experiences as immigrants. In effect, it is as though the Korean immigrant whose experience was with life in the hinterlands of America have nothing but their ethnicity in common with those Korean immigrants whose experience was gained from life in the cities of America. While they were working, they probably never gave serious thought to what they would do after they retired. Certainly, they never thought that they would find their fellow Korean immigrants to be so unlike themselves in interests, activities, and hobbies. In short, they were surprised to find themselves strangers among their fellows: a situation they never anticipated.

There are those who wish to return to Korea when they are financially independent. These immigrants say the only reason they came to America was to make money. They see no reason to stay in America after they have achieved their goal. One of the immigrants who thinks this way says: "In America, you get no respect, no recognition, and you always feel isolated. Furthermore, this is a joyless place; making money is everything." In one case, after living in America for eight years, a woman immigrant's desire to return to Korea was so overwhelming that she seriously considered leaving her husband and children in America and going back to Korea alone. She says: "I feel so lonely living in America. Others, who are financially independent, see there is no reason to stay in America; they are just waiting for their children to become adults. Then they plan to go back to Korea." Another immigrant adds: "After working so many years, I can now live comfortably in Korea on the money I receive from my pension. I have even bought a burial site reserved for American immigrant returnees by the Korean government."

In their study of assimilation patterns of Korean immigrants in the Chicago area, Hurh and his associates found that 65.8 percent of their sample of

283 said they desire to spend their retirement years in Korea. The predominant reasons given for returning to Korea were their continuing problems with adjustment to life in America and their emotional, social, and political attachment to Korea. Some of the statements made by the Korean immigrants and gathered by Hurh and his associates were: "I want to bury my bones in Korea"; "I want to be with my relatives and friends for the rest of my life"; "I want to help Korea with what I have learned in this country."[1] Among these Korean immigrants are those who wish to return to Korea, not necessarily because they are unwilling to adjust to life in America, but because they don't feel they belong. To them, America is a big, beautiful, plentiful country, but one which only native-born American whites or Europeans can enjoy. Such feelings are shared by any number of Korean immigrants. No matter how long they have lived in America, they still feel like outsiders. As a result, for them, Korea will always be where their heart is, and their wish is to follow their heart.

The third category of immigrants consists of those who have no desire to live out their lives in the United States and who are determined to go back to Korea. They are usually traditionalists—the immigrants who make frequent trips to Korea and talk about Korea in glowing terms. In their minds, there is no doubt they will leave America as soon as they find the right opportunity to do so. These are the people who usually claim America is for white people; who assert that racism is rampant; that minorities are forever second-class citizens; that the crime rate is too high; that morality is in decline, and so forth. They feel they are lucky to have Korea as a refuge. When they return to Korea, they believe they will be able to live like "human beings," with dignity and respect. Many of them are from the Los Angeles area and experienced at first hand the Los Angeles riots in 1992. They are the ones who have become very disenchanted with living in America. Abelmann and Lie cite cases of some Korean immigrants who hate the United States and want to go back to Korea desperately, but they cannot: "Even if you come here with lots of money, it all gets tied up in debts—house, car, and so on—it's different from Korea: you can't leave." They report an immigrant as saying: "I have absolutely no interest—even though I know I could—in getting an American citizenship because it doesn't mean a damn thing in the United States. In the United States, the ideology is 'whites-are-the-best.' This government does absolutely nothing for minorities so there is no point to citizenship."[2] Although Korean immigrants who belong to the third category is small in number, these are the Korean immigrants who stay in America purely for economic reasons: their loyalties rest with Korea. An immigrant says: "Living in America is a constant struggle. I try to tough it out, but it is becoming very difficult." Another immigrant, anxious to go back to Korea, is even disappointed with his children's education. A father says: "I am concerned about my children's education in America. What good is education without the foundation of Korean nationality?"

Korean immigrants in both the second and the third categories expressed their conviction that someday they will return to Korea. However, the difference between these two categories is that those in the second category have actually made some long-range plans, while those in the third category seem to have done little beyond expressing their dislike for living in America. One should keep in mind, however, that many Korean immigrants who say they are planning to return to Korea probably will not carry through with their plans. They will settle in America, get involved with their businesses, their relatives and friends, and share vicariously in their children's education. As the years go by, and as they become more familiar with the English language and American culture, Korea will slowly recede into the past. Their wish to return to Korea will diminish. It used to be a common practice among those Korean parents who planned to return to Korea to send their children to schools in Korea during the summer so that they would not forget their heritage. Many have now given up this practice after realizing that their children will probably never go back to Korea, and that they themselves will never return to Korea if it means leaving their children in America.

It does appear, however, that the immigrants' desire to return to Korea is very strong, at least in the initial phase of their early adjustment difficulties in America. According to Hurh and his associates' study, a high percentage of Korean immigrants revealed that they hope to retire in Korea, but that may be largely due to the fact that the sample's average length of residence in the United States was only 4.76 years.[3] Had they interviewed Korean immigrants who have resided in America for a much longer period of time, the percentage of Korean immigrants who expressed a desire to retire in Korea would have been much lower.

Korean immigrants who came to America as part of a family do not always function as a family unit in planning their future lives after living in America for a while. Children grow up, become Americanized, secure their independence, and move out of their parents' homes. Wives also become economically independent and sometimes pursue their own careers. Even elderly parents become independent as they discover the generous benefits the state and federal governments provide: SSI, Medicaid, subsidized housing, for instance. To show how the elderly are becoming independent, Min cites the example of an elderly woman who decided to remain in Flushing,

N.Y. instead of joining her son in Long Island: "My son wanted me to move in together. But I decided to remain in Flushing because for my social life my Korean friends here are far more important than my children. I did not want to lose my friendship networks by moving to Long Island. Also, I thought it was almost impossible for me to live away from the Flushing Korean ethnic community where all kinds of Korean foods and services are available." [4] Decisions about the future more and more are being left to the individual rather than to the family unit, even among the elderly.

It happens, sometimes, that no matter how much a husband may wish to return to Korea for better opportunities, his wife cannot, or will not, follow him because of her own career or their children's education. When husbands return alone to Korea to work, their marriage becomes an "international commuter marriage," or "transnational family," as Min refers to it.[5] In such cases, husbands and wives maintain their relationship with phone calls and frequent visits. As transportation and telecommunication between Korea and the United States became readily available at a reasonable cost, Korean immigrants have been quick to take advantage of the opportunities to keep in touch with their spouses, relatives, and friends. To some Korean immigrants, the issue of whether they intend to reside permanently in America or Korea is not important to their plans. An immigrant in Los Angeles comments: "Living in Los Angeles is like living in Korea as I mostly interact with Koreans, shop for groceries at a Korean supermarket, and participate actively in Korean affairs. When I feel like visiting Korea to see my relatives, I just fly over there. To me the demarcation between Korea and the United States is not clear. I can live in either one." On the other hand, there are other Korean immigrants, who, after realizing the difficulty of being accepted by other Americans and becoming assimilated into American society, want a definite plan about where they want to spend the rest of their lives. Korea is no longer a developing country. While it is still culturally traditional for the most part, it is becoming highly industrialized and developed, even though it is under constant threat from North Korea. For some Korean immigrants, returning to Korea to live is becoming a more attractive alternative; especially when they consider all the difficulties they have had to overcome to live in America.

NOTES

1. Won Moo Hurh, Hei Chu Kim, and Kwang Chung Kim, *Assimilation Patterns of Immigrants in the United States: A Case Study of Korean Immigrants in the Chicago Area* (Washington, D.C.: University Press of America, 1979), 41.

2. Nancy Abelmann and John Lie. *Blue Dreams: Korean Americans and the Los Angeles Riots* (Cambridge: Harvard University Press, 1998), 37.

3. Hurh, Kim, and Kim, *Assimilation Patterns of Immigrants in the United States*, 19.

4. Pyong Gap Min. *Changes and Conflicts: Korean Immigrant Families in New York* (Boston: Allyn and Bacon, 1998), 88.

5. Ibid., 114.

APPENDIX: QUESTIONNAIRE

Dear Friend:

I am sorry to bother you in your busy schedule. I am a sociology professor at Lycoming College in Williamsport, PA and currently conducting research on patterns of adjustment of Korean immigrants in the United States. Like you, I am a Korean immigrant. I would be grateful if you would answer the following questions and return the questionnaire to me at your earliest convenience. If recording your answers on a cassette is more convenient for you than writing, please do so. I will gladly reimburse the cost of the recording. Again, I thank you for your time and effort in answering the questions. If you would like to have a copy of result of the research, please include your home address with this questionnaire.

Sincerely,

Moon H. Jo, Ph.D.
Department of Sociology
Lycoming College

1. Please describe the circumstances surrounding your emigration to the United States. Specifically, what motivated you to come to the United States?

2. It is assumed that most Korean immigrants encountered difficulty in adjusting to the new society at some point after their arrival to the United States. Some experienced difficulty in finding employment, while others encountered difficulty in raising their increasingly Americanized chil-

dren. What was most difficult for you in your period of adjustment? Please describe in some detail?

3. How difficult has it been for you to accept American ideas, values, morals, customs, and traditions? If some of these elements of culture are not suitable to you, please explain why.

4. How well do you feel that the Korean immigrant group is accepted by the host society? Do you feel that the host society welcomes you as an immigrant? Have you or your family members ever encountered discrimination or prejudice in any particular situations? If so, please describe some of these incidents?

5. How would you assess your overall current status as an immigrant in the United States? At this point, what is the prospect of your future in this country?

6. Please circle or answer the following:

(a) Sex:—Male—Female—(Please circle one)

(b) Age:

(c) Marital status:—Single—Married—Divorced—Other—(Please circle one)

(d) Date of arrival in the United States:

(e) Highest educational level achieved in Korea. (Please circle one)
   High school attended
   High school graduated
   College attended
   College graduated
   Graduate school attended
   Graduate school (including professional schools) graduated

(f) The highest educational level achieved in the United States.
   (Please write)

(g) The type of occupation you held in Korea right before you emigrated to the United States. (Please specify the nature of the work)

(h) Current occupation. (Please specify the nature of the work)

BIBLIOGRAPHY

Abelmann, Nancy, and John Lie. *Blue Dreams: Korean Americans and Los Angeles Riots.* Cambridge: Harvard University Press, 1995.

Bach, Robert L., and J. B. Bach. "Employment Patterns of Southeast Asian Refugees." *Monthly Labor Review* (October 1980): 31–38.

Barringer, Herbert, Robert W. Gardner, and Michael J. Levin. *Asian and Pacific Islanders in the United States.* New York: Russell Sage Foundation, 1993.

Bogardus, Emory. "Comparing Racial Distance in Ethiopia, South Africa, and the United States." *Sociology and Social Research* 52 (1968): 149–156.

———. *Social Distance.* Yellow Spring, Ohio: Antioch Press, 1959.

Bonacich, Edna. "Theory of Middleman Minorities." *American Sociological Review* 38 (1973): 583–94.

Bonacich, Edna, Ivan Light, and Charles Wong. "Koreans in Small Business." *Society* 14 (1977): 54–59.

Bouvier, Leon F., and Robert W. Gardner. "Immigration to the U.S.: The Unfinished Story." *Population Bulletin* 41 (1986).

Cabezas, Amado, Tse Ming Tam, Brenda M. Lowe, Anna Wong, and Kathy Owyang Turner. "Empirical Barriers to Upward Mobility of Asian Americans in the San Francisco Bay Area." In *Frontiers of Asian American Studies: Writing, Research and Commentary*, eds. Gail Nomura, Russel Endo, Stephen H. Sumida, and Russel C. Leong. Pullman: Washington State University, 1989.

Cain, Bruce E., and D. Roderick Kiewiet. *Minorities in California.* Pasadena: California Institute of Technology, 1986.

Carvajal, Doreen. "Oldest Profession's Newest Home." *The New York Times*, May 26, 1996.

Chan, Sucheng. "European and Asian Immigration into the United States in Comparative Perspective, 1980s to 1920s." In *Immigration Reconsidered*, ed. Virginia Yans-McLaughlin. New York: Oxford University Press, 1990.

Chang, Edward T. "New Urban Crisis: Korean-Black Conflicts in Los Angeles." Ph.D. dissertation, University of California, Berkeley, 1991.

Chang, Yunshik. "Women in a Confucian Society: The Case of Chosun Dynasty Korea (1392–1910)." In *Traditional Thoughts and Practices in Korea*, eds. Eui-Young Yu and Earl H. Phillips. Los Angeles: Center for Korean-American and Korean Studies, California State University, 1983.

Choy, Bon-youn. *Koreans in America.* Chicago: Nelson Hall, 1979.

Corwin, Miles. "Packing Up and Going Back Home." *Los Angeles Times*, March 4, 1993.

Daniels, Roger. *Coming to America.* New York: HarperCollins, 1990.

Desruisseaux, Paul. "Foreign Enrollment Rises Slightly at Colleges in the United States." *The Chronicle of Higher Education*, December 12, 1997.

Dickerson, Debra. "Racial Fingernail Politics." *U.S. News and World Report*, April 14, 1997.

Dovidio, John. "Aversive Racism and the Need for Affirmative Action." *The Chronicle of Higher Education*, July 25, 1997.

Eu, Hongsook. "Health Status and Social and Demographic Determinants of Living Arrangements Among the Korean Elderly." *Korea Journal of Population and Development* 21 (1992): 197–223.

Fairchild, Henry P. *Greek Immigration to the United States*. New Haven: Yale University Press, 1991.

Frazier, Franklin E. *Black Bourgeoisie: The Rise of a New Middle Class*. New York: Free Press, 1957.

Gabaccia, Donna. *From the Other Side: Women, Gender, and Immigrant Life in the U.S. 1980–1990*. Bloomington: Indiana University Press, 1994.

Goldberg, Jeffrey. "The Overachievers." *New York*, April 10, 1995.

Gonzales, Juan L. *Racial and Ethnic Families in America*. Iowa: Kendall/Hunt Publishing Co., 1992.

Hays, Constance. "Asian-American Groups Call for Breslin's Ouster Over Racial Slurs." *New York Times*, May 7, 1990.

Higher Education Research Institute. *Race and Ethnicity in the American Professoriate*. Los Angeles: Graduate School of Education and Information, 1997.

Hughey, A. M. "The Incomes of Recent Female Immigrants to the United States." *Social Science Quarterly* 17 (1990): 383–390.

Hurh, Won Moo. "Marginal Children of War: An Exploratory Study of American-Korean Children." *International Journal of Sociology of the Family* 2 (1972): 10–20.

Hurh, Won Moo, and Kwang Chung Kim. *Korean Immigrants in America*. Madison, New Jersey: Fairleigh Dickinson University Press, 1984.

————. "Uprooting and Adjustment: A Sociological Study of Korean Immigrants' Mental Health." Final report submitted to the National Institute of Mental Health. 1988.

Hurh, Won Moo, Hei Chu Kim, and Kwang Chung Kim. *Assimilation Patterns of Immigrants in the United States: A Case Study of Korean Immigrants in the Chicago Area.* Washington, D.C.: University Press of America, 1979.

Immigration and Naturalization Service. *Annual Reports.* Washington, D.C.: U.S. Government Printing Office, 1960–1979.

————. *Statistical Yearbook.* Washington, D.C.: U.S. Government Printing Office, 1979–1997.

Jeong, G. J., and W. Schumm. "Family Satisfaction in Korean/American Marriage: An Exploratory Study of the Perceptions of Korean Wives." *Journal of Comparative Family Studies* 21 (1990): 352–335.

Jo, Moon H. "The Putative Political Complacency of Asian Americans." *Political Psychology* 6 (1984): 583–605.

————."Korean Merchants in the Black Community: Prejudice Among the Victims of Prejudice." *Ethnic Racial Studies* 15 (1992): 396–411.

Jo, Moon H., and Daniel Mast. "Changing Images of Asian Americans." *International Journal of Politics, Culture and Society* 6 (1993): 417–441.

Kalton, Michael. *Korean Ideas and Values.* Elkins Park, Pa.: Phillip Jaison Memorial Foundation, Inc., 1979.

Karnow, Stanley, and Nancy Yoshihara. *Asian Americans in Transition.* New York: The Asian Society, 1992.

Kim, Bok-Lim. "Casework with Japanese and Korean Wives of Americans." *Social Casework* 53 (1972): 273–279.

————. "Asian Wives of U.S. Servicemen: Women in Shadows." *Amerasia Journal* 4 (1977): 91–115.

Kim, David S. *Korean Small Businesses in the Olympic Area.* Los Angeles: School of Architecture and Urban Planning, University of California, 1975.

Kim, Dong Soo. "How They Fared in American Homes: A Follow-up Study of Adopted Korean Children." *Children Today* 6 (1977): 2–6, 31.

Kim, Dong Soo, and Sookja P. Kim. "A Banana Identity: Asian American Adult Adoptees in America." Paper presented at the annual program meeting of the Council on Social Work Education, Washington, D.C., February 17, 1985.

Kim, Elaine. "They Armed in Self-Defense." *Newsweek*, May 18, 1992.

Kim, Elaine H., and Eui-Young Yu. *East to America: Korean American Life Stories.* New York: The New Press, 1996.

Kim, Eun-Young. "Career Choice Among Second-Generation Korean Americans: Reflections of Cultural Model of Success." *Anthropology and Education Quarterly* 24 (1993): 224–248.

Kim, Illsoo. *New Urban Immigrants: The Korean Community in New York: The Korean Community in New York.* Princeton, N.J.: Princeton University Press, 1981.

Kim, Kwang Chung, and Won Moo Hurh. "Employment of Korean Immigrant Wives and the Division of Household Tasks." In *Korean Women in Transition: At Home and Abroad,* eds. Eui-Young Yu and Earl H. Phillips. Los Angeles: Center for Korean-American and Korean Studies, California State University, 1987.

————. "Two Dimensions of Korean Immigrants' Sociocultural Adaptation: Americanization and Ethnic Attachment." Paper presented at the Annual Meeting of the American Sociological Association, Atlanta, Georgia, 1988.

Kim, Kwang Chung, Won Moo Hurh, and Shin Kim. "Generational Differences in Korean Immigrants' Life Conditions in the United States." *Sociological Perspectives* 36 (1993): 258–270.

Kim, Warren Y. *Koreans in America.* Seoul: Po Chin Cahi Printing Co., 1971.

Kitano, Harry H. L., and Roger Daniels. *Asian Americans: Emerging Minorities.* Englewood Cliffs, N.J.: Prentice Hall, 1995.

Kitano, Harry H. L., Wai-tsang Yeung, Lynn Chai, and Herb Hatanaka. "Asian American Interracial Marriage." *Journal of Marriage and the Family* 46 (1984): 179–190.

Korean Ministry of Education, 1965–90. *Statistical Yearbook of Education (Kyoyuk Tonggye Yon'gam).* Seoul, Korea.

Kwak, Dong Chung, "Mending Broken Immigrant Lives." *Los Angeles Times,* June 24, 1995.

Lee, Daniel B. "Marital Adjustment Between Korean Women and American Servicemen." *Korean Observer* 20 (1989): 321–352.

Lee, Don Chang. *Acculturation of Korean Residents in Georgia.* San Francisco, Calif.: R and E Research Associates, 1975.

Lee, Joann Faung Jean. *Asian Americans.* New York: The New Press, 1992.

Light, Ivan, and Edna Bonacichi. *Immigrant Entrepreneurs: Koreans in Los Angeles 1965–1982.* Berkeley, University of California Press, 1988.

Lozano, Juan A. "Professor's Win Could Spur Change." *Albuquerque Journal.* April 12, 1998.

Mangiafico, Luciano. *Contemporary American Immigrants: Patterns of Filipino, Korean, Chinese Settlement in the United States.* New York: Praeger, 1988.

Melendy, Brett. *Asians in America: Filipino, Koreans, and East Indians.* Boston: Twayne Publishers, 1977.

Min, Pyong Gap. "From White-Collar Occupations to Small Business: Korean Immigrants' Occupational Adjustment." *The Sociological Quarterly* 25 (1984): 333–352.

————— . "An Exploratory Study of Kin Ties Among Korean- Immigrant Families in Atlanta." *Journal of Comparative Family Studies* 25 (1984): 59–75.

————— . *Ethnic Business Enterprises: Korean Small Business in Atlanta.* New York: Center for Migration Studies, 1988.

————— . "Korean Immigrant Entrepreneurship: A Multivariate Analysis." *Journal of Urban Affairs* 10 (1989): 197–212.

————— . "Some Positive Functions of Ethnic Businesses for an Immigrant Community: Koreans in Los Angeles." Final report submitted to the National Science Foundation. Department of Sociology, Queens College of CUNY, N.Y. 1989.

————— . "Korean Americans." In *Asian Americans: Contemporary Trends and Issues*, ed. Pyong Gap Min. Thousand Oaks, Calif.: Sage Publications, 1995.

————— . *Caught in the Middle.* Berkeley: University of California Press, 1996.

————— . *Changes and Conflicts: Korean Immigrant Families in New York.* Boston: Allyn and Bacon, 1998.

Mints, John, and Peter Pae. "The High Price of Success." *Washington Post*, September 7, 1998.

Nugent, Walter. *Crossings: The Great Transatlantic Migration, 1870–1914.* Bloomington: Indiana University Press, 1992.

Owen, Carolyn, Howard C. Eisner, and Thomas R. McFaul. "A Half- Century of Social Distance Research: National Replication of the Bogardus Studies." *Sociology and Social Research* 66 (1981): 80–99.

Pang, Keum-Young Chung. *Korean Elderly Women in America: Everyday Life, Health, and Illness.* New York: AMS Press, 1991.

Park, Insook Han, and Lee-Jay Cho. "Confucianism and the Korean Family." *Journal of Comparative Family Studies* 24 (1995): 117–134.

Park, Insook Han, J. T. Fawcett, Fred Arnold, and Robert Gardner. *Korean Immigrants and U.S. Policy: A Predeparture Perspective.* Honolulu: East-West Population Institute, 1990.

Ratliff, B. W., H. F. Moon, and G. H. Bonacci. "Intercultural Marriage: The Korean American Experience." *Social Casework* 59 (1978): 221–226.

Shin, Eui Hang. "Interracially Married Korean Women in the United States: An Analysis Based on Hypergamy-Exchange Theory." In *Korean Women in Transition: At Home and Abroad*, ed. Eui-Young Yu and Earl H. Phillips. Los Angeles, Calif.: Center for Korean-American and Korean Studies, California State University, 1990.

Shin, Eui Hang, and Kyung-Sup Chang. "Peripherization of Immigrant Professionals: Korean Physicians in the United States." *International Migration Review* 22 (1988): 609–626.

Song, Young I. *Silent Victims: Battered Women in Korean Immigrant Families.* San Francisco, Calif.: Oxford Press, 1987.

Sowell, Thomas. *Race and Culture.* New York: Basic Books, 1994.

Strosnider, Kim. "N.Y. Public College Aims to Raise Funds." *The Chronicle of Higher Education*, March 14, 1997.

Taft, Philip, Jr. "Policing the New." *Police Magazine*, July 1982.

Takaki, Ronald. *Strangers from a Different Shore: A History of Asian Americans.* Boston: Little, Brown and Company, 1989.

Tang, Joyce. "Asian American Engineers: Earnings, Occupational Status, and Promotions." Paper presented at the Annual Meeting of the American Sociological Association, Cincinnati, Ohio, August 1991.

Turner, Jonathan, and Edna Bonacich. "Toward a Composite Theory of Middle-man Minorities." *Ethnicity* 7 (1980): 144–158.

Um, Shin Ja. *Korean Immigrant Women in the Dallas-Area Apparel Industry.* New York: University Press of America, 1996.

U.S. Bureau of Census. "1990 Census of Population, Asians and Pacific Islanders in the United States. Washington, D.C.: U.S. Government Printing Office, 1992.

———. *1990 Census of Population, General Population Characteristics, United States.* Washington, D.C.: U.S. Government Printing Office, 1992.

U.S. Census of the Population and Housing. *Foreign Born Immigrants: Koreans.* Washington, D.C.: U.S. Government Printing Office, 1984.

U.S. Commission on Civil Rights. *Recent Activities Against Citizens and Residents of Asian Descent.* Washington, D.C.: U.S. Government Printing Office, 1986.

———. *Civil Rights Issues Facing Asian Americans in the 1990s.* Washington, D.C.: U.S. Government Printing Office, 1992.

U.S. Department of Commerce. *Statistical Abstract of the United States: The National Data Book.* Washington, D.C.: U.S. Bureau of the Census, 1990.

Woodhams, Fred. "Minority Medical Professors Are Less Likely to Hold Senior Post, Study Finds." *The Chronicle of Higher Education.* September 18, 1998.

Yim, Sun Bin. "Korean Battered Wives: A Sociological and Psychological Analysis of Conjugal Violence in Korean Immigrant Families." In *Korean Women in a Struggle for Humanization*, eds. Harold Hakwon Sun-woo and Dong Soo Kim. Memphis, Tenn.: Association of Korean Christian Scholars in North America, 1978.

———. "The Changing Significance of Ethnic and Class Resources in Immigrant Business: The Case of Korean Immigrant Businesses in Chicago." *International Migration Review* 25 (1990): 303–332.

Yoon, In-Jin. *The Social Origin of Korean Immigration to the United States from 1965 to the Present.* Honolulu: East-West Population Institute, 1993.

———. *On My Own: Korean Businesses and Race Relations in America.* Chicago: University of Chicago Press, 1997.

Yu, Eui-Young. "Occupation and Work Patterns of Korean Immigrants." In *Koreans in Los Angeles: Prospects and Promises,* eds. Eui-Young Yu, Earl

H. Phillips, and Eun Sik Yang. Los Angeles: Center for Korean-American and Korean Studies, California State University, 1982.

————. "The Activities of Women in Southern California Korean Community Organizations." In *Korean Women in Transition: At Home and Abroad,* eds. Eui-Young Yu and Earl H. Phillips. Los Angeles: Center for Korean American and Korean Studies, California State University, 1987.

————. "Korean Community Profile: Life and Consumer Patterns." *Korea Times*, 1990.

Yun, Yo-Yun. "Early History of Korean Immigration to America." In *The Korean Diaspora,* ed. Hyung-Chan Kim. Santa Barbara, Calif.: Clio Press, 1979.

Zaldivar, R. A. "Immigrants Find English Skills Rising in Importance." *Albuquerque Journal*, June 8, 1997

Zenner, Walter. "Middleman Minority Theories: A Critical Review." In *Sourcebook on the New Immigration*, ed. Roy Simon Bryce-Laporte. New Brunswick, N.J.: Transaction, 1980.

INDEX

About the Author

MOON H. JO is a retired Professor of Sociology at Lycoming College, in Williamsport, Pennsylvania. His research on matters related to Asians has been published in a number of journals, including *Political Psychology*, *Ethnic and Racial Studies*, *International Social Science Review*, and *International Journal of Politics, Culture and Society.*

ISBN 0-313-30918-3

90000>

EAN

9 780313 309182

HARDCOVER BAR CODE